AMIDST REVOLUTION

by

EMILIO CASTRO

CHRISTIAN JOURNALS LIMITED
BELFAST

First English edition 1975 by Christian Journals
Limited, 2 Bristow Park, Belfast BT9 6TH

ISBN 0 904302 07 5

Translated from the Spanish
by James and Margaret Goff

Cover by Blaise Levai

Made and printed in Ireland by
CAHILL & CO., DUBLIN

Contents

A Letter to God

Dear Lord,

It has been a long time since I wrote to you. Today I feel a real need for you and your presence, perhaps because of the nearness of death or the relative failure of the struggle. You know that I have tried to be faithful to you—always and by all means—consistent with my whole being. That is why I am here. I understand love as the urgency of helping to solve the problems of the "other person"—in whom you are present.

I left what I had and came here. Perhaps today is my (Maundy) Thursday and tonight my (Good) Friday. Because I love you I surrender everything I am into your hands, without limit. What hurts me is the thought of leaving those I most love—Cecy and my family—and perhaps not being here to participate in the triumph of the people—their liberation.

We are a group full of true, "Christian" humanity, and I think we will change the course of history. The thought of this comforts me. I love you and I give you myself and ourselves, completely, because you are my Father. No one's death is meaningless if his life has been charged with significance: and I believe this has been true of us, here.

Chau, Lord! Perhaps until that heaven of yours, that new world we desire so much!

NESTOR PAZ

Many Latin American Christians think like Nestor Paz, who was killed in 1970. He understood his commitment to armed conflict in his native Bolivia as an evangelical imperative when all else failed. This letter is part of his continual conversation with God.

I Cry in the Night from the Torture Chamber

Psalm 129   Ernesto Cardenal

From the depths, I cry to you oh Lord:
I cry in the night from the prison cell
and from the concentration camp
From the torture chamber
in the hour of darkness
hear my voice
            my S.O.S.

If you were to keep a record of sins
Lord, who would be blameless ?
But you do pardon sins
you are not implacable as they are in their Investigation !

I trust in the Lord and not in leaders
Nor in slogans
I trust in the Lord and not in their radios !

My soul hopes in the Lord
more than the sentinels of dawn
more than the way one counts the hours of night in a prison cell.

While we are imprisoned
            they are enjoying themselves !
But the Lord is liberation
the freedom of Israel.

Ernesto Cardenal is from the Central American country of
Nicaragua where he was a resistance fighter prior to becoming
a Trappist monk. He lives in a Trappist community which he
founded and sees this a more appropriate way of fighting
injustice and dictatorship. For him the spiritual power of God
is greater than the guns and bullets of man.

CHAPTER I

Amidst Revolution

This is a subject of interest both to those who are concerned about the revolutionary process in the world and to those concerned about the life of the Church.

Because the Church is immersed in the human situation it influences what people do; and what people do influences the Church. A revolutionary process is shaking the Church out of its routine and presenting it with various options. The Church must become an 'agent of action' within the process, or it will inevitably be reactionary against it. At the same time, in those parts of the world where the Christian presence is numerically important, it will be difficult to think of real and permanent changes in society without the participation of the members and leaders of the Christian church.

Particularly in Latin America the subject is timely and urgent. A few years ago at President Nixon's request, Nelson Rockefeller undertook a tour of the continent to study the situation and to advise on US foreign policy in Latin America. Rockefeller mentioned the hidden revolutionary potential within the

Church and recommended that it be given careful attention. This experienced politician saw that seeds of discontent and a passion for justice were germinating within a body which traditionally had been allied to the *status quo* and that ferment in the Church would soon have an effect on all aspects of Latin American society. While the politician lamented this fact, young people in Latin America saw it with very different eyes. A few years earlier it was normal for young people to be indifferent to religion, believing that from the Church, as from ancient Nazareth, nothing new or nothing good could come. Today they look eagerly toward the old church institution from which they hope a word might come that will lead to liberating action.

The subject may also be important for the situation in the developed world where the Church has either been an adornment of society or has existed on its margins. Where it has maintained a biblical tradition in which justice and human solidarity are fundamental categories, however, it may at any moment nourish itself on the seeds of the counter-culture that challenges the surrounding tranquility. When this happens it is newsworthy. Thus, for example, when the World Council of Churches took sides in the racial struggle in South Africa and in the Portuguese colonies the European press gave echo to the reaction. The old problem of the relationship between Church and society is again up for discussion, no longer as a theoretical problem of theology but as a concrete option between obedience to or betrayal of the Gospel.

Logically, I am interested in the problem of the efficacy of Christian participation in the social area. On this efficacy will depend the quantity of love that can be translated into justice in community affairs and the possibility of rapid reconciliation in social organizations that are dying because of internal divisions. I am also interested in establishing church participation on a firm basis of Christian conviction supported by biblical witness. This does not mean a quick escape into political action, but subjection to the intellectual discipline of testing, investigating, and eventually justifying that action in the light of clearly established Christian convictions.

There can be no Christian reflection that is not reflection on what it means to be 'on the Way' and committed. As Albert Schweitzer said at the end of his book, *Quest of the Historical Jesus*, 'He comes to us as One unknown, without a name, as of old, by the lake-side, He came to those men who knew Him not. He speaks to us the same word: "Follow thou me!" and sets us to the task which He has to fulfil for our time. He commands. And to those who obey Him, whether they be wise or simple, He will reveal Himself in the toils, the conflicts, the sufferings which they shall pass through in the fellowship, and, as by ineffable mystery, they shall learn in their own experience who He is.' The truth of Christian doctrine can be known by judging it where men suffer and sometimes hope and rejoice. Therefore, a description of the Latin American situation as general background and basic data is needed for theological reflection. I do not believe the Latin American situation to be normative for other areas, rather it is the only area in which I can be immersed with some authenticity. It will not be difficult for you to extrapolate this situation and apply the reflection to your own historic circumstances. A brief description of Latin American churches is also necessary.

I will then proceed to a theological study of the mission of the Church in the plan of God. And I will try to show how that saving and liberating mission of God which includes all of humanity is projected toward the limits of history, and awaits the service of a Christian community which presently symbolizes the goal toward which it aspires, and which seeks to interpret those human aspirations related to the highest destiny to which God calls mankind. Then I will consider the various possibilities for action that the Church is currently facing in Latin America and describe in terms of obedience the possibilities which are open to it.

Appended is a series of statements that justify the various theses advanced in the body of the book and illustrate the positions of official bodies or representative persons of the Latin American Christian community.

My hope is that this book will contribute to the knowledge of the Latin American situation, to theological reflection on the task of the Church today in other parts of the world and, in some measure, to the inspiration and encouragement of those who, in obedience to their Christian calling, dream and struggle for a new day for their people.

HUMAN BACKGROUND

The overwhelming fact is external dependency. My own country, Uruguay, for example, exists by virtue of arbitration carried out by England, Argentina and Brazil, establishing a bottom state that assured free entry for the European metropolis to the River Plate and its broad commercial opportunities. It is possible to see in Latin America how everything is directed toward the port—the linking point of the colony with the metropolis—while the interior remains completely orphan to all developments. This would also explain,

Latin Americans would say, some of the internal characteristics of Latin American society.

For one thing, the Spanish conquest established the authority of the conquerors over the natural resources and over the nationals. The land was distributed to the *conquistadores*, the mines assigned to them, and they became practically owners and lords of the life of the inhabitants of the region. A model of paternalistic society was established.

In the second place, the interest of the paternalistic land-owners was united with the interest of the merchants of the metropolis overseas. Thus was produced a minority oligarchy that dominated the sources of national production and made them function according to their own interest and to the interest of the foreigners.

Today this assumes modern forms: it is the alliance of land-owners, bankers, exporters, who, in general, are branches of international monopolies. But their origins can be traced in colonial practices continued later through trade relations with, first, England, and later the United States. This will explain also the foreign influence in the thinking of educated Latin American minorities.

'The worst injustices the people of Latin America suffer stem from the multiform economic dependency of the nations on the periphery of world economy—the underdeveloped ones—in relation to the highly developed *centre* countries. This is so with the Western monetary system, in which the ninety-six poor countries have neither voice nor vote in decisions that directly affect them, with the serious reduction from twenty-one per cent to seventeen per cent in Latin American participation in international commerce; with the "international division of labour" and the inevitable negative trend of the trade terms of the raw materials and manufactured products (unless agreements like those of oil-exporting countries were extended to other raw materials); and this is the case with the so-called "brain drain" that draws from underdeveloped nations thousands of their best talents, largely for the benefit of developed nations, where they go for specialization and where so many of them remain for ever.' [1]

The distortion produced by the presence of foreign capital is multiplied in the distortion of the economy of each country. Thus Chile has been condemned to be the great producer of copper, Bolivia of tin, Brazil of coffee, Central American countries of fruit.

Today, when the great international private investors come, attracted by the possibility of an effective Latin American Common Market, they invest in areas of production that would never mean economic independency, nor integral development of the country, but greater and more rapid profit for foreign capitalists who hope to recover their investment rapidly. Thus aid plans become new chains which bind the receivers to the lenders, since they usually come conditional to the good political conduct of those that receive the help. Receiving countries are to follow the counsel dispensed by the great developed powers and buy products from the same powers.

In this manner Latin America is confronted by the fact that, instead of aid, its 'credit' goes to help the economy of the country which 'helps'. The Economic Commission of the United Nations for Latin America has proved that year by year more capital leaves Latin America than enters. The payment for interest and fees for this debt is a tremendous handicap to accumulating the necessary funds for the financing of internal development of the Latin American countries.

To complete the picture two social facts must be taken into account: one, the accelerated population growth, which places Latin America as the continent of most rapid demographic expansion. It is interesting to note that in Latin America birth control presents genuine ideological disputes. It is not just the negative attitude of the Catholic Church, which might be catalogued as reactionary or conservative, but also there are more progressive groups, including the most radically leftist, which attack the policy of limiting population because they think of it as an instrument of the local dominant oligarchs and foreign powers for controlling and suppressing manifestations of popular discontent.

'One hundred and twenty million children are in the middle of this storm. Every minute a child dies from sickness or hunger. But in the year 2000 there will be six hundred and fifty million Latin Americans; half of them will be under fifteen years of age: a time bomb.' (2)

Instead of getting at the root of structural problems that produce cultural and material poverty, the effort is applied to slowing down population growth so as not to burden the new generations of the world with additional problems of education and employment.

This population growth brings to fifty per cent the people under nineteen years of age. A revolutionary potential, this, as youths seek educational and work opportunities and find that there is no room for them. It must also be remembered that throughout Latin America illiteracy is still about fifty per cent.

The second fact, the impossible situation in the rural areas which results in an exodus toward the cities. 'Half of the Latin Americans are rural workers, but while the estates larger than a thousand hectares (one per cent) cover more than 370,000,000 hectares (sixty-two per cent), three times the agricultural land of China, 70,000,000 small land-owners with farms smaller than twenty hectares are truly "medieval serfs". This is not all. At the very brink of despair we find the sombre army of 8,000,000 rural families— 50,000,000 men, women and children—hungry, shoeless, illiterate, without a single piece of land of their own, workers on somebody else's land for miserable wages, deprived of schools, hospitals, security or personal dignity; they are poorer and more vulnerable than the African peasants, who are protected to a certain extent by their tribal organizations, no longer existing among us. "Twelve miles beyond the last street lamp of the Latin American cities rural poverty is worse than in Africa," says Father Roger Vekemans, founder of the Centre for Social and Economic Development in Latin America (DESAL).' (3)

In general the phenomenon of urbanization is more important than that of industrialization. Instead of multiplication of opportunities for all, there is multiplication of belts of slums around Latin America's large cities. The Brazilian *favelas*, Montevideo's *canttegriles*, Argentina's *villas miserias*, Chile's *callampas* are just so many ways of pointing out the existence of a phenomenon visible in the outskirts of all our cities. This again highlights that mass unemployment which is a potential menace to the stability of the system. Urban concentration has produced, logically enough, a greater popular organization. Thus trade unions are becoming aware and achieving power and their demands are beginning to be heard. A situation of lessening production, with a great reluctance to make profit for foreign business, and with an unequal distribution of national income,

16

added to the great growth in population, makes for permanent and explosive instability. To control this alarming situation recourse is made to a policy repressive at every level. This repression is one of the most outstanding characteristics of Latin America today, and it is thoroughly co-ordinated. In many Latin American countries the military force held by the police for this kind of political control is much greater than that of the army for the national defence, and it costs much more than the amounts budgeted for education or social services. At the same time the armies are increasingly being trained to repress any kind of protest.

Consequently violence is an ever present fact in all major Latin American cities. It is born of that institutional violence which imposes subhuman living conditions on large sections of the population. It is influenced by repressive violence applied to all manifestations of popular discontent. It is multiplied by the people's counter violence, the expression of desperation, spear-headed by groups steeped in ideology who feel they can undermine the present situation and prepare the way for radical change, even if they cannot hope for immediate revolutionary success.

We must remember that the North American presence is in evidence throughout the whole continent. It would be almost impossible to land at any Latin American airport and not find United States military air-force planes there. United States military missions operate in every country with the single exception of Cuba. The traumatic experience of Santo Domingo, while not the first, is a most telling example. The legitimate government elected by a free and democratic vote was under serious threat from an attempted military *coup*. When the ensuing struggle seemed to be going the government's way, a massive landing of US marines swung the balance in favour of the military. This episode is not forgotten by Latin Americans, effecting caution in some, and desperation in others. Of course, this dependency, exercised through the local oligarchies, is manifested not only in the economy of the continent, but in every aspect of Latin American life. So, for example, in the area of mass-communication, Mario Kaplún gives the following picture : 'If we go to the cinema in any Latin American country there is a two-to-one chance that we will see a picture made in the USA because fifty-five per cent of the films shown in cinemas in Latin America come from the USA. If we turn on the TV the experience will be no different. The investigation carried out by UNDA/AL in December 1970 revealed that programmes of North American origin take up an average of thirty-four per cent of total TV time in Latin America. In some countries, such as Guatemala and Nicaragua, the average reaches fifty per cent and surpasses the time occupied by local programmes. At the same time programmes originating in Latin America itself are given nine per cent of TV time over the area as a whole. According to *Vision* magazine, America, in spite of its poverty, underdevelopment and lack of foreign currency for necessary imports, nevertheless spends over thirty-three million pounds annually on North American TV series and films. If we go to a news-stand in any Latin American country to buy a magazine, we will find it literally covered with comic books (Superman, cowboys, and the apparently innocuous Donald Duck). All this material which the well known USA "cultural industry" produces in series and translates into Spanish or Portuguese is massively consumed by children, Latin American youth and even adults. Through all this sub-literature is portrayed an image of the USA as the mecca of Goodness and Progress, while our underdeveloped peoples are presented as lazy, incapable and therefore deserving of their condition of dependency.

'But we have not gone to the news-stand to buy the adventures of Roy Rogers but to seek a popular magazine dealing with current issues and news relevant to all of Latin America. Does one exist ? Yes, only one. It is not a Latin American magazine, but a Yankee magazine, *Selections from Readers Digest* which covers all of Latin America, with nine sub-regional editions (eight in Spanish), which, according to calculations, surpasses two million copies. Almost all of the material, from USA sources, is contrary to the authentic interests of our peoples. Is there then no popular magazine circulated in Latin America and published by Latin Americans ? No, lamentably there is not.

'Besides economic colonialism, **Latin America also** suffers from informative and cultural colonialism. But what are the reasons for this situation ? When the causes are investigated one of the first things that comes into view, with regard to information, is that two agencies virtually control the flow of news : United Press International (UPI) and Associated Press (AP), both North American agencies.

'Thus the principal forms of mass communication belong to those least interested in transforming the society. The owners of the large agricultural, commercial and financial enterprises — that is to say, those favoured by the present *status quo*—are usually also the owners of the principal media of communication, and therefore to inform truthfully what is happening in Latin America and in their own country is contrary to their interests.'

A GIANT AWAKENS

To characterize in general terms the Latin American continent at this moment : it is a giant which is beginning to search tentatively for its next steps towards the future. Whereas up to about 1960 the general tone, with some exceptions, was that of quietism and resignation in situations considered unchangeable, at the present moment the dominant characteristic is the hunger for change, the assurance that there is something new and different that can be created to-morrow. There is an awakening of man to the possibilities that history offers. So far this awakening is uneven. Students, in the first place, and organized labour in the second, have taken the lead. But it would now be difficult to persuade any section that the philosophies and the situations of yesterday should be preserved.

So the situation is not static. . . . active currents of protest can be detected. The common demoninator of the groups that make up the first is the "will for revolution", the frontal attack against the existing social systems. It is composed of labour organizations, generally with a Marxist orientation, but more recently with a Christian inspiration as well; a large sector of youth, especially university students; and relatively numerous groups of intellectuals, professionals, technicians, and representatives of the Church in growing numbers. They have not yet reached a con-census as to the necessary means to overthrow and to replace the old traditional society, but it is only a matter of time for all these groups to converge in agreement on goals and means to reach them.'

'There is no Latin American country where this phenomenon, which shocks many people and gives hope to many others — the commitment of the

Christians and the Church to revolution——has failed to express itself. It has become somewhat a matter of routine to see repression, jail, exile, torture and also death reaching Catholic priests and nuns.'(5)

In this situation various experiments have been tried in a search to move the Latin American common people toward the possibilities of a better life. Social experiments have been carried out in Bolivia, Cuba, Peru, and more recently in Chile. From each of these experiences there is something for all to learn.

In 1952 Bolivia passed through a true people's revolution. In the previous year the opposition candidate won the presidential election. Rather than let the winner take office, the incumbent turned power over to a military *junta*. However, an alliance of workers and peasants in a frontal combat with enormous bloodshed destroyed the army and gained power for the common people. This was followed by the nationalization of mines and agrarian reforms that gave land to the peasants who worked it. The failure of this revolution in economic terms was due to the fall in the price of tin on the international market and a drastically reduced agricultural production caused by a lack of training by the Indian peasants to operate in a money market. However, this popular movement had permanent human consequences. The Indian who for the first time had a plot of land felt like a 'man' after four centuries of submission. With the entrance into political life of the peasant masses the whole Bolivian political panorama has changed. Bolivia now suffers under a military government whlch uses repression to keep workers and peasants in submission. Nevertheless, in the midst of this situation there are signs of a permanently living hope. There may be temporary submission but the people are not resigned.

21

Their hope of being the protagonists of their own national destiny is not dead. The first way, then, is that of popular insurrection. At present it seems to be frustrated.

The second revolutionary phenomenon of recent times is the Cuban revolution. The story of the group of guerilla fighters who from the Sierra Maestra were first able to neutralize the government army and then to overcome it with arms is well known. Later, real reconstruction of the country began with the nationalization of foreign property and agrarian and urban reform.

The success of the Cuban revolution in 1959 played an important part in galvanizing the people of Latin America through the example of the small group of revolutionaries with a cohesive radical programme. The necessity for Cuba to move more and more towards orthodox Marxism and to depend on Soviet help, limits the experiment as a working model for Latin America. Indeed the American blockade on the one hand and Russian aid on the other make it well nigh impossible to judge the merits or demerits of the Cuban phenomenon. However, that a tiny country ninety miles from the United States has been able to maintain its independence and its way of life is of great significance. Furthermore that it continues to determine its own internal economic, social and political relationships, places Cuba in a position of moral leadership to small Latin American countries, giving them encouragement and hope. Nobody is trying to imitate Cuba, but many have been inspired by what they see as Cuba's heroism and tenacity.

But the Cuban situation is unique. Post 1959 Latin American history has conclusively shown that no other guerilla style action has been able to overcome existing structures of power. In country after country the guerillas have been defeated. There seems no way by which they can provide the justice so urgently sought by the Latin American masses.

In the case of Peru it has been the army, which like all Latin American armies is more and more technical and technocratic, that took over the government. It did so in terms of a demanding nationalism that brought it up against those elements which placed reliance on foreign forces and led it to question the power structures within the country. Although there is no clear socialist ideology in the military revolution in Peru, nevertheless, starting from a comprehension of national needs, and with a greater government participation in the economic life, including a policy of expropriation of large landed estates and large natural riches, they proclaim their desire to favour more participation by the people in the making of decisions. It still remains to be seen how far this regimen is capable of creating the institutional mechanisms that permit the incorporation of the common people in the power structure. It is evident that what has been accomplished is very important, and shows up as a possibility on the Latin American horizon.

Unhappily, the actions of the army in Brazil, Uruguay and Chile do not leave much hope for the possible repetition of this kind of way forward in the near future of Latin America.

If the Chilean experiment had been allowed more time to prove its usefulness, it might have become the alternative model for many situations where at present the only hope of progress seems to be centred on violence. With the overthrow of the elected government by the army, however, a bitter campaign has been mounted against the forces of progress. This has had far-reaching consequences throughout the length and breadth of Latin America, because it has killed the hope of serious social change by democratic means.

The situation in Latin America could then be summarized as follows :

> Although Latin America is no longer a colony, its status is nevertheless being determined by its continuing dependence on external powers. Its liberation and growth are hampered by mounting debts, by a malformed internal economy, and by patterns of development imposed from without by the great industrial forces. The policy of aid, investments and loans serves to strengthen the bonds of dependence.
>
> Rapid increases in population throw into the study and work market millions of human beings who cannot be properly absorbed. In their frustration they become potential material for revolution.
>
> There is a new and critical awareness of the Latin American situation. The fact of under-development and the need for fundamental structural changes have been authoritatively established by specialized agencies of the United Nations and by university research teams. Their statistics, interwoven with a nationalistic ideology, have strengthened demands for revolutionary change which will at the same time destroy external dependence and the internal structures of capitalism and privilege.
>
> Repression increases both at national and continental level in an effort to control the revolutionary potential of the young, and to eliminate from the list of visible options those that are postulated by the continent's intellectual vanguard.
>
> As a consequence there is violence in practically all the countries; it is the response of the people, especially of the students, to the violence inherent in the social structures and exercised by the forces dedicated to the preservation of the *status quo.*
>
> The Latin American peoples hunger for what is new. The march from countryside to city is the modern exodus of the farm labourer, seeking like the Hebrew people, the

promised land, the land of hope, the new tomorrow. The impossibility of repressing all popular movements is a fact, the chaos, the anarchy, to be seen in many Latin American countries at the present time is indicative of the struggle of peoples seeking their better destiny, and the resistance they encounter.

We know, then, the Latin American hope and we know the realities of popular frustration. For many, the solution is individual—to escape, to migrate. Australia, for example, is becoming a strong attraction for the university graduates. For the ruling élites, the only solution is a fascist type of government and repression. But at the popular level, there is a reality of hope; and here, between hope and frustration, between expectancy and repression, the Church should find a real mission. Here, in encouragement of that hope, and in helping to implement this hope for real change, lies an important task for Christians to undertake.

CHAPTER II

The Churches in Latin America

Latin America has been considered Christian ever since the conquest. The Roman Catholic Church evangelized the indigenous population practically in its entirety. The Protestant world considered Latin America a Catholic continent. The Edinburgh Conference of 1910, despite its ecumenical character, had no Latin American delegates. Latin America was to be the private holding of the Catholic Church.

It is interesting to note that within Catholicism this thought dominated in some sectors even up to 1948, when the concordat between the Catholic Church and the Colombian Government reserved two thirds of the national territory for missionary action. Other denominations were prohibited from working there as it was feared the indigenous population might be too easily influenced by Protestant proseletyzing.

Catholicism was introduced to Latin America by the conquerors through a strange mixture of military imposition, evangelism and cathechizing. It resulted in a popular religiosity which was a syncretism compounded of ancient religious practice and Catholic doctrine, forms and liturgy. With the passing of the years, different philosophic influences came to the continent; some of them (including some Protestant thought) gradually produced the phenomenon of secularization and opened up the possibility of religious plularism.

Nevertheless, account must be taken of the Catholic character of the continent as a major and predominant fact. The struggle for national independence at the beginning of the nineteenth century placed the Church in a difficult situation. Some brilliant priests made the cause of the patriots their cause and openly joined the ranks. Others favoured holding to the traditional *status quo.* The revolution won out in practically all the Latin American countries, but the alliance between Church and State persisted, and the new Latin American State took over the right of sponsor that the Vatican had granted the Spanish Crown. Even today, for example, the Argentine Government nominates to the Vatican the candidates for the Bishops there. In general terms the long colonial period and the first century of independence found the Catholic Church on the side of the rulers, with the humanitarian task of softening the worst defects of the reigning system. Thus, very early, Bartolomé de las Casas took over the protection of the American Indian, and the Jesuit Missions of Paraguay tried to redeem the situation of the natives. But, beginning with the second half of the last century, liberal currents, French positivism, the upsurge of Masonry, the coming of Protestantism, all drove the Church to a defensive position of looking for state protection and demanding the continuation of a type of authoritative society incapable of resisting the attacks of the incipient modernity. Consequently, the rise of liberalism is answered by excommunication, Protestantism by persecution, and modernity—and later, Marxism

—by a spirit of fear that sought shelter in anathema as a way of preserving its continental Catholic integrity.

All this traditional picture is now being submitted to total revision and truly revolutionary changes. The process that leads to these changes can be found in several causes.

At the end of the Second World War Pope Pius XII encouraged the evangelization of Latin America, which he saw in a world perspective as the spiritual reserve of Catholicism. Therefore, there was a call to multiply the missionary vocation in the United States, Canada and Europe towards Latin America, a continent that is recognized as especially lacking in ecclesiastical vocation. This invasion of foreigners, basically North Americans, produced a situation of dependency of the Catholic Church on foreign countries. At the same time it brought with it an element of change, of modernity that shook the prevailing routine. The theological currents of renewal in the countries from which the missionaries came filtered through and stirred up problems sometimes foreign to Latin America. Nevertheless, there were initiated processes which shaped a new generation of theologians, who later used the same intellectual structure for analysing their continental situation and for defining forms of witness and mission relevant to the new situation.

One result of this eagerness for modernity is the appearance of the Latin American Council of Bishops, CELAM, in 1955. It still had at that time a defensive attitude, but it was trying to develop a national conscience on a continental scale and to institute a programme for action.

The most fundamental episode of all was the

Second Vatican Council. In the words of a Latin American Bishop, the sessions of the Council were the real theological seminary in which the Latin American bishops studied. Coming from more or less traditional situations they were exposed to the thought and the opinions of the most illustrious theologians of Christianity. They had to live together with the Protestant and Orthodox observers. Their horizons were widened, and the Council's resolutions opened up the institutional possibility of carrying out experiments in a search for new forms of fidelity.

Another factor to be considered is the awakening of a revolutionary consciousness in Latin America, which had its symbolic expression in the victory of the Cuban Revolution. From that very moment the problems of the construction of a different Latin America were presented for the consideration of every institution, and the Church could not keep apart.

CROSSROADS

In Medellin in 1968 the Conference of Latin American Bishops assumed a radically revolutionary posture and adopted the motto *liberacion* as its imposing word and imposing task, challenging today's Catholics in our continent.

What the Reformation meant for European Christendom, Medellin means for Roman Catholicism. In the future it will be impossible to understand the history of the Church or the history of the continent without reference to this starting point as fundamental to contemporary Catholicism. It is there that it is recognized that 'Latin America seems to live still under the tragic emblem of underdevelopment, which separates the brethren from the joy not only of material goods, but also of the very human fulfilment.

In spite of the efforts that are made the results are hunger and poverty, widespread sickness, infant mortality, illiteracy and sub-human living, great inequalities in income and tensions between social classes, outbreaks of violence, and minimal participation of the people in the management of the common welfare.

'Recognizing this fact, and facing it' — says Medellin — 'the Church, as a part of the Latin American being, in spite of its limitations, has lived with our peoples in the process of colonization, liberation and organization. Our contribution does not wish to compete with the efforts for solution made by other national Latin American and world organizations, and certainly we do not reject them, nor overlook them. Our proposal is to encourage those efforts and accelerate their fulfilment, and deepen their content in the processes of change by applying Gospel values to them. We want to offer the collaboration of Christians compelled by their baptismal responsibilities and by the gravity of the moment. We do not want technical solutions nor infallible remedies. We want to feel the problems, perceive the demands, share the anguish, discover the road ahead, and co-operate in the solutions.

'The new image of the Latin American man demands a creative effort. The public powers, furthering energetically the supreme demands of the common welfare, the technicians planning the measures to be taken, the families and educators awakening and encouraging responsibilities, the peoples joining the common effort towards realization, the Spirit of the Gospel encouraging with the dynamic of love, offer the possibility of a transforming and personalizing redemption.

'Our most urgent commitment is to purify ourselves in the Spirit of the Gospel, all of us members of the Catholic Church. We should end the separation between faith and life, for "if we are in union with Christ—the only thing that counts is faith active in love".

'This commitment demands that we live a genuine Biblical poverty expressed in authentic manifestations which can be seen as clear signs for our people. Only a poverty of that quality will reveal Christ Saviour of men, and discover Christ, Lord of history.

'Our thoughts have clarified the dimensions of other commitments, which, though in a different mood, will be assumed by all of God's People :

—Inspire, encourage and urge a new order of justice, which will incorporate all men in the management of their own communities;

—Promote the constitution and the efficacy of the family, not only as a sacramental human community, but also as an intermediate structure to achieve social change.

—Make education more dynamic in order to accelerate the training of mature men for their responsibilities to the present hour.

—Promote workers' professional organizations, without doubt decisive elements in socio-economic transformation.

—Encourage a new evangelization and a new and intensive cathecism to reach both the élite and the masses and achieve a lucid and committed faith.

—Renew or create new structures in the Church which institutionalize dialogue and channel collaboration between bishops, priests, those in religious orders and laymen.

—Collaborate with other Christian confessions, and with all men of goodwill who are dedicated to an authentic peace rooted in justice and love.' (6)

Medellin highlights a radical opening to the world, and a definite opening to ecumenism. All the reports of several committees indicated the task in Latin America must be undertaken in relation to all the other Christian communities in the continent.

But it is obvious that an Assembly, no matter how important it is, is only a meeting producing documents until the latter are implemented in practice. Medellin postulated the doctrine, the ideology, the call to freedom. The implementation, the interpretation and the application of these resolutions in the local parishes have placed the Catholic Church in its most important hour of ferment. The internal tension is seen in every country, and it would be difficult to find a Latin American newspaper that made no reference to this type of problem on practically any day. There are still islands of conservatism in several Latin American dioceses. It is even possible that conservative forces could prevail. But the tendency is clearly towards a public engagement for a radical social change. For example, in relation to the electoral victory of Marxism in Chile in 1970, the Declaration of the Bishops of Chile says :

'We have co-operated, and we want to co-operate with the changes, especially with those that favour the poorest. We know that the changes are difficult, and that they bring great risks to all. We understand that it is hard to give up privileges. Therefore, we would do well to remember the teachings of Christ regarding the urgency of the brotherhood of men, which demands unselfishness and a better distribution of material goods.'

We can see that, in general, they go along with the process of change in society, even when the ecclesiastic institution maintains a policy of moderation and prudence. But in these countries there have sprung up clerical groups that take a much more radical position. Thus, for example, there is the movement called 'Young Church'. In reaction to the victory of Salvador Allende, they said :

'We have a great and historic task before us: to incorporate the Christian people in the creating of a new society on all work fronts. We will give our lives, if necessary in defence of the people's government and the consolidation of the new society.'

In Argentina the movement called 'Priests of the Third World' is resolved to join the revolutionary process, choosing a Latin American solution, which implies necessarily the socializing of the means of production, of economic power, of politics, and of culture.

In Colombia, the 'Golconda Priests' say :

'The energetic reprobation we make regarding neo-colonial capitalism, incapable of solving the pressing problems that trouble our people, encourages us in our actions and efforts looking towards the achievement of a socialist society which would permit the suppression of all forms of exploitation of man by man such as now happens in response to the historical tendencies of our time and the idiosyncracy of colonial man.'

Well known is the attitude of Helder Camara, Archbishop of Recife, denouncing the tortures and the situation of opprobrious poverty in his country, and demanding radical changes in society. In his case

33

is the added demand that non-violence be the method of action for attaining social change, a demand that is not given with the same urgency in the other movements we have cited.

All this makes the Catholic Church at the present time a creative ferment in Latin American society, and a positive promise for its future.

PROTESTANTISM

As for Protestantism, we must note that it has several origins that condition its history and its contemporary reality. We must realize that there are various Protestantisms. There is an immigrant Protestantism that came to Latin America to serve foreign citizens who brought their culture and their religion with them. The first churches were built in the coastal cities to minister basically to the spiritual needs of the English sailors and traders. Along the Latin American coast one can find the Anglican Churches, many of them now abandoned, signs of the commercial English presence that predominated for one hundred and fifty years. We also find the rural communities of German, Swiss and Italian origin. These churches long maintained their character of cultural islands in the sea of Latin American culture. Their point of reference was to be found in a far country. Their connexion was provided in the ancestral language. Their larger cultural possibility enabled them rapidly to prosper economically, and become, in most cases, groups of middle or upper class, who naturally are fearful of the situation of social change which they see approaching.

The leaders of these churches today are well aware of their pertinence to the Latin American situation, and that their future lies in the Spanish and Portuguese languages, in their incarnation in the national community, and that they must be open to contacts and to inter-church possibilities. Nevertheless, it is hard to overcome long-time habits of separation, defensive attitudes, and sometimes pride in relation to the surrounding community. The greater cultural possibility to which I have referred makes these groups an important potential contribution to the development of Latin America to the extent that they continue in a process of responsible integration in the surrounding community. This is a frontier to be grant-ed priority in the witness of the Church in Latin America.

The second sector of Latin American Protestantism is the product of missionary endeavour, fundamentally North American, but also British and Scandinavian.

Because of the ecumenical reticence manifested in Edinburgh, the historic missions did not enter Latin America with much enthusiasm. On the contrary, this region became the only mission field in which North American Fundamentalist groups have a notable pre-dominance in the number of missionaries sent and churches founded. Consequently, Latin American Protestantism is characterized by an evangelistic zeal which gives absolute priority to the numerical growth of the Church. Here the Churches had the greatest difficulty in regard to ecumenism with Roman Catholicism. Many were afraid that friendship with that Church would put a brake on the evangelistic thrust, which they consider essential to the Gospel.

Thus, just as the immigrant churches amount to cultural islands, these mission churches became sub-cultures separated from the rest of the world, bringing unconsciously certain values of the Saxon cultures and isolating their members from the rest of the continent. To save themselves from the surrounding sin they sought their protection and their sanctity in the Church. Since all should be evangelists, nobody had time for any other kind of activity in society. In this way there developed a Protestantism strongly individualistic, pious, and centred in the Bible, which was read as the bearer of a personal and devotional message.

From one of these groups, the Methodist Church in Chile particularly, and some missions from Scandinavia and the United States, the Pentecostal movement arose. One group in Chile, separated at the beginning of this century from the Methodists, has grown so much that, whereas the Methodist Church continues with 7,000 members, the Pentecostal movement which sprang from it, has about 700,000. This movement is characterized by a large group which is dynamic and has popular participation. It is made up largely of people who have lost their former roots in the countryside, who came to the cities in search of new horizons. The Church becomes for them the centre for personal and social integration. With emphasis on total salvation, which includes health, these Pentecostal groups are responding to the more intimate and felt needs of the common people. They can be criticized for repeating traditional sacral norms; that is, the Pastor assumes the roles that in the traditional patriarchal society were filled by the owner of the fief. It is he who blesses and curses, supplying salvation or judgment to the members of his congregation. In this respect the participation within a Pentecostal Church could be considered a continuing of submission, and an ignoring of what is happening in the world, all so characteristic of traditional society.

But this situation is rapidly changing. Second and third generation Protestant church people are realizing their full participation in the Latin American society. In fact the numerical growth means that the society itself is calling to the Protestant churches asking for a definition and relation to the basic problems of the human community. Even the Pentecostal Churches are realizing that they belong to the proletariat, the masses of oppressed people in Latin America who are also beginning to dream and to work for a new day. The ecumenical movement has surely been instrumental in this, through travels, scholarships, books, grants to seminaries, a process of theological reflection in action has taken place that is challenging the behaviour of the churches and is also challenging the realities of the society in Latin America. New ecumenical action groups have emerged in almost every country, where the traditional distinction between Protestant and Roman Catholics are overcome by a sense of common allegiance to the Christian faith in a particular human situation where that Christian faith demands action for the liberation of mankind. Christians, Catholics and Protestants are participating equally in the hopes and fears of Latin American society. It could be said that in several countries Christians are more exposed to the repression against challenging ideas because of the growing fear of the potential of the Church for social renewal. A *prioi* they cannot any longer be considered as allied to the *status quo.* The Roman Catholic Church has taken a more independent stance in relation to the State and the Protestant Churches are coming out of their isolation in sub-cultures. All of them are in the arena where a new Latin America is being forged. What could be the contribution of these churches, what should it be ? That is my next concern. But in order to be able to describe the vocation of the churches today, we must have a clear picture of our theological conviction concerning the history of mankind in general and the history of Latin America in particular.

CHAPTER III

Mission of the Church in Latin America

The mission of the Church cannot be understood except in the broader context of the mission of God.

The questions therefore are the following : What is God's purpose in the creation of humanity ? What is the goal toward which God is leading the human adventure ? What is the end, the meaning, the purpose of man's life on earth ? When those questions are answered the question of the particular role of the Church in the fulfilment of this divine plan can be discussed.

Of course, when one talks about the mission of God in terms of the purpose of history, one must beware of the temptation of making a philosophy or natural theology out of history, trying to interpret human events so as to draw from them a key or general conclusion that will indicate the direction to follow and the destiny assured. Throughout the centuries, every time that this effort has been made a heresy has resulted. It inevitably means applying to the interpretation of historical events a criterion that has been accepted *a priori* and that was extracted, consciously or unconsciously, from the philosophy that dominated the historian's perspective. One must recognize that there has always been an *a priori* criterion but it should be looked for in the revelation that is from God in the person of Jesus Christ and in the testimony of the scriptures. From there I will proceed to analyze the present Latin American situation to discover the specific mission of the Church in Latin America.

In Jesus Christ man discovers that God's concern is for the whole human person. In other words, God's mission does not deal with only one aspect of life that might be called the spiritual; it is a concern for the totality of the human being. Jesus Christ is not incarnate in an idea, in a spiritual being, but is incarnate-spirit, a human being totally subject to the limitations of the flesh; in that totality God grants man the supreme honour of being recognized as his son. The whole attitude of Jesus and his teaching confirms this lesson about his own personality. He not only seeks to change man's mind, he seeks to change the conditions of his life. He feeds the multitude, cures the sick, comforts the afflicted. The ethical judgments that he makes are based chiefly on the way in which men serve one another in the whole of their being : 'As you did it to one of the least of these my brethren'. The purpose of God therefore concerns the whole person.

In Jesus Christ we have God's supreme sacrifice for the benefit of the world and of all humanity. 'For the Son of man came to give his life as a ransom for many.' 'For God so loved the world that he gave his only Son.' 'God was in Christ reconciling the world to himself.' While there are phrases in the Gospel that speak to us of judgment and the seriousness of the decision that men make regarding the fact of

Jesus Christ, it is entirely clear that the intention of the Gospel is not limiting but inclusive; it wants 'all men to be saved and to come to the knowledge of truth'. Human evil is recognized, but there is divine acceptance which overcomes it : 'Father, forgive them for they know not what they do.'

The reconciliation that comes through Jesus Christ is a cosmic act; his death opens a new stage in the history of humanity. This is the stage of the preaching of the Gospel to be sure, the Messiah having come to describe the purpose of God for humanity. It is also the stage in which humanity is called to participate in carrying out this purpose, in the sure knowledge that nothing or nobody can frustrate the purpose of God.

In Judeo-Messianic thought the coming of the Messiah means the end of history, with the establishment of peace, the *shalom* of God in the world. In the Christian concept, the coming of the Messiah opens the eschatological period in which the peace of God is announced and the basis of that peace established in the assurance of pardon and reconciliation to God. Man is invited, however, to participate in the making of history, to seek in the spirit of the Messiah the establishment of peace on earth. 'If any man would come after me, let him deny himself and take up his cross and follow me.' 'As the Father has sent me, even so I send you.'

This concern of God in Christ for the entire person and for all human history confirms the best tradition of the Old Testament. The covenant of God with Noah after the flood includes all humanity in the promise of God that never again will waters totally cover the earth; the seasons are to follow one another in sequence. The natural environment of human activity is assured by God. In the election of the Hebrew people in Abraham the intention of God to benefit all humanity is also clear. 'In you all the families of the earth will be blessed.' This does not mean that God chooses a people to make them the object of his personal interest while he forgets the rest of humanity. Throughout the centuries God has always had a witness in every people. But he chooses one people for a particular mission : to reveal his name, to decipher the meaning of history, to be the bearer of the promises for humanity. This mission is one of suffering in favour of all mankind.

In the Old Testament there is the beginning of that specific vocation of one sector of humanity in favour of the whole that becomes evident in the person of Jesus Christ.

That the people of Israel has been chosen for *one* mission does not mean that God may not choose other people, other groups, other circumstances, to fulfil other forms of his mission which may serve the overall purpose: to establish the unity of mankind, peace on earth.

One day it will be Cyrus who through his military conquests will determine history in such a way that it fulfils the plan of God. Another day it will be Rome that will establish the conditions in which the Gospel can be preached. But whether the agent works in direct and dynamic relation with the people that bear the revelation and the promise, or whether it acts in the antipodes of the planet creating more human conditions with no historic connexion to the people of the Promise, in one or another case, these peoples, these historic agents, are also actors in the great purpose of God for humanity and consequently co-workers with God. We might say it this way : in the

42

light of the Scriptures the purpose of God for humanity is clear — to gather all things together in Christ, the total recapitulation that implies the establishment of *shalom*, peace, one of the dominant concepts of the whole Bible.

This *shalom*, or peace, is not a concept with a merely spiritual connotation. It incorporates a series of values that today we would call material, but which in the scriptural understanding are deeply spiritual. The image of *shalom* that the Old Testament gives us is that of the man who is seated under the vine and receives his friends and entertains them with the fruit of the vine. He is a man who enjoys the tranquility of his family, who sees the fruit of his work and who is able to live in a harmonious relation of security and communication with his neighbour.

Security, family, work, human fellowship — these are the basic elements that the idea of *shalom*, the notion of peace, embodies. Everything that leads humanity in the direction of this peace, everything that brings people closer to each other is a form of contribution to, a progression toward, and an orientation in the direction of, that history, which is the gathering together of all things in Jesus Christ. A reconciliation on the plane of political life, some progress in the struggle for justice, all these are ways to contribute to God's mission, to be involved in fulfilling his will. In the light of what God shows us in Jesus Christ of his purpose for humanity these events cease to be secular and become profoundly sacred and deeply religious events. It is in such events that God's saving interest for all humanity is manifest.

The salvation which Christ brought, and in which we participate, offers a comprehensive wholeness in this divided life. We understand salvation as newness of life— the unfolding of true humanity in the fulness of God. It is

43

salvation of the soul and the body, of the individual and society, mankind and 'the groaning creation'. As evil works both in personal life and in exploitative social structures which humiliate humankind, so God's justice manifests itself both in the justification of the sinner and in social and political justice.

As guilt is both individual and corporate so God's liberating power changes both persons and structures. We have to overcome the dichotomies in our thinking between soul and body, person and society, humankind and creation. Therefore we see struggles for economic justice, political freedom and cultural renewal as elements in the total liberation of the world through the mission of God. This liberation is finally fulfilled when 'death is swallowed up in victory'. This comprehensive notion of salvation demands of the whole of the people of God a matching comprehensive approach to their participation in salvation.

BIBLICAL PARADIGMS

Two biblical paradigms have become classics in Latin America: the Exodus and the Babylonian Captivity. The Hebrew people come to Egypt looking for protection and soon fall into salvery. Their condition grows steadily worse as they are dominated and subjected. To this people God sends Moses, a liberator and agitator. Moses calls the people to leave for a promised land. He breaks the existing relations within which the people had accepted their situation of oppression. Moses has to work hard to convince a people accustomed to oppression that there is a new day for them. The struggle of the leader is not merely with Pharaoh; it is primarily with a people whom he has to mobilize. In Exodus Chapter 5 we find the people saying to Moses: 'The Lord look upon you and judge.' It is as if they are saying, 'May God punish you for coming here to complicate our lives, since you have made us abominable before Pharaoh and his servants, putting the sword in their hand to kill us.' When the word gets out that this people wants to become free, the repression and oppression are made harder and more difficult. The people want to give up and stop struggling. Moses tries to name the hunger for bread, for freedom, for land, for new life, for national and independent life, that is dormant in the domesticated people. He has to show how the secular act of freedom that they seek is rooted in God's will and is the response to a biblical call.

It is only in the perspective of this faith that the simple people, even without understanding it all, begin their march through the desert in search of the promised land.

If there had been on Mount Sinai a historian, a sociologist or an anthropologist who looked at that tattered people, he would have said that it was a purely social event, just one more tribe seeking the possibility of a better life. So it is today, the country people, the mountain people and immigrants from another country come to the outskirts of the cities. They are those who, just like the Hebrew people, motivated by material hunger and hunger for freedom seek something of greater worth in life, something that the captivating lights of the city symbolize.

Moses knew how to give guidance and how to show the strong vocation of that people's march. The Church in Latin America today is facing popular movements and has to sharpen its vision of faith to see them, not only as social phenomena, describable by social, political and economic co-ordinates, but also as a march toward the tomorrow that God promises, as a hunger for a worthwhile life, as a response of the simple Latin American people to the hunger for eternity that God put in their hearts. Thus the Church in Latin America today is ready to call the people to march and to encourage them on that march. But the wave of repression that sweeps the continent makes me think seriously of another biblical paradigm.

In chapter 29 of the book of the prophet Jeremiah there is the letter he writes to those who have been carried into captivity. The prophet gives the captives advice which does not seem very revolutionary :

> Build houses and live in them; plant gardens and eat their produce. Take wives and have sons and daughters; take wives for your sons, and give your daughters in marriage, that they may bear sons and daughters; multiply there, and do not decrease. But seek the welfare of the city where I have sent you into exile, and pray to the Lord on its behalf, for in its welfare you will find your welfare. For thus says the Lord of hosts, the God of Israel : Do not let your prophets and your diviners who are among you deceive you, and do not listen to the dreams which they dream, for it is a lie which they are prophesying to you in my name; I did not send them, says the Lord. For thus says the Lord : When seventy years are completed for Babylon, I will visit you, and I will fulfil to you my promises and bring you back to this place. For I know the plans I have for you, says the Lord, plans for welfare and not for evil, to give you a future and a hope.

Jeremiah is saying that God has his time. The response of people who want to obey God is not exactly the same in all historic circumstances. There are times when patience is the test of faithfulness and times when the march, the exodus, the search for liberty is the proper action. But at all times the promise of liberation is present. Even the words sent by Jeremiah to the captives presuppose that the waiting and working is to be done for the sake of a new tomorrow that God is promising. The day will come when the voice in Isaiah will speak saying : 'Speak tenderly to Jerusalem, and cry to her that her time of service is ended, that her iniquity is pardoned.'

46

THE KAIROS

Alongside the well-known 'Theology of Liberation' in Latin America there is beginning to emerge a 'Theology of Captivity'. In both cases we find that the intention is to discover the *Kairos*, the moment of God.

In the confusion of our time the Latin American Church has to discern where the search for the peace that God promises us is leading. The Church has to inspire the people's hopes and at the same time protect those hopes with a big dose of realism. It has to maintain a capacity to live in the midst of circumstances that seem mutilated and the ability to dream and plan in the midst of days that appear to have no tomorrow.

Latin America lives between hope and fear, between enthusiasm and repression, between the hallelujah of the manifestation and the darkness of oppression. In these circumstances the Church of Jesus Christ that knows the secret of the divine purpose for human history is called upon to fulfil a mission: to maintain a dimension of humanity, to keep open to the people the possibility of the new day. It must find the specific role that belongs to the people of faith in this historic span.

As Miguel Brun says, 'the mission of the Church is none other than to serve God in the fulfilment of his promise of total liberation for the world. The mission, therefore, is not the Church's but God's. It is not the Church that frees, it is God through Jesus Christ. The mission of the Church is to act instrumentally, moved by the Spirit of God, in favour of his liberating action'. (8) Our problem is to try to define the specific functions of the Church. In Moses the political and religious tasks coincide, but this coinci-

47

dence does not occur in general in Hebrew-Christian history. The Church, as a community of faith, is not concerned with the conquest of power, nor is that its vocation. God has other instruments for the exercise of power among men. On the other hand, it is very difficult to make a distinction of planes between the Church, the community of faith and the secular community in exercising a joint responsibility for the welfare of people. The Bangkok Conference 1973 recognized that for the community of faith there are different priorities for the common ministry in the same hope of salvation.

'But there are historical priorities according to which salvation is anticipated in one dimension first, be it the personal, the political or the economic dimension. These points of entry differ from situation to situation in which we work and suffer. We should know that such anticipations are not the whole of salvation, and must keep in mind the other dimensions while we work. Forgetting this denies the wholeness of salvation. Nobody can do in any particular situation everything at the same time. There are various gifts and tasks, but there is one spirit and one goal. In this sense, it can be said, for example, that salvation is peace for the people in Vietnam, independence in Angola, justice and reconciliation in Northern Ireland and release from the captivity of power in the North Atlantic community, or personal conversion in the release of a submerged society into hope, or of new life styles amid corporate self-interest and love-lessness.' (9)

In an effort to clarify the general thinking let us start from the biblical text : 'As the Father has sent me, even so I send you.' (John 20:21). Some assume that the mission of the Church is the prolongation in time of the mission of Christ. In other words, the specific mission of the Church must be fulfilled according to Christ's historical model. But one is not dealing with an imitation of one's personal mission to give one's life for the salvation of the world but with the acceptance of one's missionary style as a standard for the community of the faith. Thus, it will help in organizing one's thought to describe for the Church the tasks that correspond to the traditional roles that belong to Jesus Christ—prophet, priest and servant king.

CHAPTER IV

The Church as Prophet

The image of the prophet in the Old Testament is generally that of a solitary person who struggles against the established order in the name of a vision or a word from God. Generally he has no social authority. However, the Church in Latin America must assume its prophetic role from a position of influence and social prestige. It cannot evade responsibility for the institutional influence of the Church. The traditional alliance between the Church and its milieu is symbolized by the presence of imposing Church buildings in the farthest corners of the continent and by the continuation even today of Church participation in civic acts that invest those acts with a certain sacredness.

The traditional Church-State alliance led to a paradoxical situation in Chile after the military *coup.* On September 18, the Chilean National Independence Day, it is customary to celebrate a *Te Deum* of thanksgiving for the nation with the attendance of the civic authorities. In 1973, although the military *coup* and the death of President Allende were very recent memories, the military *junta* as a whole was present in the cathedral for the service. The *Te Deum* was an

ecumenical event and its organizers made clear that
they wanted to dedicate it to national peace and
reconciliation. But the nation's press, functioning only
with the new government's permission, emphasized
the element of thanksgiving in the service and, consequently sought to show Church approval of the new
military government. The illustration shows the
participation of the masses in religious life and the
abiding presence of the Church in Latin American
civic life.

Events in the church community have repercussions
in secular life. The Church is not the only decision-
making centre for Latin American problems.
Economic, political and military forces also participate, as does the omnipresence of foreign dependency. However, because of its social presence and
the religious loyalty of the masses the Church is an
element of coercion of social protest that is essential
in the building of Latin America's future.

Holding to this view I believe that theological positions which choose a status of political asepsis for
the Church are seeking an impossibility.

There are religious groups that are growing rapidly
in Latin America. Some eleven million people in Brazil
participate in spiritist cults which are forms of escape
from the surrounding reality. But the Church cannot
escape. Its convictions about its responsibility for all
human life and its own social position makes it an
element of action or reaction in the community.

In his book, *A Theology of Liberation*, Gustavo
Gutierrez says it this way :

> The 'social problem' or the 'social question' has been
> discussed in Christian circles for a long time, but it is
> only in the last few years that people have become clearly
> aware of the scope of misery and especially of the
> oppressive and alienating circumstances in which the great

majority of mankind exists. This state of affairs is offensive to man and therefore to God. Moreover, today people are more deeply aware both of personal responsibility in this situation and the obstacles these conditions present to the complete fulfilment of all men, exploiters and exploited alike.

People are also more keenly and painfully aware that a large part of the Church is one way or another linked to those who wield economic and political power in today's world. This applies to its position in the opulent and oppressive countries as well as in the poor countries, as in Latin America, where it is tied to the exploiting classes. Under these circumstances, can it honestly be said that the Church does not interfere in 'the temporal sphere'? Is the Church fulfilling a purely religious role when by its silence or friendly relationships it lends legitimacy to a dictatorial and oppressive government ? We discover, then, that the policy of non-intervention in political affairs holds for certain actions which involve ecclesiastical authorities, but not for others. In other words, this principle is not applied when it is a question of maintaining the *status quo*, but it is wielded when, for example, a lay apostolic movement or a group of priests holds an attitude considered subversive to the established order. Concretely, in Latin America the distinction of planes model has the effect of concealing the real political option of the Church—that is, support of the established order. It is interesting to note that when there was no clear understanding of the political role of the Church the distinction of planes model was disapproved of by both civil and ecclesiastical authorities. But when the system—of which the ecclesiastical institution is a central element—began to be rejected, this same model was adopted to dispense the ecclesiastical institution from effectively defending the oppressed and exploited and to preach a lyrical spiritual unity of all Christians. The dominant groups, who have always used the Church to defend their interests and maintain their privileged position, today—as they see 'subversive' tendencies gaining ground in the heart of the Christian community—call for a return to the purely religious and spiritual function of the Church. (10)

The churches, at least on the level of declarations of purpose, seek a new identification with the people, a close experience with reality, which will enable them to act prophetically.

Jesus Christ made the lot of the poor of the earth his own by being born in a manger and living in a proletarian home. He made the death of the despised his own by being raised up on a cross in the company of two others condemned to death.

As the Medellin meeting says :

> Christ, our Saviour, not only loved the poor, but rather being rich He became poor, He lived in poverty. His mission centred on advising the poor of their liberation and He founded His Church as the sign of that poverty among men.

> The Church itself has always tried to fulfil that vocation, notwithstanding 'very great weaknesses and flaws in the past'. The Latin American Church, given the continent's conditions of poverty and underdevelopment, experiences the urgency of translating that spirit of poverty into actions, attitudes and norms that make it a more lucid and authentic sign of its Lord. The poverty of so many brothers cries out for justice, solidarity, open witness, commitment, strength and exertion directed to the fulfilment of the redeeming mission to which it is committed by Christ.

> The present situation, then, demands from bishops, priests, religious and laymen the spirit of poverty which, 'breaking the bonds of the egotistical possession of temporal goods, stimulates the Christian to order organically the power and the finances in favour of the common good'.

> The poverty of the Church and of its members in Latin America ought to be a sign of the inestimable value of the poor in the eyes of God, an obligation of solidarity with those who suffer. (11)

Identification is made not only on the poverty level but also on the level of hope. The Church is beginning to realize that it belongs in the culture of poverty and it sees in that culture the possibility of a new formulation of the Gospel more faithful to the action of the living God in Latin America. From that awareness all kinds of liturgical experiments are taking place in order to express a new identity with the people of Latin America.

But the prophet not only lives in the midst of his people and makes their lot his own, he fulfils a conscientising role. Moses had to perform the task of *conscientisation* of an oppressed people; he had to help them understand the possibilities of their situation by virtue of the promise of divine help. In a more secular language, today's Christian practises his vocation by helping people to be aware of the limitations that oppress them and of the historical possibilities of changing them.

From this point of view, one of the most creative and fruitful efforts which has been implemented in Latin America is the experimental work of Paulo Freire, who has sought to establish a 'pedagogy of the oppressed'. By means of an unalienating and liberating 'cultural action', which links theory with praxis, the oppressed person perceives—and modifies—his transfer from a 'naive awareness'—which does not deal with problems, gives too much value to the past, tends to accept mythical explanations and tends towards debate—to a 'critical awareness', which delves into problems, is open to new ideas, replaces magical explanations with real causes and tends to dialogue. In this process, which Freire calls *conscientisation*, the oppressed person rejects the oppressive consciousness which dwells in him, becomes aware of his situation, and finds his own language. He becomes, by himself, less dependent and freer, as he commits himself to the transformation and building up of society. Let us specify, also, that this critical awareness is not a state reached once and for all, but rather a permanent effort of man who seeks to situate himself in time and space, to exercise his creative potential, and to assume his responsibilities. Awareness is, therefore, relative to each historical stage of a people and of mankind in general. (12)

Next in importance is the task of building a critical consciousness of society within the Christian community. Even in repressive situations it is possible to structure channels of communication in the Church and to help small groups become aware of their problems and search for solutions. For example, in Brazil it is practically impossible to find the name of Archbishop Helder Camara of Recife in the press or on radio or TV. All news that relates to him is censored. However, by virtue of internal channels of communication in the Church his thought and example are known by millions. The Church is thus an institution with potential to challenge, to a certain extent, conditions established by the *status quo* and to reach important sectors of the population which otherwise would be moulded by the mass media.

A third endeavour in the prophetic task is the desacralization of existing structures by theological criticism.

When private ownership is held to be a sacred right, the Church's discussion of property ownership rights——because God is the sole owner of the earth——desacralizes the issue, destroys barriers and frees collective consciousness to create alternatives. When the Church discusses and analyzes the praxis and reality of the people in Latin America in theological texts it contributes an element which challenges the prevailing situation. On the popular level the Church has an acceptance greater than that of competitive parties or groups. It is harder to undermine the Church's position by accusing it of communism or marxism than it is to undermine secular political groups. In this sense theological reflection on the surrounding reality, if it is projected beyond the inner church framework, is a prophetic contribution to the discussion of Latin America's present and future.

But 'prophetic denunciation' in the Bible means something more. Its task is one of *conscientisation;*

it also performs the work of teaching and training a group of close followers of the Prophet. It puts forth principles or guidelines of God's action in history; it culminates in the condemnation of existing conditions and assumes the risks that go with denunciatory action.

In Latin America the Church and Christian groups have made their voice heard clearly with reference to specific situations and problems. Christians have had to pay, and are paying, the price of martyrdom for this witness.

See, for example, what the small Methodist Church of Bolivia says in a manifesto which was delivered to the President of the nation by church leaders.

> In the background of this situation stand oppressive international structures such as imperialism and the economic and warmongering interests of the great powers. Like the rest of the Third World, we are obliged to sell raw materials at low prices and buy back goods manufactured by workers abroad who receive ten, twenty, or even thirty times the wages which Bolivian workers receive. Foreign investors seek to exploit our resources under conditions which are unacceptable in other countries and which are injurious to our national sovereignity and dignity.
>
> There are also internal exploiters, privileged Bolivian minorities who act in connivance with international and anti-national interests. The truth is that not only do they buy us, but we sell ourselves. The will power and heavy bureaucracy of state organizations; the mercenariness of politicians and functionaries; the eagerness for rapid wealth; the lack of responsibility and discipline; the cowardliness that hinders our committing ourselves responsibly; the lack of courage and hope to work for the future; the instability of our governments; the inconsequence of opposition groups and political parties; and the lack of continuity in effort——these are also undeniable causes of our backwardness.
>
> As Christian and Bolivian citizens, we are disturbed by some aspects of our present government : the excessive placement of military personnel in key positions of all

areas of the government, with a consequent duplication of salaries; the lack of participation by the people, even at the municipal level; the indefinite suspension of the Constitution and the absence of a representative legislative body; the precarious existence of the judicial power in relation to the *de facto* government; the uncontrolled verticality of government decisions. There is an apparent inconsistency between nationalist declarations and some practices, such as the unfulfilled promise of amnesty and political liberty for political leaders who intended to return to the country.

To be Christian does not make us infallible, but it does obligate us to speak out even at the risk of making mistakes. We must give the present Bolivian government opportunity to carry out its programme according to its declared platform. It is necessary to overcome the immaturity of repeatedly starting abortive 'revolutions'. At the same time, the government must be sensitive to the reality of this present moment in history. It must be willing to listen, to rectify, and to open the deepening revolutionary process to the participation of all the Bolivian people. Only thus will it be able to fulfil the historic role that it wants to undertake. (13)

This statement makes what Gustavo Gutierrez has to say understandable :

Frequently in Latin America today certain priests are considered 'subversive'. Many are under surveillance or are being sought by the police. Others are in prison, have been expelled from their country (Brazil, Bolivia, Colombia, and the Dominican Republic are significant examples), or have been murdered by terrorist anti-communist groups. For the defenders of the *status quo*, 'priestly subversion' is surprising. They are not used to it. The political activity of some leftist groups, we might say, is—within certain limits—assimilated and tolerated by the system and is even useful to it to justify some of its repressive measures; the dissidence of priests and those of religious orders, however, appears as particularly dangerous, especially if we consider the role which they have traditionally played. (14)

CHAPTER V

The Church as Priest

The prophetic function of the Church is related to the structural problems of Latin American society. Thus *conscientisation*, internal communication, the theological analysis of social problems and the specific word are described as a commitment of the Church which originates from its identification with the poor, the marginal and the exploited.

This description may be criticized as too secular and out of character with the Church's specific vocation to reconcile and unite all things to God. But the prophet begins to speak, from an awakening of consciousness, of a relationship to the Eternal and from that his value judgments on surrounding situations emerge. The prophet is not a sociologist although he works with data from sociology and the social sciences. He is a man of faith and on the basis of faith speaks out from the midst of human life on personal and social conditions that restrict humanity's fulfilment and keep the abundant life promised by Jesus Christ from being a reality for people and society.

Therefore, my division into chapters is artificial and is only useful for explanation. When one speaks of the Church in its priestly function the prophetic mission is not forgotten. Of course, one cannot speak of a prophetic function without the existence of a community called to the priesthood; neither can one speak of the priesthood unless there are signs of the Church's prophetic action.

By the Church's priestly action I understand the task of linking man to God and man to man. It is the creation of peace with God and peace with one's neighbour.

It may seem that now I am using more pious and traditional language. When one tries to bind the whole life of a community more closely to the life of God there must come a time when this intent to bind is done consciously. There must be a symbolic moment which somehow represents the entire scope of concern. Liturgy or worship cannot be a substitute for militancy or service to God expressed in work and concern for our neighbour. Every good work sings praises to the Lord. But worship, a conscious encounter with the community of faith as it tries to co-ordinate its life with the divine purpose, fulfils a vicarious, representative and symbolical function. It is the moment when one stops to be aware that life has meaning when seen in the perspective of divine will and in the context of obedience to that will as it is known in Jesus Christ.

Worship may be defined as the conscious attempt of the community to relate the life of all society to its Lord. It is a moment, a happening, an event, an occasion to which one comes with expectation, opening oneself to the mystery, trusting that the Holy Spirit will act and prepare Christians to receive judgment and inspiration from God.

Some Marxists will state that religion is the

'opiate of the people' since oppressed people create religion to soften their existence and enable themselves to endure the oppression they suffer. They promise themselves a reward in the future while they endure the present situation. But the experience of worship can be dynamite when it becomes contemplation on the God who acts in history and invites us to see his action in everyday life.

When God is praised for his creative acts and the Lord of history is worshipped the attention of Christians will concentrate on secular events. For a Church that reads Latin American history and sees in that history the hand of God leading people to a new stage of humanization and freedom, for a Church that wants to co-operate with the coming of a new day for Latin American people, worship is the moment when all that expectation, hope and concern is brought and placed before God.

When God is seen as one who is concerned for all of human life, as his passion and concern to be a servant show him to be, Christians fall to their knees confessing their sin.

Of course 'sin' refers to its full manifestation, at both the individual and the institutional levels. As a young person said, 'the churches have been obsessed with sexual sins and have often protested against them, but they have forgotten to ask, "How can we love our neighbour, the neighbour who is suffering under present social conditions?"'

Thus, the experience of worship is an element of popular *conscientisation*, a deepening of individual vocation and the presentation of the events of human history before the throne of Grace, in the hope that thereby divine wisdom and inspiration may become manifest.

In Latin America liturgy is not confined to large church institutions. It emerges as well in grassroots communities as small groups of Christians meet for prayer, Bible reading and meditation. In these circles a climate of confidence is created which permits frank discussion of the commitment of the Christian Church and of each member of the group.

The Church in performing this priestly function of joining the life of the individual with society is performing its specified vocation and rendering an important service to society. It disseminates information, stimulates consciences, summons people to a vocation, purifies intentions, inspires courage and nourishes hope.

Evangelization, another fundamental task of the Church, also demonstrates the importance that church life has for the future of the Latin American people, since in the call to conversion, repentance and discipleship there is a summons to work for liberation. If the biblical message of union with the missionary God, the liberating God, the God whose purpose we know in Christ, sounds forth we are unable to escape to a private religion.

Christians are called to an obedience that incorporates them into the community of faith and into the secular human communities where they must give witness to the faith in sacrificial service.

In the hard Latin American situation, face to face with oppression and repression, it is important for those who fight for the cause of justice to be rooted in a worshipping community. They need a personal experience of encounter with the God who liberates, to understand that even their historical failures are not the final word, but that they are enrolled in the service of a God who knows the secret of history and knows how to use even failures to carry history to its goal.

The priestly task of the Church is not exhausted in the evangelistic task of calling to discipleship nor in the communal task of worship in which the encounter of God with the world is symbolized in depth; it also has to do with the encounter of persons and their reconciliation.

Of course, there is an important presupposition here : that the absence of conflict is not synonymous with peace, that conflict is not in itself destructive of the basic communion which unites us, but rather can help our communion to reach a firm basis. Faith forbids that we cry 'Peace !' when there is no peace. Jesus did not hesitate to call the powerful of his time 'whitened sepulchres'. He rejected the possible roads to compromise suggested by his apostles or even by Pilate himself.

In as much as Christ challenges us to take a stand with the disinherited of the earth, it is He who leads us towards division. Of course, we can be mistaken in our interpretation of the signs of the times and our judgments as to the best ways of raising the disinherited to their central role in history. But the seriousness of our choice is offered in obedience to Jesus Christ. This means that conflict within the Christian Church not only repeats to a certain degree the divisions which exist in secular societies, it also deepens them, since the passion and loyalty which mark us as Christians are also present in the various choices we make.

We cannot see the destiny of our neighbour as a marginal issue; it is a basic choice : we either serve Christ or reject him. Christian conversion—the orientation of our lives based on acceptance of the pardon and salvation which God offers us in Christ—demands militant discipleship in the service of our neighbour. But it is in the fulfilment of that discipleship that the divisions arise. Hence the burden of the pain which accompanies them. Hence also the creative possibilities within the conflict which oblige us to live with the tension until we find a means of solution.

Thus, it is not because the Church may be above conflicts that it offers the service of reconciliation.

The Church has a long tradition as mediator in social conflicts. Over the centuries its presence has provided solace at times of great human tension. It has been assumed that to a certain extent the Church would be above the conflicts which divided society at any given moment.

But the word 'reconciliation', the Christian Church's gesture of solidarity, can only be credible when it bears the marks of the Cross, when the Church has not remained outside the conflict but has participated in the destiny of the dispossessed.

In God's purpose all things are to be summed up in Jesus Christ. That is our goal, and the basis of our life. We move in this eschatological tension, amid the conflict which we aim to overcome, in the hope of that reconciliation, whose foundation God has placed in Jesus Christ and whose consummation we will see in the fulness of this Kingdom. Since we participate in God's mission, pursuing its way amidst the activities of men in history, we live out each situation of conflict in the hope that it will reveal its full liberating potential; at the same time, we have to establish signs of reconciliation, those symbolic actions which will allow men to believe that the conflict is not final, not absolute, that beyond it lies a promise of reconciliation and fulfilment to which we can aspire.

Traditional social service activities of the churches, often criticized for dealing only with the consequences of social evil without attacking its roots, can also be understood as a means of establishing symbols of the reconciliation we seek, not just as a means of patching up the situation by postponing necessary conflict. We have to recognize, however, that there are many situations which simply do not allow the kind of conflict which offers hope of human liberation. Although this judgment has perhaps more to do with political tactics than with theology, we would be blind if we did not recognize the fact that in some semi-closed situations it is premature to try to achieve a truly liberating conflict. The only realistic possibility might be to create partial human encounters bringing about temporary reconciliation in the existing situation. This might be the only way if we are truly searching for a social and emotional basis from which the radical nature of the problems and the resulting conflict can eventually be faced. Indiscriminate social service—such as Red Cross-type

63

activities—can raise up signs of humanity amid situations of aggressivity, bearing in mind our common participation in man's ultimate need for livelihood and survival. Social service can also preserve social groups from total submission to enslaving circumstances. When there is no prospect of conditions favourable to the conflict which could bring about radical change in the structure of society and thus in the oppression men suffer, there can still be interim situations in which men can regain courage and become aware of the human dignity which will eventually allow them to face the basic problems. In this sense, 'reconciliation', by rescuing man from servility, submission and resentment, and by helping him to become aware of his situation, will be a liberating factor, although at the same time we recognize that such 'reconciliation', while it offers possibilities for pursuing more deeply the necessary social dialogue, may also by that same token make the conflict all the more serious.

In other words, the violence implicit in the social situation can be made less acute by Christian social service which eliminates one dimension of social hate. At the same time, however, that same social service can awaken the consciousness of the oppressed to the magnitude of their problems and equip them to raise the questions and indeed pursue the demands which will lead to their liberation.

Continual intercession for peace in situations of conflict, which can similarly be criticized as premature pacification, can be equally seen as a truly liberating possibility. To implore God to intervene, which we criticize if it is taken to mean that the battle will go differently under God's supervision, provides nevertheless an opportunity to calm our spirits and see the conflict in its true dimensions. Social experience—at least in Latin America—has taught us the importance conflicting groups can on occasion give to the church as providing a certain breathing space in the situation. This can permit the struggle to be humanized and can help avoid the most desperate solutions. To live out reconciliation in the light of the Cross should at least prevent religious intolerance from taking a part in our social conflicts. By religious intolerance I do not mean the hatred generated by religious loyalties, but rather the state of emotional exaltation in which hatred becomes the guiding power of human action. To do away with hatred as a

key factor in social struggle would be a significant liberation of the combatants. For the struggle for liberty is not
carried out only at the level of outward opposition between
men, but within each human conscience. To the extent
that we believe that men have a common destiny, a tomorrow towards which we all strive and which has been
affirmed by God in Jesus Christ—in which we shall have
to meet as brothers—we are already helping to eliminate
irrational factors in our conflicts. (15)

This situation is exemplified by the service that the
Churches in Chile are rendering in the present situation. They were the first group that could organize
for the protection of foreign political refugees threat-
ened with a rapid expulsion to their countries of
origin. Through the work of the Churches an immediate human service was performed which laid the
basis for a new beginning of community dialogue
within Chile.

This situation illustrates quite well what the
Bishops said in Medellin :

Peace is, above all, a work of justice. It presupposes and
requires the establishment of a just order in which men
can fulfil themselves as men, where their dignity is respected, their legitimate aspirations satisfied, their access to
truth recognized, their personal freedom guaranteed; an
order where man is not an object, but an agent of his own
history. Therefore, there will be attempts against peace
where unjust inequalities among men and nations prevail.
Peace in Latin America, therefore, is not the simple
absence of violence and bloodshed. Oppression by the
power groups may give the impression of maintaining
peace and order, but in truth it is nothing but the 'continuous and inevitable seed of rebellion and war'.

Peace can only be obtained by creating a new order which
carries with it a more perfect justice among men. It is in
this sense that the integral development of man, the path
to more human conditions, becomes the symbol of
peace. (16)

CHAPTER VI

The Church as Servant

In traditional theology the offices of Christ are those of prophet, priest and king. I use the translation servant in our title because I understand it as the best way to describe the royal character of Jesus Christ according to the Gospel and the best way to present a model of action and life for the Christian Church.

When the sons of Zebedee come asking for the first places in the kingdom Jesus tells them : 'You know not what you ask'. His throne will be a cross; the two first places will be other crosses. Because he is the Lord he takes the towel and the basin to wash his disciples' feet. Because he is the Lord, he takes upon himself the burden of service and the suffering of the world.

The Church will have authority to the degree that it renounces human power. Only in the function of a total surrender of power to the service of God in its neighbour can the Church again find a dimension of spiritual and moral authority effective even in the social circumstances of Latin America.

What then will be the servant emphasis that the

Church should make in Latin America today ? I do not propose to enter into a discussion of the subject of Christian social service or how the solution of structural problems is to be sought, or whether the action of the Church goes to the roots or whether it is purely remedial assistance. It is very difficult to establish a dividing line in general terms and much more difficult to apply it to concrete situations where perhaps the only possibility is immediate assistance to keep alive those who some day will have a chance to confront the structural problems.

In Latin America projects have been classified so as to show the various possibilities : projects of Christian charity that imply immediate service for a need without regard to ideological problems : reformist or modernizing projects which, while they do not confront the radicality of the problem, have some elements of conscientisation and are open to the future : revolutionary projects which go to the root of Latin American dependency : and projects that are frankly reactionary and maintain a situation of oppression, and consequently should be rejected. Welfare charity, reform and revolution — here are the great possibilities for Christian action in Latin America.

But it is important to point out some fundamental priorities of the present time. First, one must refer to the life and sacrificial presence of Christians within Latin American society. Groups that preach and practise non-violent methods of social change in the continent are performing small but symbolic acts of presence in relation to the problems that afflict the people. It is too soon to state whether they offer clear options for the present situation, but in view of the failure of various violent and even electoral solutions it is worth asking if non-violence as a method of appealing to the community conscience to change social structures might not have a right to be tried.

In this sense the task of Archbishop Helder Camara has found international backing. How many groups can be formed which will assume responsibility for the fullness of personhood for Latin Americans and at the same time surrender to suffering, sacrifice and 'death' itself, with the desire to avoid an increase in the level of violence that prevails in society ? In the urgency of the Latin American situation there is no time to lose in discussions on violence and non-violence. Those who are committed to non-violence should prove the efficiency, the validity of their approach not by discussing with those who do not share that conviction, but by struggling with the factors of oppression in society. Christians may make a contribution by incorporating into structures of social struggle spiritual values that can mean real challenges to prevailing situations. All non-violent action carries with it a dimension of martyrdom to which the churches are now called. When the risen Lord appears to the disciples they can only recognize him because he shows his wounded side and pierced hands. These are the signs of his participation in the suffering of the people and the acceptance of a major role in the sacrifice of the people who will authenticate the work of the Church in all spheres, whether of charity, reform or revolution.

The Latin American Church must offer the service of hope; it must be the people of hope; it must transmit hope. The Apostle Paul would say that in hope we were saved, that 'we hope against hope'. When the horizon is dark and there is a temptation to resignation, Christians who know the resources of God have to lift up the utopia of faith as an inspiration to maintain openness to the opportunities of history. Moses had to speak of the land that flows with milk and honey because in that vision the exhausted Israelites found energy to keep marching in the desert of Sinai.

Insofar as the Latin American Church arouses a dimension of hope the people can be called to action which is coherent with that hope.

The formation of utopias, conceived as the description of another *topos*, another place to create, one which challenges the present, is fundamental in the community organization of popular will. Without a dream toward which to point, without hope from which to act, there is no possibility of the popular mobilization which is necessary for effective historical action.

But at the present time Christians are in a situation of involution in the liberation process, a situation that can be defined as 'captivity'. Popular longing and hope for a new type of society are buried by the brutality of power relationships in the Latin American scene. And then comes the question : What life style corresponds to a situation of captivity ? Is it possible to speak of hope even in this situation ? Is there an element of salvation which comes from the presence of a hope in the midst of repression ?

There are biblical paradigms that can help. In Psalm 137 there is a picture of the courage of the Hebrews carried into captivity. The ridicule of their oppressors who ask them for songs of their lost land is such that the Hebrews' desperation becomes hatred. They utter a terrible benediction : 'Happy shall he be who takes your little ones and dashes them against the stones.'

Contemporary versions of this attitude can be found in manifestations of terrorism; while they may well express the anger of a sector of society, in no way do they serve in creating a social utopia. For many people the death of hope gives place to hatred, slavery and fear. Others, perhaps the majority, experience a spiritual withdrawal. They are the mass of people resigned to a social situation which they can neither understand nor change. The biblical paradigm for their situation would be the Hebrew people in Egypt. Moses had more difficulty convincing his own people than he did struggling with Pharaoh. There are extremes of misery in which even the ability to protest is lost. There are extremes of suffering in which the only possible temptation is to submit and forget.

Jeremiah expressed another possibility in his well-known letter to the captives in Babylon : (Jeremiah 29: 4-7 and 10-11). It is the understanding of God's time, the assurance of a tomorrow that must come, that lets them go on building, and working, and growing in family life and in organization so as to be ready for the 'day of the Lord'.

Also there remains the hope of faith. At least in Latin America and in the special Chilean situation basic importance must be given to the existence of a popular religiosity centred in the Christian Gospel. This popular faith is where the construction of a hopeful attitude may begin even in the present repressive circumstances.

It is here that the description of the content and the quality of hope assumes fundamental importance. Because the Christian hopes in the resources of God he overcomes the limitation that the forces of repression impose. He knows that throughout history, and especially under the sign of the cross, instruments of evil and oppression have been transformed into sources of blessing for the people. It was thus that the prevailing evil in the historical circumstances of the people of Israel could never be considered as definitive, but always as carrying with them an element of purifying judgment and at the same time a new way of looking forward to the plentitude of the divine promise.

In the same way the worship experience permits Christians to project themselves beyond the socio-economic-political reality, limited as it is to resources present in the very economy of the Universe. Then they can return to deal with the existing socio-economic limitations.

The Christian, as well as the Marxist, has an interpretation of history which lets him look forward in hope. The difference is that the Christian hope is based on a worship experience to which the common people of Latin America have access. The experience of worship, prayer and personal reflection is a foretaste of hope, an early enjoyment of the presence of God which comes from the presence of His Kingdom. It acts as manna, as daily food to maintain hope in the present while looking forward to the future. The Christian community has to live its hope by functioning as a messianic community. It is the suffering servant that carries the sorrows, the sufferings, the sins of humanity, in order to create new possibilities for human life.

Another basic service is that of providing possibilities for human life In the midst of situations that are constantly on the brink of the destruction of all that merits the name 'human'. I refer to consideration of the individual who needs encouragement, understanding, motivation and training to interpret what happens and who needs help in order to become an actor in the process of changing his environment. In the midst of concern for great collective movements and ideological struggles the Church is the place where small communities can meet. There people discover they are human beings. Façades and official attitudes disappear; there people meet on the totally human level, as brothers, beggars, pilgrims, before the throne of Grace.

The importance of man feeling that he is man in some moment of his existence cannot be over-emphasized. When one lives in situations of intense ideological struggle where the borderline between the battle of ideas and the battle of persons is hard to discern, or when situations of oppression are such that hatred befuddles conscience, or when actions become so ambiguous that one is constantly at risk of living hypocritically, one's well-being requires the encounter of man with man, openness to the mystery of the infinite and life in a community of forgiveness. In summary there must be a dimension of personal encounter if a dimension of humanity is to be restored.

Recently certain theologians have spoken of play as a possibility for humanization in repressive situations. When sport, social games and art are expressions whereby surrounding tension is relieved, they fulfil an important function. But all dimensions of human culture have to be undergirded by a vision that relates the community and personal action to God's ultimate purpose in order that these expressions may not be just ways to escape from reality. Theatre, music and sport are vehicles through which one can express a hunger for humanity, friendship, authenticity and freedom under circumstances where it is impossible to express them otherwise.

Their effect will be humanizing if they are rooted in that vision of history which certifies that hatred and oppression do not have the final word and there is a new day for which one must be hoping, looking and waiting.

If dancing, play, celebration and wonder become substitute-gratifications they will sublimate the creative intention of the community. For creation to take place, suffering and hope cannot be separated. Suffering is the thorn that makes it impossible for us to forget that there is a political task still unfinished—still to be accomplished. And hope is the star that tells the direction to follow. The two, suffering and hope, live from each other. Suffering without hope produces resentment and despair. Hope without suffering creates illusions, naiveté, and drunkenness. (17)

The Church as prophet raises levels of awareness, contributes to the process of communication, participates in intellectual discussion of the big issues of every nation and preaches a true word or performs a symbolic action for specific times and events.

The Church as priest lifts up before God overall problems, the dreams of human dignity and the effects of calling and supporting individuals in their efforts to transform prevailing unjust situations.

The Church as priest seeks to bind men together in their constant hunger for reconciliation, not betraying its prophetic dimension but intelligently implementing it.

The Church as a royal body and a servant people is called to assume the suffering of Latin America. It must try all possible methods of non-violent action, and from its wealth of Christian expression help solve the continent's problems. The Church offers a ministry of hope by raising the banner for the now day that God promises and enabling his people to survive in critical situations as they search for an exit from the tunnel they are in. The Church serves as a community of faith where man has both a historical and an eternal dimension. There barriers of human pretension break down, the weakness of Christians and the power of God's promise appear and there can be human and humanizing life always and everywhere. Apart from the Church's success or failure in co-operating with the liberation process in Latin America, it has an important vocation to carry on, an important service to render and an important offering to give to God.

BY WAY OF CONCLUSION

Latin America is in an explosive situation: poor people, student elites and labour leaders are eager for freedom; sectors who hold economic power and are also dependent on commercial power centres in developed countries fear change and use repression. The Church enters the new situation with deep internal divisions and makes an enormous institutional sacrifice in order to be of service.

What is the Church's future in this revolutionary situation ? Even though it is tempted to go back to the role of a religious chaplaincy with concentration on classic religious problems the return is impossible. It is undeniable that liturgy also has political significance. Even though there are some voices that recall a past that they think was happy and want to go back to a situation that overlooks the collective destiny of Latin American peoples, intellectually articulate defenders of this position will be hard to find. This leads to a discussion of necessary and possible new lines of action.

The tasks mentioned previously are necessary and possible to some degree. Their unity and relevance should be emphasized. However, Latin America's present and future situation has given rise to a committed ecumenical movement that affects all churches equally. As Gustavo Gutierrez says :

> On the other hand, meetings between Christians of different confessions but of the same political option are becoming more frequent. This gives rise to ecumenical groups, often marginal to their respective ecclesiastical authorities, in which Christians share their faith and struggle to create a more just society. The common struggle makes the *traditional* ecumenical programme seem obsolete (a 'marriage between senior citizens' as someone has said) and impels them to look for new paths toward unity. (18)

The alienation of these groups f r o m church authority is a fact. It is also true that their influence is felt at all levels of church life. Their publications are read; their experts are consulted; and their struggle is followed closely with mixed feelings of criticism and hope.

In this ecumenical encounter and ecumenical reality strategic options must be made.

Apparently Latin America's situation resembles the one Vietnam went through. For years to come repression will be seen alongside struggle. In such circumstances what can be done ? What are the priorities ?

In *The End of Our Time*, a small book written in 1923, Nicolas Berdyaev, the Russian philosopher, contemplates the fall of western civilization. He calls on Christianity to assume its responsibility to rediscover the paths of obedience characteristic of the medieval age. Christianity's refuge in monastic orders during the barbarian invasions may have made possible the missionary effort of the early Middle Ages that came out of the monasteries. The concentration of faith in those centres, which provided a refuge with Christian charity and teaching, was then considered an escape from society, but did it not provide the real opportunity for intelligent service to recreate a culture and design new social structures for the New Age ? Perhaps Latin Americans must learn to reflect and rediscover the importance of the small group which dedicates itself to religious discipline, has a clear vocation that steadfastly maintains the dimension of faith, and keeps a ministry of refuge accessible in the hope that some day the doors will open again for missionary work that can permeate all society.

Along this line the Brazilian theologian Rubem Alves asks Latin Americans to recognize that they are not living in a time of liberation but in a state of captivity. What must Christians learn in order to maintain some degree of humanity when submitted to captivity ? How can they be free and also be captive ? Here a theme is recovered that appears in Paul's letters and also in Martin Luther's writings. 'A Christian man is the most free lord of all, and subject to none; a Christian man is the most dutiful servant of all, and subject to everyone'.

In the previous chapter alternatives inherent in that paradox were discussed. If they are elements in the Christian Church's vigil as it awaits the dawn of the new day they will perform a valuable service.

Perhaps Berdyaev and Alves are trying to say what the Apostle Paul said : 'Hope against hope'. While the anguish of Latin Americans is shared, while the tension and division in the church community is endured, while daily sacrificial action is undertaken, our imagination to search for opportunities that correspond to the mystery and wisdom of God is opened in order to create a new day in Latin America.

76

The facts have already passed their verdict on the desires of the heart. They are defeated. Yet—this is the word that makes all the difference—one moves toward the future in the certainty that the present has not said all that is to be said. And one literally bets one's life on this coming but still unseen creative event. It seems to me that this is what faith in God is all about. It is not the knowledge that there is a Being who lives somewhere in or outside this universe. For the Bible, to believe in God is the same as to believe that, contrary to our realistic assessment of the situation, something new and unexpected will suddenly erupt, thus changing completely the possibilities of human life and fulfilment. (19)

Perhaps, in the expression of Helder Camara, "the moment has arrived for Abrahamic minorities to appear!" Those groups, conscious that they are responding not only to the dictates of secular history but also to a divine call, make the fate of the Latin American people their own. Thus they can suffer with them, hope with them and struggle with them.

NOTES

1 Radomiro Tomic, *Worldwide*, volume 16, no 7, July 1973, Latin America, 'No Room for Illusion', p.21; Council on Religion and International Affairs.

2 Eduardo Galeano, *Open Veins of Latin America : Five Centuries of the Pillage of a Continent* (trans. Cedric Belfrage), p.14.

3 Radomiro Tomic, *Op. cit.*, p.18.

4 *WACC Journal*, volume XIX, no 4, 1972, Latin America, *Latin America incommunicado*, pp. 12-15; World Association for Christian Communication.

5 Radomiro Tomic, *Op. cit.*, p.20.

6 Second General Conference of Latin American Bishops, *The Church in the Present-Day Transformation.*

7 Report of the World Conference on *Salvation Today*, Bangkok, December 29, 1972 - January 8, 1973.

8 *ibid.*

9 *ibid.*

10 Gustavo Gutierrez, *A Theology of Liberation: History, Politics and Salvation;* Maryknoll, New York: Orbis Books, 1973; trans. and ed. Sister Caridad Inda and John Eagleson.

11 Second General Conference of Latin American Bishops, *Op. cit.,* 'Doctrinal motivation', pp. 215-216.

12 Gustavo Gutierrez, *Op. cit.,* Chapter VI B, pp. 91-92.

13 Methodist Evangelical Church in Bolivia, *Manifesto to the Bolivian Nation,* III, 'Our Bolivian Situation', pp. 4-6.

14 Gustavo Gutierrez, *Op. cit.,* Chapter A2, p.106.

15 Second General Conference of Latin American Bishops, *Op. cit.,* Book II, 'Conclusions'.

16 *ibid.*

17 Rubem Alves, *Tomorrow's Child,* p.203.

18 Gustavo Gutierrez, *Op. cit.,* p.104.

19 Rubem Alves, *Op. cit.,* pp. 194-195.

Appendix 1

MESSAGE TO THE PEOPLE OF LATIN AMERICA

from the Roman Catholic Bishops meeting in Medellin, August 26 - September 6, 1968

Our Word, a sign of commitment

The Second General Conference of the Latin American Episcopate to the peoples of Latin America: "Grace and peace from God, our Father, and from the Lord Jesus Christ".

Upon finishing the work of this Second General Conference we wish to direct a message to the peoples of our continent.

We want our word as pastors to be a sign of commitment.

As Latin American men we share the history of our people. The past definitively identifies us as Latin Americans; the present places us in a decisive crossroads, and the future requires of us a creative labour in the process of development.

Latin America, a community in transformation

Latin America, in addition to being a geographical reality is a community of peoples with its own history, with specific values and with similar problems. The confrontation and the solutions must acknowledge this history, these values and these problems.

The continent harbours very different situations, but requires solidarity. Latin America must be one and many, rich in variety and strong in its unity.

Our countries have preserved a basic cultural richness, born from ethnic and religious values that have flourished in a common conscience and have borne fruit in concrete efforts towards integration.

Its human potential, more valuable than the riches hidden in its soil, makes of Latin America a promising reality brimming with hope. Its agonizing problems mark it with signs of injustice that wound the Christian conscience.

The multiplicity and complexity of its problems overflow this message.

Latin America appears to live beneath the tragic sign of underdevelopment that not only separates our brothers from the enjoyment of material goods, but from their proper human fulfilment. In spite of the efforts being made, there is the compounding of hunger and misery, of illness of a massive nature and infant mortality, of illiteracy and marginality, of profound inequality of income, and tensions between the social classes, of outbreaks of violence and rare participation of the people in decisions affecting the common good.

**The Church, the history of Latin America and
our contribution**

As Christians we believe that this historical stage of Latin America is intimately linked to the history of salvation.

As pastors, with a common responsibility, we wish to unite ourselves with the life of all of our peoples in the painful search for adequate solutions to their multiple problems. Our mission is to contribute to the integral advancement of man and of human communities of the continent.

We believe that we are in a new historical era. This era requires clarity in order to see, lucidity in order to diagnose, and solidarity in order to act.

In the light of the faith that we profess as believers, we have undertaken to discover a plan of God in the "signs of the times". We interpret the aspirations and clamours of Latin America as signs that reveal the direction of the divine plan operating in the redeeming love of Christ which bases these aspirations on an awareness of fraternal solidarity.

Faithful to this divine plan, and in order to respond to the hopes placed in the Church, we wish to offer that which we hold as most appropriate: a global vision of man and humanity, and the integral vision of Latin American man in development.

Thus we experience solidarity with the responsibilities that have arisen at this stage of the transformation of Latin America.

The Church, as part of the essence of Latin America, despite its limitations, has lived with our peoples the process of colonization, liberation and organization.

Our contribution does not pretend to compete with the attempts for solution made by other national, Latin American and world bodies; much less do we disregard or refuse to recognize them. Our purpose is to encourage these efforts, accelerate their results, deepen their content, and permeate all the process of change with the values of the Gospel. We would like

81

to offer the collaboration of all Christians, compelled by their baptismal responsibilities and by the gravity of this moment. It is our responsibility to dramatize the strength of the Gospel which is the power of God.

We do not have technical solutions or infallible remedies. We wish to feel the problems, perceive the demands, share the agonies, discover the ways and co-operate in the solutions.

The new image of the Latin American man requires a creative effort: public authorities, promoting with energy the supreme requirements of the common good; technicians, planning concrete means; families and educators, awakening and orienting responsibility; the people incorporating themselves in the efforts for fulfilment; the spirit of the Gospel, giving life with the dynamism of a transforming and personalizing love.

The challenge of the present moment :
Possibilities, values, conditions

Our peoples seek their liberation and their growth in humanity, through the incorporation and participation of everyone in the very conduct of the personalizing process.

For this reason, no sector should reserve to itself exclusively the carrying out of political, cultural, economic or spiritual matters. Those who possess the power of decision-making must exercise it in communion with the desires and options of the community. In order that this integration respond to the nature of the Latin American peoples, it must incorporate the values that are appropriate to all and everyone, without exception. The imposition of foreign values and criteria would constitute a new and grave alienation.

We count upon elements and criteria that are profoundly human and essentially Christian, an innate sense of the dignity of all, a predilection to fraternity and hospitality, a recognition of woman and her irreplaceable function in the society, a wise sense of life and death, the certainty of a common Father in the transcendental destiny of all.

This process requires of all of our nations the surmounting of mistrust, the purification of exaggerated nationalism and the solution of their conflicts.

We consider it irreconcilable with our developing situation to invest resources in the arms race, excessive bureaucracy, luxury and ostentation, or the deficient administration of the community.

The firm denunciation of those realities in Latin America which constitute an affront to the spirit of the Gospel also forms part of our mission.

It is also our duty to give recognition to and to stimulate every profound and positive attempt to vanquish the existing great difficulties.

Youth

In this transformation, Latin American youth constitute the most numerous group in the population and show themselves to be a new social body with their own ideas and values desiring to create a more just society.

This youthful presence is a positive contribution that must be incorporated into the society and the Church.

Commitments of the Latin American Church

During these days we have gathered in the city of Medellin, moved by the spirit of the Lord, in order to orient once again the labours of the Church in a spirit of eagerness for conversion and service.

We have seen that our most urgent commitment must be to purify ourselves, all of the members and institutions of the Catholic Church, in the spirit of the Gospel. It is necessary to end the separation between faith and life, "because in Christ Jesus . . . only faith working through love avails".

This commitment requires us to live a true scriptural poverty expressed in authentic manifestations that may be clear signs for our peoples. Only poverty of this quality will show forth Christ, Saviour of men, and disclose Christ, the Lord of history.

Our reflections have clarified the dimensions of other commitments, which, allowing for modifications, shall be assumed by all the People God :

— To inspire, encourage and press for a new order of justice that incorporates all men in the decision-making of their own communities;

— To promote the constitution and the efficacy of the family, not only as a human sacramental community, but also as an intermediate structure in function of social change;

— To make education dynamic in order to accelerate the training of mature men in their current responsibilities;

— To encourage the professional organizations of workers, which are decisive elements in socio-economic transformation;

— To promote a new evangelization and intensive catechesis that reach the elite and the masses in order to achieve a lucid and committed faith;

—To renew and create new structures in the Church that institutionalize dialogue and channel collaboration between bishops, priests, religious and laity;

—To co-operate with other Christian confessions, and with all men of good will who are committed to authentic peace rooted in justice and love.

The concrete results of these deliberations and commitments we give to you in detailed and hopeful form in the Final Documents which follow this Message.

A final call

We call to all men of goodwill that they co-operate in truth, justice, love and liberty, in this transforming labour of our peoples, the dawn of a new era.

In a special way we direct ourselves to the Church and Christian communities that share our same faith in Jesus Christ. During this Conference our brothers of these Christian confessions have been taking part in our work and in our hopes. Together with them we shall be witnesses of this spirit of co-operation.

We wish also to caution, as a duty of our conscience, as we face the present and future of our continent, those who direct the destinies of public order. In their hands is the possibility of an administrative conduct that liberates from injustice and acts as a guide to an order having for its end the common good, that can lead to the creation of a climate of confidence and action that Latin American men need for the full development of their lives.

By its own vocation, Latin America will undertake its liberation at the cost of whatever sacrifice, not in order to seal itself off but in order to open itself to union with the rest of the world, giving and receiving in a spirit of solidarity.

We find dialogue with our brothers of other continents who find themselves in a similar situation to ours to be most important for our work. United in difficulties and hopes, we can make our presence in the world a force for peace.

We remind other peoples who have overcome the obstacles we encounter today, that peace is based on the respect of international justice, justice which has its own foundation and expression in the recognition of the political, economic and cultural autonomy of our peoples.

Finally, we have hope that the love of God the Father, who manifests Himself in the Son, and who is spread abroad in our hearts by the Holy Spirit, will unite us and always inspire our actions for the common good.

Thus we hope to be faithful to the commitments that we have made in these days of reflection and common prayer, in order to contribute to the full and effective co-operation of the Church in the process of transformation that is being lived in our America.

We hope also to be heard with understanding and goodwill by all men with whom we commune in the same destiny and the same aspiration.

All our work and this same hope we place under the protection of Mary, Mother of the Church and Patroness of the Americas, in order that the reign of God may be realized among us.

We have faith :
>in God
>in men
>in the values
>and the future of Latin America.

"The grace of Our Lord Jesus Christ, the charity of God and the fellowship of the Holy Spirit be with you all."

Medellin, 6 September, 1968

Appendix 2

MANIFESTO TO THE BOLIVIAN NATION

Methodist Evangelical Church in Bolivia*

I WHO WE ARE

We are the Methodist Evangelical Church in Bolivia, that is to say, members of the pilgrim people of God, initiated by Jesus Christ, who broke into history through the events of the Cross and the Resurrection —events which Christians the world over celebrate this week.

Christians and Protestants

We are not merely of today or yesterday. We are part of the Universal Church, constituted under the authority of the Holy Scriptures for the fundamental purpose of bearing witness to Jesus Christ. We do not pretend to be possessors of an exclusive truth, nor do we feel called to a sectarian or proselytizing labour. We consider ourselves to be heirs of a long history in which many churches and Christian groups participate.

---

*Translated from "Manifesto a la Nación Boliviana", (La Paz, Bolivia: Iglesia Evangélica Metodista en Bolivia, March 29, 1970). Mimeographed.

We are heirs, in particular, of the evangelical movement which burst forth in the 16th century with the Protestant Reformation, and of the Methodist spiritual renewal movement which began in England in the 18th century and which has produced a family of millions of Christians in Africa, Asia, Europe and America.

Loyalty to Christ and to Man

Above all, our loyalty is to Jesus Christ and his gospel, an integral gospel destined "for all men and for the whole man", according to the happy phrase of John XXIII. Consequently, our loyalty is also to man, specially to the Bolivian man to whom this liberating gospel is directed and whom we wish to serve in the name of Christ.

For this reason the Methodist Evangelical Church in Bolivia from its beginning early in this century interested itself in the needs of the Bolivian man: in education, introducing new methods and systems in the schools, creating primary and vocational schools in rural areas, and participating in the renewal of Bolivian education at all levels; in the medical field, establishing clinics and health centres, reaching into the most forgotten places of the nation, founding the first nursing school in Bolivia, and launching out in programmes of public health, especially in new zones of colonization. During the last sixty-five years, in eight Departments of the country, Methodist congregations have grown up and they now lead service programmes such as vocational and basic adult education, student centres, co-operative enterprises, and various forms of community development.

An Autonomous Church

All this labour was carried on by Bolivian and foreign Christians. As it grew and was consolidated a growing national leadership was prepared. Finally the Bolivian Methodist community felt that the moment had come to break the flowerpot in which the plant of Christianity had come in order to transplant the gospel in Bolivian soil and let it produce its own version of Christianity. The Methodist Evangelical Church in Bolivia, by the unanimous decision of its members and with the approval of its sister churches in other countries, declared itself autonomous, drafted its own statutes, determined its own structures, and elected its own authorities.

II   OUR REASON FOR BEING

Our reason for being is in the gospel of Jesus Christ, a gospel which implies the full humanization of man, the realization of God's purpose for the man he has created and redeemed. This gospel brings a liberation, a salvation that reaches man's whole being: his soul and eternal destiny, and also his historical, material, individual, and social being. God's concern is for the whole man and not for just a part of him. This is the biblical message that we proclaim and seek to incarnate.

Christian Humanization

Jesus Christ is the prototype of man as God means for him to be: the integral man, free, fully developed in his calling, his mission, and his destiny; man completely obedient to God and wholly committed to mankind. In the measure in which men are like him and commit themselves to him to be transformed they determine their true humanization.

Man, however, is alienated and dehumanized. He is alienated from himself, a prisoner of fear, of superstition, of selfishness, or in a word, of sin. He has no clear understanding of his origin; he does not comprehend his present state; it is hard for him to discover his mission in life, and he fumbles in search of his destiny. He is alienated from his neighbour whom he sees more as a competitor, a rival, or an enemy, than as a brother. Even in the most intimate circle of family and friends misunderstanding, hostility, distrust, and even hate appear. Man is alienated from society when he does not comprehend his rights and duties, when he has not awakened to human solidarity and common responsibility. Man learns to be a social being or he becomes dehumanized. And the men who exploit and oppress others are as much dehumanized as the ones who are exploited and oppressed.

Dehumanizing Conditions

Not only are there dehumanizing tendencies within man himself, there are dehumanizing forces built into society. Sin has an objective social dimension. The social, political, cultural, and economic structures become dehumanizing when they are not at the service of "all men and the whole man", in a word, when they are structures that perpetuate injustice. Structures are the product of human activity but they assume an impersonal, even demonic character, and put themselves beyond the reach of individual action. Collective concerted effort is necessary to change these structures; there are no structures that are sacred or unchangeable.

The God we know through the Bible is a liberating God, a God who destroys myth and alienations; a God who intervenes in history to break down the structures of injustice and who raises up prophets to point the way to justice and mercy. He is the God who frees slaves (Exodus), who makes empires fall, and lifts up the oppressed (Magnificat, Luke 1:52).

This is the message of hope and liberation in the gospel: "The Spirit of the Lord is upon me, because he has anointed me to preach good news to the poor. He has sent me to proclaim release to the captives and recovering of sight to the blind, to set at liberty those who are oppressed, to proclaim the acceptable year of the Lord" (Luke 4:18-19). Our obligation is to proclaim this message if we do not want to be found unworthy of our mission and our name.

The Christian church cannot covenant with any force that oppresses or dehumanizes man.

The Easter observance is nothing more or less than the celebration of the liberating acts of God.

III OUR BOLIVIAN SITUATION

When we look at our Bolivian situation in the light of the gospel we are faced with the spectacle of a chronic, heart-rending, dehumanization: a country with immense resources overwhelmed with backwardness and under-development; a people living in under-consumption with the lowest per capita income in all of Latin America; "the miners' cemeteries", macabre witnesses of generations of men sacrificed in the prime of life, leaving, after a short period of productivity, their orphans and widows abandoned to the most complete helplessness, while the minerals extracted from the earth at the cost of their lives go to enrich a small minority and benefit the industry and commerce of the rich countries of the earth; three million peasants, the basic population of the nation, marginated by illiteracy and poverty and treated as mere disposable objects by the insensitive bureaucracy and political leadership; thousands of children without schools, desks, or teachers; thousands of university students pushing to enter classrooms, only to feed into the interminable lines of the unemployed, or become political appointees, aspirants to scholarships, or migrants to other countries.

Oppressive Structures

In the background of this situation stand oppressive international structures such as imperialism and the economic and warmongering interests of the great powers. Like the rest of the Third World, we are obliged to sell raw materials at low prices and buy back goods manufactured by workers abroad who receive ten, twenty, or even thirty times the wages which Bolivian workers receive. Foreign investors seek to exploit our resources under conditions which are unacceptable in other countries and which are injurious to our national sovereignty and dignity.

There are also internal exploiters, privileged Bolivian minorities who act in connivance with international and anti-national interests. The truth is that not only do they buy us, but we sell ourselves. The will power and heavy bureaucracy of state organisms; the mercenariness of politicians and functionaries; the eagerness for rapid wealth; the lack of responsibility and discipline; the cowardliness that hinders our committing ourselves responsibly; the lack of courage and hope to work for the future; the instability of our governments; the inconsequence of opposition groups and political parties; and the lack of continuity in effort—these are also undeniable causes of our backwardness.

We have to fight against the foreign powers that are choking us and fencing us in and also against the tendencies that undermine and corrode the inner strength of our society.

Our Points of Strength

We are not pessimists; there are great values in our people and in our land. Some of these are the following : the strength and work habits of our rural people; the courage and stoicism of our miners; the eagerness for learning and self-improvement on the part of the new generations of country and city; the initiative and vision in our colonists who go to the Yungas and the Eastern Regions and in the developers of new agriculture, cattle raising, and small industry; the invaluable experience of our Bolivian technologists who work in COMIBOL, YPFB*, and other state agencies; and a nationalist and revolutionary spirit that is taking form today among military personnel, workers, and university students.

The Present Government

As Christians and Bolivian citizens we are disturbed by some aspects of our present government : the excessive placement of military personnel in key positions of all areas of the government, with a consequent duplication of salaries; the lack of participation by the people, even at the municipal level; the indefinite suspension of the Constitution and the absence of a representative legislative body; the precarious existence of the judicial power in relation to the *de facto* government; the uncontrolled verticality of government decisions. There is an apparent inconsistency between nationalist declarations and some

---

*COMIBOL (Corporación Minera de Bolivia) is the Bolivian State Mining Corporation; YPFB (Yacimientos Petrolíferos Fiscales Bolivianos) is the Bolivian State Petroleum Corporation.

practices, such as the maintenance of the North American Mission and Military Aid, and the unfulfilled promise of amnesty and political liberty for political leaders who intended to return to the country.

On the other hand, we honestly recognize a highly positive balance in the present revolutionary government. Precisely because we see signs of humanization for our people we back measures such as the following : the nationalization of our natural resources and the effort to create a national metallurgical and petrochemical industry; the repealing of the Law of State Security and of Union Reglamentation; the withdrawal of armed forces from the mines and the reinstatement of workers dismissed for political reasons; the disposition of the government to enter into dialogue with students, workers, *entrepreneurs*, and other vital sectors of the nation; the movement to renew diplomatic relations with Chile and to proceed with regional and Latin American continental integration; participation in the government by civilians of recognized nationalist and revolutionary tendencies; the formation of the National Ethical Commission; the sustained defense of our exports, foreign exchange and national currency; the pledge to back educational reform and initiate a large-scale literacy programme in the coming years; the declared intention to work with a national revolutionary model that is not merely a copy or importation of other ideological systems; and the plan to carry out administrative and tax reforms that will put our country on the road to efficiency and modernity for better service to the Bolivian people, etc.

Obligated to Speak Out

To be Christian does not make us infallible, but it does obligate us to speak out even at the risk of making mistakes. We must give the present Bolivian government opportunity to carry out its programme according to its declared platform. It is necessary to overcome the immaturity of repeatedly starting abortive "revolutions". At the same time, the government must be sensitive to the reality of this present moment in history. It must be willing to listen, to rectify, and to open the deepening revolutionary process to the participation of all the Bolivian people. Only thus will it be able to fulfil the historic role that it wants to undertake.

IV   TOWARD THE FUTURE

As the newly autonomous Methodist Evangelical Church in Bolivia we wish to participate in this constructive process of preparing a new tomorrow for Bolivians.

At the Service of the Bolivian People

We place ourselves, with all our human, material, and spiritual resources, at the service of our people. And we seek to perform our task in collaboration with all Bolivian Christians and even with those who are not Christians but who feel the same call to work together for a more dignified human life.

We are already under way. In an endeavour to achieve excellence and democratization in education we have entered into agreements with the Ministries of Education and Peasant Affairs to operate jointly our educational institutions and to put them at the service of the least privileged. Also, we are jointly operating with the Ministry of Public Health and the municipality of Montero the public hospital of that city which serves as a regional public health centre for the north of Santa Cruz. Our Evangelical School of Nursing with is specialized personnel and present resources this year is integrating with the National School of Nursing to form a unique University School of Nursing which will be part of the School of Medicine of the Universidad Mayor de San Andrés.

The Awakening of Consciousness

Since the needs of our people are so great and urgent no one should withhold his effort and resources. As long as we are able to do so, we shall continue to promote such programmes as literacy work, healing, teaching, and community development which we presently maintain on the Altiplano, the Alto Beni, Yapacaní and the Chapare. We will put all the experience and capability of our Bolivian personnel into these tasks and will try to interest other Christian organizations abroad to collaborate through personnel, equipment and donations.

We feel, however, that this labour is not enough. We must work for radical and profound changes in the structures of society that affect human life. We must work for complete liberation. Hence we assign a priority to the task of forming a critical consciousness (conscientisation) in our people. The liberation of man will not be accomplished unless he is first freed from his alienations, his complexes, his admiration of his oppressor, and his imitation of foreigners.

Formation of the New Man

Our best contribution as a Christian church is to participate in the formation of the new Bolivian man, truly humanized by the gospel of Jesus Christ. In our Protestant churches we have aimed at forming a moral man, irreproachable in his conduct, freed from vices, a useful element in society, honest, hard-working, and a good father. But the Christian man is much more than the prototype of sobriety. He is a free man, without alienations, conscious of his possibilities and of the responsibility of taking his destiny into his own hands. He is the passionate man with a "hunger and thirst for righteousness", who, like his Master, "has not come to be served, but to serve and give his life a ransom for many". He is the reconciled and reconciling man who has received a ministry of reconciliation from him who on a Cross "was reconciling the world unto himself". Finally, he is the man born to a hope that rejects resignation as a false virtue; he fights against every unjust structure that tends to make man a one-dimensional being with no hope for the future.

Evangelism correctly understood—the proclamation of the Good News and the confrontation of man with the liberating gospel of Jesus Christ— puts man on the road to his full humanization. But it is necessary to complement that task of proclamation and confrontation with a sustained and systematic effort for the education and conscientisation of the Bolivian man. Therefore, we consider that the formation of a critical consciousness in the Bolivian people and the opening of paths of hope to the marginated sectors of our society are parts of the mission that God has entrusted to us. Therefore, we assign a fundamental role to the future massive literacy campaign to which the government has committed itself. We promise our fullest support in this campaign.

Call and Commitment

We call upon all Christian churches, civic groups, university students, workers, and every man of good will, to work together in this task of conscientisation and liberation of our people. Let us seek to overcome all our suspicions, divisions, and resentments. Leaving behind every feeling of opportunism let us launch forth with confidence into the common task that awaits and challenges us. The opportunity is ours to go down in history as the generation that assumed the responsibility, honestly and without excuses, to extract Bolivia from its emaciation, sharing with sister nations of America the struggle for the liberation of the Latin American man.

Let the Bolivian people know that our Christian community shares in this struggle for liberation and hope.

For the Methodist Evangelical Church in Bolivia,

MORTIMER ARIAS, Bishop.

La Paz, Bolivia
Easter Sunday, March 29, 1970.

Appendix 3

I HAVE HEARD THE CRY OF MY PEOPLE

Statement of Bishops and Religious Superiors Northeast Brazil, May 6, 1973

I have seen the affliction of my people and have heard their cry because of their oppressors; I know their suffering (Ex. 3:7).

These words from Exodus, spoken by God to Moses, are a fitting expression of our feelings in these days. Before the suffering of our people, humbled and oppressed for centuries, we feel called by the Word of God to take up a position, a clear position on the side of the poor, a position taken in common with all those who commit themselves to the people for their true liberation.

Following in the steps of Moses, we want to fulfil, together with the people of God, our mission as pastors and prophets. We are summoned to speak by the Word of God, which judges the events of history. In this light we have tried to understand the cry of our people, the daily facts and events of a suffering people — phenomena which recommend themselves to a serious study of our human situation.

In the awareness of our frequent omissions and uncertainties in the course of the history of our Church in Brazil, we feel powerless and awed before such a huge task. We spontaneously repeat the question asked of Yahweh by Moses : Who am I that I should go to Pharaoh ? But we also feel a strength from above, the grace of the One who has called and sent us : 'God answered : I will be with you' (Ex. 3: 11-12).

Statements on Human Rights

This is why in this anniversary year of the Universal Declaration of Human Rights and on the tenth anniversary of Pope John XXIII's encyclical letter *Pacem in Terris*, the bishops and major superiors of the Northeast of Brazil, in accordance with the conclusions and appeals of the XIIIth General Assembly of the National Bishops' Conference of Brazil (CNBB) held in February of this year (cf. IDOC 73/161/002), decided to make public the following statement as one of the priorities of their mission and as a contribution to the celebration of these important events.

Such a commemoration, however, should not be a matter of mere rhetoric, lacking a sense of reality and having no impact on the life of the people. 'Go, and I will be with your mouth and teach you what you shall speak' (Ex. 4:12).

Nor is it for us to abuse or use inadequately our power and duty to speak. To speak in the name of God at this moment of history, to the people of our country, inviting them to a true conversion, i.e. to a loyal examination of their human conduct and a consequent radical transformation of their life in its entirety, individually and collectively, under the guidance of the Holy Spirit—this is what has been given to us as a Strength from God, to achieve the new creation and renew the face of the earth.

Hence, searching to interpret the judgment of God

upon the reality of the world, as we believe our mission as pastors and prophets urges us to do, our word must be a summons, active and effective, like a two-edged sword, piercing through to the core of things and discerning the thoughts and intentions of the heart (cf. Heb. 4:12).

At this moment, even before talking to others, we ourselves must try to open up to the call from Jesus Christ, 'the faithful witness' (Rev. 2:4), exhorting us to faithfulness and asking us to shake the apathy of our churches. He is the One who prompts them to an irrevocable mission of presence and actualization in the course of human history. 'He who has an ear, let him hear what the Spirit says to the churches' (cf. Rev. ch. 1-3).

Let it not be said, however, that it is not our task to talk on concrete human matters and that we should limit ourselves to the so-called spiritual sphere. For us, the spiritual sphere embraces man as a whole, in all his dimensions, since he must be seen in the light of the unappealable judgment of God and the unificative action of the Spirit.

Furthermore, it is our right and duty as pastors to treat of human problems and consequently of economic, political and social problems, inasmuch as what is at stake in them is man *and* God, who has pledged himself to man.

Our Commitment

Truly, if we want to be faithful to the Gospel, our commitment is with the people. With its hope. With its liberation. Is it not to the people that God committed himself ? What is the meaning of the Bible if not to reveal to us God's commitment to the people, Yahweh's covenant with human history ? Is it not true that Christ, in whom ultimate communion is achieved, defined his life as that of the Good Shepherd who gives himself for his flock ?

In a humble attempt to take account of our mission, we ask from God the strength to raise our voice in the hope that the Lord's threat against unfaithful and negligent prophets will not fall upon our heads :

> Woe to the foolish prophets who follow their own spirit ... Because you have uttered delusions and seen lies, therefore behold, I am against you ... because they have misled my people, saying 'peace', when there is no peace ... Ho, shepherds of Israel who have been feeding yourselves !... So they were scattered because there was no shepherd; and they became food for all the wild beasts (Ez. 13: 3, 8; 34: 2, 5).

Our responsibility as pastors sets us once more before a challenge: persevering fidelity to man within his historical context.

Ministers of Liberation

We are servants, ministers of liberation 'for freedom Christ has set us free' (Gal. 5:1).

As ministers of liberation, we have need now more than ever before for continuous conversion in order to serve better. We need to listen to the cry of the man of the Northeast, crying for this ministry of liberation, pleading with us to share his 'hunger and thirst for justice'.

This man's march towards liberation challenges our society and enters into conflict with its criteria of luxury, with the distortion of statistics and other official data aimed at justifying what the 2nd CELAM Conference at Medellin called the 'institutionalized violence' in which we live. The situation in which Latin American society finds itself was characterized by our episcopal conference as 'a sinful situation'.

103

It is thus in deep consciousness of our pastoral and prophetic function that we are going to talk in this challenging hour, reviewing historical events which of themselves are already questioning us.

We will begin with official data, the findings of scientific surveys, so that our judgment in the name of God will not be based on superficial impressions or subjective attitudes. Our point of view, however, is that of man, the whole man and all men. It is that of God who, making himself man, transformed man, in Christ, the measure of all things.

There follows detailed analysis of the de facto situation in the Northeast of Brazil.

Conclusion

The Church cannot remain indifferent before all that has been exposed and a situation which, in its human configuration and in its psychological and moral aspects, is in reality still much more serious and dramatic. By divine vocation we belong to the family of those who must commit themselves to those who are marginated inasmuch as we are part of the human race, beset with weaknesses (cf. Heb. 5:2). Consequently, as in the case of Peter and John in the early Church (cf. Acts 4: 19-20), our Christian conscience does not allow us to remain silent.

We know that we will not be understood by the many who, because of their self-centred interests, cannot or do not want to understand even evident facts. They are the accommodating advocates of the *status quo.* For obvious reasons, they transform faith into a theory about our personal relations with God, without interfering in social and political action among men. They make religion something exclusive. They use it as an ideological tool, to defend groups and institutions which are not at all at the service of man and are thus opposed to God's design.

In this respect, St. James says in his epistle : 'Is it not the rich who oppress you, is it not they who drag you into court ? Is it not they who blaspheme that honourable name by which you are called ?' (James 2: 6-7).

Regretting the erroneous thinking of many well-meaning Christians in this regard, Pope John XXIII observed : 'the inconsistency between religious faith, in those who believe, and their activities in the temporal sphere, results—in great part if not entirely —from the lack of a solid Christian education' *(Pacem in Terris, part V, par. 144).*

The Church in the World

We want to re-emphasize in this final section that we cannot conceive of the Church as a reality separate from the world, as a ghetto standing on its own. The Church is at the service of the world. It is turned towards the world (cf. Conciliar Pastoral Constitution *Gaudium et Spes).* In part, it identifies itself with the world, expressing the dimension of God's grace and love in human reality which constitutes the world. This is where salvation takes place, coming from God who loves all men. It is in the heart of mankind, in the vastness of human history, that the vivifying love of Christ's Spirit is at work. How can we then absent ourselves from the world ? How can we remain indifferent or adverse, exempt ourselves from the struggle against sin, misery, slavery ?

In this way, just as the sacraments are specific signs of faith and of redeeming grace, so can human realities, in the most varied fields of activity, mediate salvation and become factors of communion with

God, through service and communion with our fellow men, with whom we share the same frailty and the same humanity.

Salvation therefore is not to be conceived of as a reality outside this world, to be reached beyond history, in a life 'beyond the tomb'. Its realization begins here. Eternal life, which is 'not yet' consummated, is 'already' given to us through the Son of God in the here and now of human life (cf. John 5: 24; 6: 40, etc.). This salvation comes from God and breaks into our humanity, within the tissue of history, and reveals itself throughout the long and complex process of man's liberation. Without forgetting the personal and internal dimension, we cannot deny that the integral liberation of man includes a political aspect in a socio-economic context. This is the reason why, according to the designs of the Father, it is being realized through and within the people, where the socio-political dimension of man is verified. God saves the individual person within a people, 'the People of God', which is the object of his love.

The Salvific Content of the People's Struggle

As in the time of Moses, any people which strives for self-fulfilment and starts shaking off the yoke of slavery, discovers an aspect of God's design and, even without knowing it, witnesses to the salvation which is being realized in it (cf. Deut. ch. 12).

It is clear that those who, like Pharaoh, maintain a people in slavery, do not recognize the salvific thrust of the people's struggle. They will not see God's presence in the unremitting energy of the poor. But the 'poor of Yahweh' are the privileged channel of God's revelation, the daily pulpit of God's Word, in events of life, in hope which is not illusive, in their longing for freedom, peace and brotherhood.

The same cannot be said of oppressors, of those who at every moment give free rein to repression. The way they argue, God is a being dragged at their side, is being used as a tool, is being put at the service of the 'established order', because this is what is most convenient for them. Nevertheless, it is the Virgin Mary herself, Mother of God and humble child of the people, who turns this ideology upside down in her description of God's wisdom : 'He has put down the mighty from their thrones and exalted the humble; he has filled the hungry with good things, and the rich he has sent away empty' (Luke 1: 52-53).

The Church Summoned to Repentance

We have to recognize in a spirit of true humility and penance that the Church has not always been faithful to its prophetic mission, to its evangelical role of being at the side of the people. How many times, involved in the mesh of evils existing in this world, the Church, under deceitful disguises, whether due to ingenuousness or captiousness, in a sad deformation of the evangelical message, has played the game of the oppressors and received favours from those who hold the power of money and of politics against the common good ? But at each hour of its existence the Word of God is sent to the Church and invites it to repent, to be converted, to return to its 'fervour of the first days' (Rev. 2:4).

We are convinced that this is the hour for an option for God and for the people. This is the time for fidelity to the mission. It is certain that the price of such a choice has always been persecution from those 'who think that they are so offering a service to God' (John 16:2). But it seems clear to us that the road to follow is that described by our Lord in his missionary instructions to the disciples and related to us by Matthew in chapter 10 of his Gospel. We know that the words of Christ, Lord of the Church, in the Book of Revelation are also directed to us : 'Do not fear what you are about to suffer. Behold the devil is about to throw some of you in prison, that you may be tested . . . Be faithful unto death and I will give you the crown of life' (Rev. 2:10).

The Church and the Poor

Under the light of faith and in the awareness of the injustice characterizing the socio-economic structures of our country, we want to undertake a profound revision of our attitude of love for the oppressed, whose poverty is the reverse side of the wealth of the oppressors.

The prevailing socio-economic structures in Brazil are built upon oppression and injustice resulting from a capitalism dependent on large international power centres. Within our country, a small minority of people, associated with international capitalism in its service, are committed to maintain by all means possible a situation which was created in their favour. A situation has arisen that is neither human nor Christian.

What we are witnessing today is that a social project conceived to bolster the efficiency of our resources in an effort against underdevelopment does not meet the present requirements for the liberation of the oppressed. A scientific comprehension of reality reveals the present need for a global historical transformation of society.

It is not enough to make a comprehensive scientific diagnosis of this reality. Christ taught us by his example to live what he proclaimed. He taught that human brotherhood and love must inspire all social structures and, above all, he lived his message of liberation to its ultimate consequences. The powerful saw in his message and in the effective love with which he announced it a real danger for their economic, social, political and religious interests, and they condemned him to death. But his Spirit, active today as yesterday, gives his impulse to history and manifests himself in the solidarity of those who struggle for freedom, in a true expression of love for their oppressed brothers.

Institutionalized Violence

The socio-economic, political and cultural situation of our people is a challenge to our Christian conscience. Undernourishment, infant mortality, prostitution, illiteracy, unemployment, cultural and political discrimination, exploitation, growing discrepancies between rich and poor, and many other consequences point to a situation of institutionalized violence in our country.

The rich become always richer and the poor always poorer in the enslaving process of economic concentration inherent in the system.

On the other hand, the necessity of repression in order to guarantee the smooth functioning and security of the capitalistic system becomes always more imperative. Repression has expressed itself in many ways : curtailing of the constitutional prerogatives of the legislative branch of government; the depoliticising of the rural and urban trade unions; the elimination of student leadership; the establishment of censorship; persecution of workers, peasants and intellectuals; harassment of priests and members of active groups of the Christian churches—all this in various forms of imprisonment, torture, mutiliation and assassination.

The burden of this tragedy, which falls more heavily on the Northeast, far from being the ineluctable resort of natural deficiencies is, now more than ever before, the consequence of a process fixed by the will of men committed to international capitalism. This made possible the construction of an unjust society and the maintenance of its crushing weight in order to defend, nurture and increase its privileges. The injustice created by this situation has its foundation in the capitalistic system of production which necessarily produces a class society characterized by discrimination and injustice.

International capitalism and its allies in our country —the dominant class—impose by the media of communication and education a dependent culture. They use this to justify their domination and dissimulate the oppressive system which sustains them. At the same time they attempt to lull asleep vast strata of the population, aiming at the formation of a type of man resigned to his alienation. The present model of economic growth, whose results remain of no use to working and oppressed classes, aims at emptying our people of true global objectives for the transformation of society.

The historical process of class society and of capitalistic domination necessarily leads to a fatal confrontation of classes. Even though this fact becomes clearer every day, it is still denied by the oppressors—and is confirmed by their denial. The oppressed masses of workers, peasants, and underemployed know this and deepen their growing liberative consciousness.

Social Ownership of the Means of Production

The dominated class has no other road to freedom except the long and difficult trek now under way, in favour of social ownership of the means of production. This is the principal foundation of the gigantic historic project for the all-inclusive tranformation of society, for a new society where it will be possible to create the objective conditions allowing the oppressed to recover their stunted humanity, to throw off the chains of their suffering, to overcome class antagonisms, and finally to win freedom. The Gospel is calling us, Christians and all men of goodwill, to become engaged in this prophetic undertaking.

Christian hope, which points to a new mankind, reconciled with itself and united with the Universe, does not allow us to remain inert, passively awaiting the hour of the restoration of all things, 'the final liberation from bondage to obtain the glorious liberty of the children of God' (Rom. 8: 18-22), but demands an unremitting and active presence, capable of eliciting, in the course of history, the signs of the future.

Brothers, the assurance given by Jesus in his eschatological discourse is an incomparable strength for us in this hour of darkness laden with promise :

Revive and lift up your head
because the time of your liberation is at hand.

Northeast, 6 May, 1973

As of this date, the following bishops and major religious superiors have been able to sign this statement :
Hélder Pessoa Câmara, *Archbishop of Olinda and Recife, Pernambuco*
José Lamartine Soares, *Auxiliary Bishop of Olinda and Recife*
Severino Mariano de Augia, *Bishop of Pesqueira, Pernambuco*
Francisco Austregésilo Mesquita, *Bishop of Afogados da Ingazeira, Pernambuco*

Walfrido Mohn, OFM, *Provincial of the Franciscans of Recife*
Hidenburgo Santana, SJ, *Provincial of the Jesuits of the North, Recife*
Gabriel Hofstede, CSSR, *Provincial of the Redemptorists, Recife*
Joao José da Motta e Alburquerque, *Archbishop of Sao Luis, Maranhao*
Manoel Edmilson da Cruz, *Auxiliary Bishop of Sao Luis*
Rino Carlesi, FSCJ, *Prelate of S. Antônio de Balsas, Maranhao*
Pascáio Rettler, OFM, *Bishop of Bacabal, Maranhao*
Francisco Hélio Campos, *Bishop of Viana, Maranhao*
Antônio Batista Fragoso, *Bishop of Cratéus, Ceará*
José Maria Pires, *Archbishop of Joao Pessoa, Paraiba*
Manoel Pereira da Costa, *Bishop of Campina Grande, Paraiba*
José Brandao de Castro, *Bishop of Propriá, Sergipe*
Timóteo Amoroso Anastácio, OSB, *Abbot of the Monastery of Sao Bento, Bahia*
Tarcisio Botturi, SJ, *Vice-Provincial of the Jesuits of Bahia*

Acknowledgments

Grateful acknowledgment is made to A. & C. Black for the quotation from Albert Schweitzer's *Quest of the historical Jesus;* to the Centro de Estudios Cristianos del Rio de la Plata, for the quotation from Miguel Brun's *Concepto Cristiano de la Salvacion Hoy;* to the Monthly Review Press for the quotation from Eduardo Galeano's *Open Veins of Latin America: Five Centuries of the Pillage of a Continent* (translated by Cerdic Belfrage); to Orbis Books for quotations from Gustavo Gutierrez's *A Theology of Liberation: History, Politics and Salvation* (translated and edited by Sister Caridad Inda and John Eagleson); to Sheed & Ward for the quotation from Nicolas Berdyaev's *The End of Our Time;* to the Division of Education of the National Council of Churches of Christ in the USA for quotations from the *Revised Standard Version;* to the Council on Religion and International Affairs for the quotations from Radomiro Tomic's article in *Worldwide;* to the World Association for Christian Communication for the quotation from the *WACC Journal;* to the Second General Conference of Latin American Bishops for quotations from their *The Church in the Present-Day Transformation;* to the Commission on World Mission and Evangelism of the World Council of Churches for the quotations from the Report of the World Conference on *Salvation Today;* to the Methodist Evangelical Church in Bolivia for the quotation from their *Manifesto to the Bolivian Nation;* to Rubem Alves for the quotations from *Tomorrow's Child.*

Jean-Paul Sartre

Intimacy

Translated by
Lloyd Alexander

Panther

Granada Publishing Limited
Published in 1960 by Panther Books Ltd
Frogmore, St Albans, Herts AL2 2NF
Reprinted 1960, 1961 (three times), 1962 (twice),
1963 (twice), 1964 (twice), 1965, 1966 (twice), 1967,
1968 (twice), 1969, 1970, 1971, 1972, 1973, 1976

First published in Great Britain by
Neville Spearman Ltd 1949
Reprinted twelve times
Made and printed in Great Britain by
Hunt Barnard Printing Ltd
Aylesbury, Bucks
Set in Intertype Times

Contents

to
Olga
Koszakiewicz

Intimacy

I

Lulu slept naked because she liked to feel the sheets
caressing her body and also because laundry was
expensive. In the beginning Henri protested : you
shouldn't go to bed naked like that, it isn't nice, it's
dirty. Anyhow, he finally followed his wife's example,
though in his case it was merely laziness ; he was
stiff as a poker when there was company (he admired
the Swiss, particularly the Genevans : he thought
them high class because they were so wooden), but
he was negligent in small matters ; for example, he
wasn't very clean, he didn't change his underwear
often enough ; when Lulu put it in the dirty laundry
bag she couldn't help noticing the bottoms were yellow
from rubbing between his legs. Personally, Lulu did
not despise uncleanliness : it was more intimate and
made such tender shadows ; in the crook of the arm,
for instance ; she couldn't stand the English with their
impersonal bodies which smelt of nothing. But she
couldn't bear her husband's negligence because it was
a way of getting himself cuddled. In the morning, when
he arose, he was always very tender toward himself,

his head full of dreams, and broad daylight, cold
water, the coarse bristles of the brush made him suffer
brutal injustices.

Lulu was sleeping on her back, she had thrust the
great toe of her left foot into a tear in the sheet : it
wasn't a tear, it was only the hem coming apart. It
annoyed her ; I'll have to fix that tomorrow, still she
pushed against the threads so as to feel them break.
Henri was not sleeping yet, but he was quiet. He often
told Lulu that as soon as he closed his eyes he felt
bound by tight, resistant bonds, he could not even
move his little finger. A great fly caught in a spider
web. Lulu loved to feel this gross, captive body against
her. If he could only stay like that, paralysed, I would
take care of him, clean him like a child and sometimes
I'd turn him over on his stomach and give him a
spanking, and other times when his mother came to
see him, I'd find some reason to uncover him, I'd pull
back the sheet and his mother would see him all naked.
I think she'd fall flat on her face, it must be fifteen
years since she's seen him like that. Lulu passed a
hand over her husband's hip and pinched him a little
in the groin. Henri muttered but did not move.
Reduced to impotence. Lulu smiled ; the word
"impotence" always made her smile. When she still
loved Henri, and when he slept, thus, she liked to imagine
he had been patiently tied up by little men like the
ones she had seen in a picture when she was a child
and reading *Gulliver's Travels*. She often called Henri
"Gulliver" and Henri liked that because it was an
English name and it made her seem educated, only he
would rather have had her pronounce it with the
accent. God, but that annoyed me : if he wanted

someone educated all he had to do was marry Jeanne
Beder, she's got breasts like hunting horns but she
knows five languages. When we were still at Sceaux,
on Sundays, I got so annoyed with his family I read
books, any book; there was always somebody who
came and watched what I was reading and his little
sister asked me, " Do you understand, Lucie ? " The
trouble is, he doesn't think I'm distinguished enough.
The Swiss, yes, they're distinguished all right because
his older sister married a Swiss who gave her five
children and then they impress him with their
mountains. I can't have a child because of my
constitution, but I never thought it was distinguished,
what he does, when he goes out with me, always going
into the *urinoirs* and I have to look at the store
windows, waiting for him, what does that make me
look like ? and he comes out pulling at his pants and
bending his legs like an old man.

Lulu took her toe out of the slit in the sheet and
wiggled her feet for the pleasure of feeling herself alert
next to this soft, captive flesh. She heard rumblings :
a talking stomach, I hate it, I can never tell whether it's
his stomach or mine. She closed her eyes ; liquids do
it, bubbling through packs of soft pipes, everybody has
them. Rirette has them, I have them (I don't like to
think about it, it makes my stomach hurt). He loves
me, he doesn't love my bowels, if they showed him
my appendix in a glass, he wouldn't recognise it, he's
always feeling me, but if they put the glass in his hands
he wouldn't care, he wouldn't think " that's hers," you
ought to love all of somebody, the esophagus, the liver,
the intestines. Maybe we don't love them because we
aren't used to them, if we saw them the way we saw

9

our hands and arms maybe we'd love them ; the starfish must love each other better than we do. They stretch out on the beach when there's sunlight and they poke out their stomachs to get the air and everybody can see them ; I wonder where we could stick ours out, through the navel. She had closed her eyes and blue circles began to turn, like the carnival yesterday, I was shooting at circles with rubber arrows and letters lit up, one at every shot and they made the name of a city, he kept me from finishing Dijon with his mania for pressing himself up behind me, I hate people to touch me from behind, I'd rather not have a back, I don't like people to do things to me when I can't see them, they can grab a handful and then you don't see their hands, you can feel them going up and down but you can't tell where they're going, they look at you with all their eyes and you don't see them, he loves that ; Henri would never think of it but he, all he thinks about is getting behind me and I know he does it on purpose to touch my behind because he knows I practically die of shame because I have one, when I'm ashamed it excites him but I don't want to think about him (she was afraid) I want to think about Rirette. She thought about Rirette every evening at the same time, just at the moment when Henri began to snuffle and grunt. But there was resistance to the thought and the other one came in her place, she even caught a glimpse of crisp black hair and she thought here it is and she shuddered because you never know what's coming, if it's the face it's all right, that can still pass, but there were nights she spent without closing her eyes because of those horrible memories coming to the surface, it's terrible when you know all of a man and especially *that*. It isn't the same

10

thing with Henri, I can imagine him from head to foot
and it touches me because he's soft with flesh that's all
grey except the belly and that's pink, he says when a
well built man sits down, his belly makes three folds,
but he has six, only he counts by twos and he doesn't
want to see the others. She felt annoyed thinking about
Rirette: "Lulu, you don't know what the body of
a handsome man is like." It's ridiculous, naturally I
know, she means a body hard as rock with muscles,
I don't like that, Patterson had a body like that and I
felt soft as a caterpillar when he hugged me against
him; I married Henri because he was soft, because he
looked like a priest. The priests are soft as women with
their cassocks and I hear they wear stockings. When
I was fifteen I wanted to lift up their skirts quietly and
see their men's knees and their drawers, it was so funny
to think they had something between their legs.

The crisp hair, the hair of a negro. And anguish in
her throat like a ball. But she closed her eyes tightly
and finally the ear of Rirette appeared, a small ear, all
red and golden, looking like a sugar candy. Lulu had
not as much pleasure as usual at the sight of it because
she heard Rirette's voice at the same time. It was a
sharp, precise voice which Lulu didn't like. "You *must*
go away with Pierre, Lulu; it's the only intelligent thing
to do." I like Rirette very much, but she annoys me
a little when she acts important and gets carried away
by what she says. The night before, at the *Côupole*,
Rirette was bent over her with a reasonable and
somewhat haggard look. "You *can't* stay with Henri,
because you don't love him, it would be a crime." She
doesn't lose a chance to say something bad about him,
I don't think it's very nice, he's always been perfect

with her ; maybe I don't love him any more, but it isn't
up to Rirette to tell me ; everything looks so simple and
easy to her : you love or you don't love any more : but
I'm not simple. First I'm used to it here and then I
do like him, he's my husband. I wanted to beat her, I
always want to hurt her because she's fat. " It would
be a crime." She raised her arms, I saw her armpit,
I always like her better when she has bare arms. The
armpit. It was half-open, you might have thought it
was a mouth ; Lulu saw purple, wrinkled flesh beneath
the curly hairs. Pierre calls her " Minerva the Plump ",
she doesn't like that at all, Lulu smiled because she
thought of her little brother Robert who asked her one
day when she had on nothing but her slip, " Why do
you have hair under your arms ?" and she answered,
" It's a sickness." She liked to dress in front of her
little brother because he made such funny remarks, and
you wondered where he picked them up. He always felt
her clothes and folded her dresses carefully, his hands
were so deft : one day he'll be a great dressmaker.
That's a charming profession, I'll design the materials
for him. It's odd for a boy to want to be a dressmaker ;
if I had been a boy I would have wanted to be an
explorer or an actor, but not a dressmaker ; but he
always was a dreamer, he doesn't talk enough, he sticks
to his own ideas ; I wanted to be a nun and take up
collections in beautiful houses. My eyes feel all soft, all
soft as flesh, I'm going to sleep. My lovely pale face
under the stiff head-dress, I would have looked distinguished. I would have seen hundreds of dark hallways.
But the maid would have turned the light on right
away ; then I'd have seen family portraits, bronze
statues on the tables. And closets. The woman comes

12

with a little book and a fifty-franc note. "Here you
are, Sister." "Thank you madame, God bless you.
Until the next time." But I wouldn't have been a real
nun. In the bus, sometimes, I'd have made eyes at
some fellow, first he'd be dumbfounded, then he'd
follow me, telling me a lot of nonsense and I'd have
a policeman lock him up. I would have kept the collection money myself. What would I have bought ?
Antidote. It's silly. My eyes are getting softer, I like
that, you'd think they were soaked in water and my
whole body's comfortable. The beautiful green tiara
with emeralds and lapis lazuli. The tiara turned and
it was a horrible bull's head, but Lulu was not afraid,
she said, "Birds of Cantal. Attention." A long red
river dragged across arid countrysides. Lulu thought
of her meat-grinder, then of hair grease.

"It would be a crime." She jumped bolt upright in
the blackness, her eyes hard. They're torturing me,
don't they see ? I know Rirette has good intentions,
but she who's so reasonable for other people, ought to
know I need to think it over. He said "You'll come ! "
making fiery eyes at me. "You'll come into my house,
I want you all for myself ! " His eyes terrify me when
he tries to act like a hypnotist ; he kneaded my arms ;
when I see him with eyes like that I always think of the
hair he has on his chest. You will come. I want you
all for myself ; how can he say things like that ? I'm
not a dog.

When I sat down, I smiled at him. I had changed my
powder for him and I made up my eyes because he
likes that, but he didn't see a thing, he doesn't look at
my face, he looks at my breasts and I wish they'd dry
up, just to annoy him, even though I don't have too

much, they're so small. You will come to my villa in Nice. He said it was white with a marble staircase, that it looked out on the sea, and we'd live naked all day, it must be funny to go up a stairway when you're naked; I'd make him go up ahead of me so that he wouldn't look at me; or else I wouldn't be able to move a foot, I'd stay motionless, wishing with all my heart he'd go blind; anyhow, that would hardly change anything; when he's there I always think I'm naked. He took me by the arm, he looked wicked, he told me " You've got me under your skin ! " and I was afraid and said, " Yes "; I want to make you happy, we'll go riding in the car, in the boat, we'll go to Italy and I'll give you everything you want. But his villa is almost unfurnished and we'd have to sleep on a mattress on the floor. He wants me to sleep in his arms and I'll smell his odour; I'd like his chest because it's brown and wide, but there's a pile of hair on it, I wish men didn't have hair, his is black and soft as moss, sometimes I stroke it and sometimes I'm horrified by it, I pull back as far as possible but he hugs me against him. He'll want me to sleep in his arms, he'll hug me in his arms and I'll smell his odour; and when it's dark we'll hear the noise of the sea and he may wake me up in the middle of the night if he wants to do it: I'll never be able to sleep peacefully except when I have my sickness.

Lulu opened her eyes, the curtains were coloured red by a light coming from the street, there was a red reflection in the mirror: Lulu loved this red light and there was an armchair which made funny shadows against the window. Henri had put his pants on the arm of the chair, and his braces were hanging in emptiness. I have to buy him new braces. Oh I don't want to, I don't want to leave. He'll kiss me all day and I'll be *his*, I'll be his pleasure, he'll look at me, he'll think, " this is my pleasure, I touched her there and there and I can do it again if it pleases me." At Port-Royal. Lulu kicked her feet in the sheets, she hated Pierre when she remembered what happened at Port-Royal. She was behind the hedge, she thought he had stayed in the car, looking at the map, and suddenly she saw him, sneaking up behind her. He looked at her. Lulu kicked Henri. He's going to wake up. But Henri said " Humph," and didn't waken. I'd like to know a hand-some young man, pure as a girl, and we wouldn't touch each other, we'd walk along the seashore and we'd hold hands, and at night we'd sleep in twin beds, we'd stay like brother and sister and talk till morning. I'd like to live with Rirette, it's so charming, women living together ; she has fat, smooth shoulders ; I was miser-able when she was in love with Fresnel, and it worried me to think he petted her, that he passed his hands slowly over her shoulders and thighs and she sighed. I wonder how her face must look when she's stretched out like that, all naked, under a man, feeling hands on her flesh. I wouldn't touch her for all the money in the world. I wouldn't know what to do with her, even if she wanted, even if she said, " I want it," I wouldn't know how, but if I were invisible I'd like to be there when somebody was doing it to her and watch her face (I'd be surprised if she still looked like Minerva) and stroke her spread knees gently, her pink knees and hear her groan. Dry throated, Lulu gave a short laugh : sometimes you think about things like that. Once she pretended Pierre wanted to rape Rirette. And I helped

him, I held Rirette in my arms. Yesterday. She had
fire in her cheeks, we were sitting on her sofa, one
against the other, her legs were pressed together, but
we didn't say anything, we'll never say anything. Henri
began to snore and Lulu hissed. Here I am, I can't
sleep, I'm upset and he snores, the fool. If he were to
take me in his arms, beg me, if he told me, "You are
all mine, Lulu, I love you, don't go!" I'd make the
sacrifice for him, I'd stay, yes, I'd stay with him all my
life to make him happy.

II

Rirette sat on the terrace of the *Dôme* and ordered a
glass of port. She felt weary and angry at Lulu:

And their port has a taste of cork, Lulu doesn't care
because she drinks coffee, but still you can't drink
coffee at apéritif time; here they drink coffee all day
or café-crême because they don't have a franc, God
that must annoy them, I couldn't do it, I'd chuck the
whole place in the customers' faces, these people don't
need to keep up with anybody. I don't know why she
always meets me in Montparnasse, it would be just as
close if she met me at the *Café de la Paix* or the *Pam-
Pam*, and it wouldn't take me so far from my work;
impossible to imagine how sad it makes me feel to see
these faces all the time, as soon as I have a minute
to spare, I have to come here, it's not so bad on the
terrace, but inside it smells like dirty underwear and I
don't like failures. Even on the terrace I feel out of
place because I'm clean, it must surprise everybody
that passes to see me in the middle of these people

here who don't even shave and women who look like
I don't know what. They must wonder " What's she
doing there ? " I know rich Americans sometimes
come in the summer, but it seems they're stopping in
England now, what with the Government we've got,
that's why the commerce-de-luxe isn't going so well, I
sold a half less than last year at this same time, and
I wonder how the others make out, because I'm the
best salesgirl, Mme Dubech told me so, I feel sorry for
the little Yonnel girl, she doesn't know how to sell, she
can't have made a franc commission this month, and
when you're on your feet all day you like to relax a
little in a nice place, with a little luxury and a little art
and stylish help. You like to close your eyes and let
yourself go and then you like to have nice soft music,
it wouldn't cost so much to go dancing at the *Ambassa-
deurs* sometimes ; but the waiters here are so impudent,
you can tell they're used to handling a cheap crowd,
except the little one with brown hair who serves me,
he's nice ; I think Lulu must like to be surrounded
with all these failures, it would scare her to go into
a chic place, fundamentally, she isn't sure of herself,
it frightens her as soon as there's a man with good
manners, she didn't like Louis ; well she ought to be
comfortable here, some of them don't even have collars,
with their shoddy appearance and their pipes and the
way they look at you, they don't even try to hide it,
you can see they don't have enough money to pay for
a woman, but that isn't what's lacking in the neighbour-
hood, it's disgusting ; you'd think they're going to eat
you and they couldn't even tell you nicely that they
want you, to carry it off in a way that would make you
feel good.

1–2 17

The waiter came: "Did you want dry port, made-moiselle?"

"Yes, please."

He spoke again, looking friendly. "Nice weather we're having."

"Not too soon for it," Rirette said.

"That's right. You'd have thought winter would never end."

He left and Rirette followed him with her eyes. I like that waiter, she thought, he knows his place, he doesn't get familiar, but he always has something to say to me, a little special attention.

A thin, bent young man was watching her steadily; Rirette shrugged her shoulders and turned her back on him; when they want to make eyes at a woman they could at least change their underwear. I'll tell him that if he says anything to me. I wonder why she doesn't leave. She doesn't want to hurt Henri, I think that's too stupid: a woman doesn't have the right to spoil her life for some impotent. Rirette hated impotents, it was physical. She's got to leave, she decided, her happiness is at stake, I'll tell her she can't gamble with her happiness. Lulu, you don't have the right to gamble with your happiness. I won't say anything to her, it's finished, I told her a hundred times, you can't make people happy if they don't want to be. Rirette felt a great emptiness in her head, because she was so tired, she looked at the port, all sticky in the glass, like a liquid caramel and a voice in her repeated, "Happi-ness, happiness," and it was a beautifully grave and tender word.

And she thought that if anybody asked her opinion in the *Paris-Soir* contest she would have said it was the most beautiful word in the French language. Did anyone think of it ? They said energy, courage, but that's because they were men, there should have been a woman, the women could find it, there should have been two prizes, one for men and one for women and the most beautiful name would have been Honour ; one for the women and I'd have won, I'd have said Happiness. Happiness and Honour. I'll tell her, Lulu, you don't have the right to sacrifice your happiness. Your Happiness, Lulu, your Happiness. Personally, I think Pierre is very nice, first, he's a real man, and besides, he's intelligent and that never spoils anything, he has money, he'd do anything for her. He's one of those men who knows how to smooth out life's little difficulties, that's nice for a woman ; I like people who know how to command, it's a knack, but he knows how to speak to waiters and maîtres-d'hotel ; they obey him, I call that a dominant personality. Maybe that's the thing that's most lacking in Henri. And then there's the question of health, with the father she had, she should take care, it's charming to be slender and light and never to be hungry or sleepy, to sleep four hours a night and run all over Paris all day selling material but it's silly, she ought to follow a sensible diet, only eat a little at one time, of course, but more often and at regular hours. She'll see when they send her to the sanatorium for ten years.

She stared perplexedly at the clock in the Montparnasse intersection, it marked 11.20. I don't understand Lulu, she's got a funny temperament, I could never find out whether she liked men or whether they disgusted her ; still, she ought to be happy with Pierre, that gives her a change, anyhow, from the one she had last year,

19

from her Rabut, *Rebut* I called him. This memory
amused her but she held back her smile because the
thin young man was still watching her, she caught him
by surprise when she turned her head. Rabut had a
face dotted with blackheads and Lulu amused herself
by removing them for him, pressing on the skin with
her nails : It's sickening, but it's not her fault, Lulu
doesn't know what a good-looking man is, I love cute
men, first, their things are so pretty, their men's shirts,
their shoes, their shiny ties, it may be crude, but it's so
sweet, so strong, a sweet strength, it's like the smell of
English tobacco and eau de cologne and their skin
when they've just shaved, it isn't . . . it isn't like a
woman's skin, you'd think it was cordova leather, and
their strong arms close around you and you put your
head on their chest, you smell their sweet strong odour
of well-groomed men, they whisper sweet words to you ;
they have nice things, nice rough cowhide shoes, they
whisper, " Darling, dearest darling " and you feel yourself fainting ; Rirette thought of Louis who left her last
year and her heart tightened ; a man in love with himself, with a pile of little mannerisms, a ring and gold
cigarette case and full of little manias . . . but they can
be rough sometimes, worse than women. The best thing
would be a man about forty, someone who still took
care of himself, with grey hair on the sides, brushed
back, very dry, with broad shoulders, athletic, but
who'd know life and who'd be good because he'd
suffered. Lulu is only a kid, she's lucky to have a
friend like me, because Pierre's beginning to get tired
and some people would take advantage of it if they
were in my place ; I always tell him to be patient, and
when he gets a little sweet on me I act like I'm not

paying attention, I begin to talk about Lulu and I always have a good word for her, but she doesn't deserve the luck she has, she doesn't realise ; I wish she'd live alone a little the way I did when Louis went away, she'd see what it was like to go back alone to her room every evening, when you've worked all day and find the room empty and dying to put your head on a shoulder. Sometimes you wonder where you find the courage to get up the next morning and go back to work and be seductive and gay and make everybody feel good when you'd rather die than keep on with that life.

The clock struck 11.30. Rirette thought of happiness, the bluebird, the bird of happiness, the rebel bird of love. She gave a start. Lulu is half an hour late, that's usual. She'll never leave her husband, she doesn't have enough will power for that. At heart, it's mainly because of respectability that she stays with Henri : she cheats on him but so long as they call her " Madame," she doesn't think it matters. She can say anything against him she wants but you can't repeat it to her the next day, she'd flare up. I did everything I could and I've told her everything I had to tell her, too bad for her.

A taxi stopped in front of the *Dôme* and Lulu stepped out. She was carrying a large valise and her face was solemn.

" I left Henri," she called from a distance.

She came nearer, bent under the weight of the valise. She was smiling.

" What ? " Rirette gasped, " you don't mean . . ."

" Yes," Lulu said. " Finished, I dropped him."

21

Rirette was still incredulous. " He knows ? You told him ? "

Lulu's eyes flashed. " And how ! " she said.

" Well, well . . . my own little Lulu ! "

Rirette did not know what to think, but in any case, she supposed Lulu needed encouragement.

" That's good news," she said. " How brave you were."

She felt like adding : you see, it wasn't so hard. But she restrained herself. Lulu let herself be admired : she had rouged her cheeks and her eyes were bright. She sat and put the valise down near her. She was wearing a grey wool coat with a leather belt, a light yellow sweater with a rolled collar. She was bare-headed. She recognised immediately the blend of guilt and amusement she was plunged in ; Lulu always made that impression on her. What I like about her, Rirette thought, is her vitality.

" In two shakes," Lulu said, " I told him what I thought. He was struck dumb."

" I can't get over it," said Rirette. " But what came over you, darling ? Yesterday evening I'd have bet my last franc you'd never leave him."

" It's on account of my kid brother, I don't mind him getting stuck up with me but I can't stand it when he starts on my family."

" But how did it happen ? "

" Where's the waiter ? " Lulu asked, stirring restlessly on the chair. " The *Dôme* waiters aren't ever there when you want them. Is the little brownhaired one serving us ? "

" Yes," Rirette said, " did you know he's mad about me ? "

22

" Oh ? Look out for the woman in the washroom then, he's always mixed up with her. He makes up to her but I think it's just an excuse to see the women go into the toilets ; when they come out he looks hard enough to make you blush. By the way, I've got to leave you for a minute, I have to go down and call Pierre, I'd like to see his face ! If you see the waiter, order a café-crême for me : I'll only be a minute and then I'll tell you everything."

She got up, took a few steps and came back towards Rirette. " I'm so happy, Rirette darling."

" Dearest Lulu," said Rirette, taking her by the hands.

Lulu left her and stepped lightly across the terrace. Rirette watched her. I never thought she could do it. How gay she is, she thought, a little scandalised, it's good for her to walk out on her husband. If she had listened to me she'd have done it long ago. Anyhow, it's thanks to me ; fundamentally, I have a lot of influence on her.

Lulu was back a few minutes later.

" Pierre was bowled over," she said. " He wanted the details but I'll give them to him later, I'm lunching with him. He says maybe we can leave tomorrow night."

" How glad I am, Lulu," Rirette said. " Tell me quickly. Did you decide last night ? "

" You know, I didn't decide anything," Lulu said modestly. " It was decided all by itself." She tapped nervously on the table. "Waiter ! Waiter ! God, he annoys me. I'd like a café-crême."

Rirette was shocked. In Lulu's place and under circumstances as serious as that she wouldn't have lost

23

time running after a café-crême. Lulu was charming, but it was amazing how futile she could be, like a bird.

Lulu burst out laughing. " If you'd seen Henri's face ! "

" I wonder what your mother will say ? " said Rirette seriously.

" My mother ? She'll be en-chant-ed," Lulu said with assurance. " He was impolite with her, you know, she was fed up. Always complaining because she didn't bring me up right, that I was this, I was that, that you could see I was brought up in a barn. You know, what I did was a little because of her."

" But what happened ? "

" Well, he slapped Robert."

" You mean Robert was in your flat ? "

" Yes, just passing by this morning, because mother wants to apprentice him to Gompez. I think I told you. So, he stepped in while we were eating breakfast and Henri slapped him."

" But why ? " Rirette asked, slightly annoyed. She hated the way Lulu told stories.

" They had an argument," Lulu said vaguely, " and the boy wouldn't let himself be insulted. He stood right up to him. ' Old asshole,' he called him, right to his face. Because Henri said he was poorly raised, naturally, that's all he can say. I thought I'd die laughing. Then Henri got up, we were eating in the kitchenette, and smacked him, I could have killed him ! "

" So you left ? "

" Left ? " Lulu asked, amazed, " where ? "

" I thought you left him then. Look, Lulu, you've got to tell me these things in order, otherwise I won't understand. Tell me," she added, suspiciously, " you really did leave him, that's all true ? "

" Of course. I've been explaining to you for an hour."

" Good. So Henri slapped Robert. Then what ? "

" Then," Lulu said, " I locked him on the balcony, it was too funny ! He was still in his pyjamas, tapping on the window but he didn't dare break the glass because he's as mean as dirt. If I had been in his place, I'd have broken up everything, even if I had to cut my hands to pieces. And the Texiers came in. Then he started smiling through the window acting as if it were a joke."

The waiter passed ; Lulu seized his arm :

" So there you are, waiter. Would it trouble you too much to get me a café-crême ? "

Rirette was annoyed and she smiled knowingly at the waiter but the waiter remained solemn and bowed with guilty obsequiousness. Rirette was a little angry at Lulu ; she never knew the right tone to use on inferiors, sometimes she was too familiar, sometimes too dry and demanding.

Lulu began to laugh.

" I'm laughing because I can still see Henri in his pyjamas on the balcony ; he was shivering with cold. Do you know how I managed to lock him out ? He was in the back of the kitchenette, Robert was crying and he was preaching a sermon. I opened the window and told him, ' Look, Henri : there's a taxi that just knocked over the flower woman.' He came right out ; he likes the flower woman because she told him she was Swiss and he thinks she's in love with him. ' Where ? Where ? ' he kept saying. I stepped back quietly, into the room, and closed the window. Then I shouted through the glass, ' That'll teach you to act like a brute with my brother.' I left him on the balcony more than an hour, he kept watching us with big round eyes, he was green with rage. I stuck out my tongue at him and gave Robert candy ; after that I brought my things into the kitchenette and got dressed in front of Robert because I know Henri hates that : Robert kissed my arms and neck like a little man, he's so charming, we acted as if Henri weren't there. On top of all that, I forgot to wash."

" And Henri outside the window. It's too funny for words," Rirette said, bursting with laughter.

Lulu stopped laughing. " I'm afraid he'll catch cold," she said seriously. " You don't think when you're mad." She went on gaily, " He shook his fist at us and kept talking all the time but I didn't understand half of what he said. Then Robert left and right after that the Texiers rang and I let them in. When he saw them he was all smiles and bowing at them and I told them, ' Look at my husband, my big darling, doesn't he look like a fish in an aquarium ? ' The Texiers waved at him through the glass, they were a little surprised but they didn't let on."

" I can see it all," Rirette said, laughing. " Haha ! Your husband on the balcony and the Texiers in the kitchenette." Several times she repeated, " Your husband on the balcony and the Texiers in the kitchenette. . . ." She wanted to find the right comic and picturesque words to describe the scene to Lulu, she thought Lulu did not have a real sense of humour, but the words did not come.

" I opened the window," Lulu said, " and Henri

came in. He kissed me in front of the Texiers and called me a little clown. ' Oh the little clown,' he said, ' she wanted to play a trick on me.' And I smiled and the Texiers smiled politely, everybody smiled. But when they left he hit me on the ear. Then I took a brush and hit him in the corner of the mouth with it : I split both lips."

" Poor girl," Rirette said with tenderness.

But with a gesture Lulu dismissed all compassion. She held herself straight, shaking her brown curls combatively and her eyes flashed lightning.

" Then we talked it over : I washed his mouth with a cloth and then I told him I was sick of it, that I didn't love him any more and that I was leaving. He began to cry. He said he'd kill himself. But that didn't work any more : you remember, Rirette, last year, when there was all that trouble in the Rhineland, he sang the same tune every day : ' There's going to be a war, I'm going to enlist and I'll be killed and you'll be sorry, you'll regret all the sorrow you've caused me.' ' That's enough,' I told him, ' you're impotent, they wouldn't take you.' Anyhow, I calmed him down because he was talking about locking me up in the kitchenette, I swore I wouldn't leave before a month. After that he went to the office, his eyes were all red and there was a piece of cloth sticking to his lip, he didn't look too good. I did the housework, I put the lentils on the stove and packed my bag. I left him a note on the kitchen table."

" What did you write ? "

" I wrote," Lulu said proudly, " the lentils are on the stove. Help yourself and turn off the gas. There's

ham in the icebox. I'm fed up and I'm clearing out.
Goodbye."

They both laughed and the passers-by turned around.
Rirette thought they must present a charming sight and
was sorry they weren't sitting on the terrace of the *Viel*
or the *Café de la Paix*. When they finished laughing,
they were silent a moment and Rirette realized they
had nothing more to say to each other. She was a
little disappointed.

" I've got to run," Lulu said, rising ; " I meet Pierre
at noon. What am I going to do with my bag ? "

" Leave it with me," Rirette said, " I'll check it with
the woman in the ladies' room. When will I see you
again ? "

" I'll pick you up at your place at two, I have a pile
of errands to do : I didn't take half my things. Pierre's
going to have to give me money."

Lulu left and Rirette called the waiter. She felt grave
and sad enough for two. The waiter ran up : Rirette
had already noticed that he always hurried when she
called him.

" That's five francs," he said. He added a little
dryly, " You two were pretty gay, I could hear you
laughing all the way back there."

Lulu hurt his feelings, thought Rirette, spitefully.
Blushing, she said, " My friend is a little nervous, this
morning."

" She's very charming," the waiter said soulfully.
" Thank you very much, mademoiselle."

He pocketed the six francs and went off. Rirette was
a little amazed but noon struck and she thought it was
time for Henri to come back and find Lulu's note : this
was a moment full of sweetness for her.

" I'd like all that to be sent *before tomorrow evening*, to the Hotel du Théâtre, Rue Vandamme," Lulu told the cashier, putting on the air of a great lady. She turned to Rirette :

" It's all over. Let's go."

" What name ? " the cashier asked.

" Mme Lucienne Crispin."

Lulu threw her coat over her arm and began to run ; she ran down the wide staircase of the Samaritaine. Rirette followed her, almost falling several times because she didn't watch her step : she had eyes only for the slender silhouette of blue and canary yellow dancing before her ! It's true, she does have an obscene body . . . Each time Rirette saw Lulu from behind or in profile, she was struck by the obscenity of her shape though she could not explain why ; it was an impression. She's supple and slender, but there's something indecent about her, I don't know what. She does everything she can to display herself, that must be it. She says she's ashamed of her behind and still she wears skirts that cling to her rump. Her tail is small, yes, a lot smaller than mine, but you can see more of it. It's all round, under her thin back, it fills the skirt, you'd think it was poured in, and besides it jiggles.

Lulu turned around and they smiled at each other. Rirette thought of her friend's indiscreet body with a mixture of reprobation and languor : tight little breasts, a polished flesh, all yellow—when you touched it you'd swear it was rubber—long thighs, a long, common body with long legs : the body of a negress, Rirette thought, she looks like a negress dancing the rhumba. Near the revolving door a mirror gave Rirette the reflection of her own full body. I'm more the athletic type, she thought, taking Lulu's arm, she makes a better impression than I do when we're dressed, but naked, I'm sure I'm better than she is.

They stayed silent for a moment, then Lulu said:

" Pierre was simply charming. You've been charming too, Rirette, and I'm very grateful to both of you."

She said that with constraint but Rirette paid no attention : Lulu never knew how to thank people, she was too timid.

" What a bore," Lulu said suddenly, " I have to buy a brassière."

" Here ? " Rirette asked. They were just passing a lingerie shop.

" No, but I thought of it because I saw them. I go to Fischer's for my brassières."

" Boulevard du Montparnasse ? " Rirette cried. " Look out, Lulu," she went on gravely, " better not hang around the Boulevard du Montparnasse, especially now ; we'd run into Henri and that would be most unpleasant."

" Henri ? " said Lulu, shrugging her shoulders. " Of course not. Why ? "

Indignation flushed purple on Rirette's cheeks and temples.

" You're still the same, Lulu, when you don't like something, you deny it, pure and simple. You want to go to Fischer's so you insist Henri won't be on the Boulevard du Montparnasse. You know very well he goes by every day at six, it's his way home. You told me that yourself : he goes up the Rue de Rennes and waits for the bus at the corner of the Boulevard Raspail."

"First, it's only five o'clock," Lulu said, "and besides, maybe he didn't go to the office: the note I wrote must have knocked him out."

"But Lulu," Rirette said suddenly. "You know there's another Fischer's not far from the Opera, on the Rue du Quatre Septembre."

"Yes," Lulu said weakly, "but it's so far to go there."

"Well, I like that; so far to gò. It's only two minutes from here, it's a lot closer than Montparnasse."

"I don't like their things."

Rirette thought with amusement that all the Fischer's sold the same things.

But Lulu was incomprehensibly obstinate: Henri was positively the last person on earth she would want to meet now and you'd think she was purposely throwing herself in his way.

"All right," she said indulgently, "let's go to Montparnasse. Besides, Henri's so big, we'd see him before he saw us."

"So what," Lulu said, "if we meet him, we meet him, that's all. He isn't going to eat us."

Lulu insisted on going to Montparnasse on foot; she said she needed air. They followed the Rue de Seine, then the Rue de L'Odéon and the Rue de Vaugirard. Rirette praised Pierre and showed Lulu how perfect he had been under the circumstances.

"How I love Paris," Lulu said, "I'm going to miss it!"

"Oh be quiet, Lulu, when I think how lucky you are to go to Nice and then you say how much you'll miss Paris."

Lulu did not answer; she began looking right and left sadly, searchingly.

When they came out of Fischer's they heard six o'clock strike. Rirette took Lulu's elbow and tried to hurry her along, but Lulu stopped in front of Baumann's florist shop.

"Look at those azaleas, Rirette. If I had a nice living room I'd put them everywhere."

"I don't like potted plants," Rirette said.

She was exasperated. She turned her head towards the Rue de Rennes and sure enough, after a minute, she saw Henri's great stupid silhouette appear. He was bare-headed, and wearing a brown tweed sports coat. Rirette hated brown: "There he is, Lulu, there he is," she said hurriedly.

"Where?" Lulu asked. "Where is he?"

She was scarcely more calm than Rirette.

"Behind us, on the other side of the street. Run and don't turn around."

Lulu turned around anyhow.

"I see him," she said.

Rirette tried to drag her away, but Lulu stiffened and stared at Henri. At last she said, "I think he saw us."

She seemed frightened, suddenly yielded to Rirette and let herself be taken away quietly.

"Now for Heaven's sake, Lulu, don't turn around again," Rirette said breathlessly. "We'll turn down the first street on the right, the Rue Delambre."

They walked very quickly, jostling the passers-by. At times Lulu held back a little, or sometimes it was she who dragged Rirette. But they had not quite reached

the corner of the Rue Delambre when Rirette saw a
large brown shadow behind Lulu; she knew it was
Henri and began shaking with anger. Lulu kept her
eyes lowered, she looked sly and determined. She's
regretting her mistake, but it's too late. Too bad for
her.

They hurried on; Henri followed them without a
word. They passed the Rue Delambre and kept walking in the direction of the Observatoire. Rirette heard
the squeak of Henri's shoes; there was also a sort of
light, regular rattle that kept time with their steps: it
was his breathing. (Henri always breathed heavily, but
never that much; he must have run to catch up with
them or else it was emotion.)

We must act as if he weren't there, Rirette thought.
Pretend not to notice his existence. But she could not
keep from looking out of the corner of her eye. He
was white as a sheet and his eyelids were so lowered
they seemed shut. Almost looks like a sleepwalker,
thought Rirette with a sort of horror. Henri's lips
were trembling and a little bit of pink gauze trembled
on the lower lip. And the breathing, always that
hoarse, even breathing, now ending with a sort of nasal
music. Rirette felt uncomfortable; she was not afraid
of Henri but sickness and passion always frightened her
a little. After a moment Henri put his hand out gently
and took Lulu's arm. Lulu twisted her mouth as if she
were going to cry and pulled away, shuddering.

Henri went " Phew ! "

Rirette had a mad desire to stop: she had a stitch
in the side and her ears were ringing. But Lulu was
almost running; she too looked like a sleepwalker.
Rirette had the feeling that if she let go of Lulu's arm

and stopped, they would both keep on running side by side, mute, pale as death, their eyes closed.

Henri began to speak. With a strange, hoarse voice he said :

" Come back with me."

Lulu did not answer. Henri said again, in the same raucous, toneless voice :

" You are my wife. Come back with me."

" You can see she doesn't want to go back," Rirette answered between her teeth. " Leave her alone."

He did not seem to hear her. " I am your husband," he repeated. " I want you to come back with me."

" For God's sake let her alone," Rirette said sharply, " bothering her like that won't do any good, so shut up and let her be."

He turned an astonished face towards Rirette.

" She is my wife," he said, " she belongs to me, I want her to come back with me."

He had taken Lulu's arm and this time Lulu did not shake him off.

" Go away," Rirette said.

" I won't go away, I'll follow her everywhere, I want her to come back home."

He spoke with effort. Suddenly he made a grimace which showed his teeth and shouted with all his might :

" You belong to me ! "

Some people turned around, laughing. Henri shook Lulu's arm, curled back his lips and growled like an animal. Luckily an empty taxi passed. Rirette waved at it and the taxi stopped. Henri stopped too. Lulu wanted to keep on walking but they held her firmly, each by one arm.

" You ought to know," said Rirette, pulling Lulu

towards the street, " you'll never get her back with violence."

" Let her alone, let my wife alone," Henri said, pulling in the opposite direction. Lulu was limp as a bag of laundry.

" Are you getting in or not ? " the taxi driver called impatiently.

Rirette dropped Lulu's arm and rained blows on Henri's hand. But he did not seem to feel them. After a moment he let go and began to look at Rirette stupidly. Rirette looked at him too. She could barely collect her thoughts, an immense sickness filled her. They stayed eye to eye for a few seconds, both breathing heavily. Then Rirette pulled herself together, took Lulu by the waist and drew her to the taxi.

" Where to ? " the driver asked.

Henri had followed. He wanted to get in with them. But Rirette pushed him back with all her strength and closed the door quickly.

" Drive, drive ! " she told the chauffeur. " We'll tell you the address later."

The taxi started up and Rirette dropped to the back of the car. How vulgar it all was, she thought. She hated Lulu.

" Where do you want to go, Lulu ? " she asked sweetly.

Lulu did not answer. Rirette put her arms around her and became persuasive.

" You must answer me. Do you want me to drop you off at Pierre's ? "

Lulu made a movement Rirette took for acquiescence. She leaned forward. " 11 Rue de Messine."

When Rirette turned around again, Lulu was watching her strangely.

" What the . . ." Rirette began.

" I hate you," Lulu screamed, " I hate Pierre, I hate Henri. What do you all have against me ? You're torturing me."

She stopped short and her features clouded.

" Cry," Rirette said with calm dignity, " cry, it'll do you good."

Lulu bent double and began to sob. Rirette took her in her arms and held her close. From time to time she stroked her hair. But inside she felt cold and distrustful. Lulu was calm when the cab stopped. She wiped her eyes and powdered her nose.

" Excuse me," she said gently, " it was nerves. I couldn't bear seeing him like that, it hurt me."

" He looked like an orang-outang," said Rirette, once more serene.

Lulu smiled.

" When will I see you again ? " Rirette asked.

" Oh, not before tomorrow. You know Pierre can't put me up because of his mother. I'll be at the Hotel du Théâtre. You could come early, around nine, if it doesn't put you out, because after that I'm going to see Mama."

She was pale and Rirette thought sadly of the terrible ease with which she could break down.

" Don't worry too much tonight," she said.

" I'm awfully tired," Lulu said, " I hope Pierre will let me go back early, but he never understands those things."

Rirette kept the taxi and was driven home. For a moment she thought she'd go to the movies but she had no heart for it. She threw her hat on a chair and took a step towards the window. But the bed attracted her, all white, all soft and moist in its shadowy hollows. To throw herself on it, to feel the caress of the pillow against her burning cheeks. I'm strong. I did everything for Lulu and now I'm all alone and no one does anything for me. She had so much pity for herself that she felt a flood of sobs mounting in her throat. They're going to go to Nice and I won't see them any more. I'm the one who made them happy but they won't think about me. And I'll stay here working eight hours a day selling artificial pearls at Burma's. When the first tears rolled down her cheeks she let herself fall softly on the bed. "Nice," she repeated, weeping bitterly, "Nice . . . in the sunlight . . . on the Riviera . . ."

III

Phew !

Black night. You'd think somebody was walking around the room : a man in slippers. He put one foot out cautiously, then the other, unable to avoid a light cracking of the floor. He stopped, there was a moment of silence, then, suddenly transported to the other end of the room, he began his aimless, idiotic walking again. Lulu was cold, the blankets were much too light. She said *Phew* aloud and the sound of her voice frightened her.

Phew ! I'm sure he's looking at the sky and the stars now, he's lighting a cigarette, he's outside, he said he liked the purple colour of the Paris sky. With little steps, he goes back, with little steps : he feels poetic just after he's done it, he told me, and he doesn't think any more about it—and me, I'm defiled. I heard him whistle under my window when he left ; he was down there dry and fresh in his fine clothes and topcoat, you must admit he knows how to dress, a woman would be proud to go out with him, he was under the window and I was naked in the blackness and I was cold and rubbed my belly with my hands because I thought I was still wet. I'll come up for a minute he said, just to see your room. He stayed two hours and the bed creaked— this rotten little iron bed. I wonder where he found out about this hotel, he told me he spent two weeks here once, that I'd be all right here, these are funny rooms, I saw two of them, I never saw such little rooms cluttered up with furniture, cushions and couches and little tables, it stinks of love, I don't know whether he stayed here two weeks but he surely didn't stay alone ; he can't have much respect for me to stick me in here. The bellboy laughed when we went up, an Algerian, I hate those people, they frighten me, he looked at my legs, then he went into the office, he must have thought, that's it, they're going to do it, and imagined all sorts of dirty things, they say it's terrible what they do with women down there ; if they ever got hold of one she limps for the rest of her life ; and all the time Pierre was bothering me I was thinking about that Algerian who was thinking about what I was doing and thinking a lot of dirtiness worse than it was. Somebody's in this room !

Lulu held her breath but the creaking stopped immediately. I have a pain between my thighs, I want to cry and it will be like this every night except tomorrow night because we'll be on the train. Lulu bit her lip and shuddered because she remembered she had groaned. It's not true, I didn't groan, I simply breathed hard a little because he's so heavy, when he's on me he takes my breath away. He said, " You're groaning." I hate people to talk to me when I'm doing that, I wish they'd forget, but he never stops saying a lot of dirty things. I didn't groan, in the first place, I can't have any pleasure, it's a fact, the doctor said so. He won't believe it, they never want to believe it, they all said : " It's because you got off to a bad start, I'll teach you " ; I let them talk, I knew what the trouble was, it's medical ; but that provokes them.

Someone was coming up the stairs. Someone coming back. God, don't let him come back. He's capable of doing it if he feels like it again. It isn't him, those are heavy steps—or else—Lulu's heart jumped in her breast —if it were the Algerian, he knows I'm alone, he's going to knock on the door, I can't, I can't stand that, no, it's the floor below, it's a man going in, he's putting his key in the lock, he's taking his time, he's drunk, I wonder who lives in this hotel, it must be a fine bunch ; I met a redhead this afternoon, on the stairs, she had eyes like a dope fiend. I didn't groan. Of course, he finally did bother me with all his feeling around, he knows how ; I have a horror of men who know how, I'd rather sleep with a virgin. They take you for an instrument they're proud of knowing how to play. I hate people to bother me, my throat's dry, I'm afraid and I have a bad taste in my mouth and I'm humiliated because they think they dominate me, I'd like to slap Pierre when he puts on his elegant airs and says, " I've got technique." My God, to think that's life, that's why you get dressed and wash and make yourself pretty and

all the books are written about that and you think about
it all the time and finally that's what it is, you go to a
room with somebody who half smothers you and ends
up by wetting your belly. I want to sleep. Oh, if I
could only sleep a little bit, tomorrow I'll travel all
night, I'll be all in. Still, I'd like to be a little fresh to
walk around Nice; they say it's so lovely, little Italian
streets and all coloured clothes drying in the sun, I'll
set myself up with my easel and I'll paint and the little
girls will come to see what I'm doing. Rot! (she had
stretched out a little and her hip touched the damp spot
on the sheet). That's all he brought me here for.
Nobody, nobody loves me. He walked beside me and
I almost fainted and I waited for one tender word, he
could have said, "I love you." I wouldn't have gone
back to him of course, but I'd have said something
nice, we would have parted good friends. I waited and
waited, he took my arm and I let him. Rirette was
furious, it's not true he looked like an orang-outang
but I knew she was thinking something like that, she
was watching him out of the corner of her eye, nastily,
it's amazing how nasty she can be, well, in spite of that,
when he took my arm I didn't resist but it wasn't *me*
he wanted, he wanted *his wife* because he married me
and he's my husband; he always depreciated me, he
said he was more intelligent than I and everything that
happened is all his fault, he didn't need to treat me so
high and mighty, I'd still be with him. I'm sure he
doesn't miss me now, he isn't crying, he's snoring, that's
what he's doing and he's glad to have the bed all to
himself so he can stretch out his long legs.

I'd like to die. I'm so afraid he'll think badly of me;
I couldn't explain anything to him because Rirette was

between us, talking, talking, she looked hysterical. Now she's glad, she's complimenting herself on her courage, how rotten that is with Henri who's gentle as a lamb. I'll go. They can't make me leave him like a dog. She jumped out of bed and turned the switch. My stockings and slip are enough. She was in such a hurry that she did not even take the trouble to comb her hair. And the people who see me won't know I'm naked under my heavy grey coat, it comes down to my feet. The Algerian—she stopped, her heart pounding—I'll have to wake him up to open the door. She went down on tiptoe—but the steps creaked one by one; she knocked at the office window.

"What is it?" the Algerian asked. His eyes were red and his hair tousled, he didn't look very frightening.

"Open the door for me," Lulu said dryly.

Fifteen minutes later she rang at Henri's door.

"Who's there?" Henri asked through the door.

"It's me."

He doesn't answer, he doesn't want to let me in my own home. But I'll knock on the door till he opens, he'll give in because of the neighbours. After a minute the door was half opened and Henri appeared, pale, with a pimple on his nose; he was in pyjamas. He hasn't slept, Lulu thought tenderly.

"I didn't want to leave like that, I wanted to see you again."

Henri still said nothing. Lulu entered, pushing him aside a little. How stupid he is, he's always in your way, he's looking at me with round eyes, with his arms hanging, he doesn't know what to do with his body. Shut up, shut up, I see you're moved and you can't speak. He made an effort to swallow his saliva and Lulu had to close the door.

" I want us to part good friends," she said.

He opened his mouth as if to speak, turned suddenly and fled. What's he doing ? She dared not follow him. Is he crying ? Suddenly she heard him cough : he's in the bathroom. When he came back she hung about his neck and pressed her mouth against his : he smelled of vomit. Lulu burst out sobbing.

" I'm cold," Henri said.

" Let's go to bed," she said, weeping, " I can stay till tomorrow morning."

They went to bed and Lulu was shaken with enormous sobs because she found her room and bed clean and the red glow in the window. She thought Henri would take her in his arms but he did nothing : he was lying stretched out full length as if someone had put a poker in the bed. He's as stiff as when he talks to a Swiss. She took his head in her two hands and stared at him. " You are pure, pure." He began to cry.

" I'm miserable," he said, " I've never been so miserable."

" I haven't either," Lulu said.

They wept for a long time. After a while she put out the light and laid her head on his shoulder. If we could stay like that forever : pure and sad as two orphans ; but it isn't possible, it doesn't happen in life. Life was an enormous wave breaking on Lulu, tearing her from the arms of Henri. Your hand, your big hand. He's proud of them because they're big, he says that descendants of old families always have big limbs. He won't take my waist in his hands any more—he tickled me a little but I was proud because he could almost make his fingers meet. It isn't true that he's impotent, he's pure, pure—and a little lazy. She smiled through her tears and kissed him under the chin.

"What am I going to tell my parents?" Henri asked. "My mother'll die when she hears."

Mme Crispin would not die, on the contrary, she would triumph. They'll talk about me, at meals, all five of them, blaming me, like people who know a lot about things but don't want to say everything because of the kid who's sixteen and she's too young to talk about certain things in front of her. She'll laugh inside herself because she knows it all, she always knows it all and she detests me. All this muck. And appearances are against me.

"Don't tell them right away," she pleaded, "tell them I'm at Nice for my health."

"They won't believe me."

She kissed Henri quickly all over his face.

"Henri, you weren't nice enough to me."

"That's true," Henri said. "I wasn't nice enough. Neither were you," he reflected, "you weren't nice enough."

"I wasn't. Ah!" Lulu said, "how miserable we are!" She cried so loudly she thought she would suffocate: soon it would be day and she would leave. You never, never do what you want, you're carried away.

"You shouldn't have left like that," said Henri.

Lulu sighed. "I loved you a lot, Henri."

"And now you don't?"

"It isn't the same."

"Who are you leaving with?"

"People you don't know."

43

"How do you know people I don't know?" Henri asked angrily. "Where did you meet them?"

"Never mind, darling, my little Gulliver, you aren't going to act like a husband now?"

"You're leaving with a man," Henri said, weeping.

"Listen, Henri, I swear I'm not, I swear, men disgust me now. I'm leaving with a family, with friends of Rirette, old people. I want to live alone, they'll find a job for me; oh Henri, if you knew how much I needed to live alone, how it all disgusts me."

"What?" Henri asked, "what disgusts you?"

"Everything!" She kissed him. "You're the only one that doesn't disgust me, darling."

She passed her hands under Henri's pyjamas and caressed his whole body. He shuddered under her icy hands but did not turn away, he only said, "I'm going to get sick."

Surely, something was broken in him.

At seven o'clock, Lulu got up, her eyes swollen with tears. She said wearily, "I have to go back there."

"Back where?"

"Hotel du Théâtre, Rue Vandamme. A rotten hotel."

"Stay with me."

"No, Henri, please, don't insist. I told you it was impossible."

The flood carries you away; that's life; we can't judge or understand, we can only let ourselves drift. Tomorrow I'll be in Nice. She went to the bathroom to wash her eyes with warm water. She put on her coat, shivering. It's like fate. I only hope I can sleep on the train tonight, or else I'll be completely knocked

out when I get to Nice. I hope he got first-class tickets ;
that'll be the first time I ever rode first class. Everything is always like that : for years I've wanted to take
a long trip first class, and the day it happens it works
out so that I can't enjoy it. She was in a hurry to leave
now, for these last moments had been unbearable.

" What are you going to do with this Gallois
person ? " she asked.

Gallois had ordered a poster from Henri, Henri had
made it and now Gallois didn't want it any more.

" I don't know," Henri said.

He was crouched under the covers, only his hair and
the tip of his ear were visible. Slowly and softly, he
said, " I'd like to sleep for a week."

" Goodbye, darling," Lulu said.

" Goodbye."

She bent over him, drawing aside the covers a little,
and kissed him on the forehead. She stayed a long
while on the landing without deciding to close the door
of the apartment. After a moment, she turned her eyes
away and pulled the knob violently. She heard a dry
noise and thought she was going to faint ; she had felt
like that when they threw the first shovelful of earth on
her father's casket.

Henri hasn't been nice. He could have got up and
gone as far as the door with me. I think I would have
minded less if he had been the one who closed it.

IV

" She did that ! " said Rirette, with a far-away look.
" She did that ! "

It was evening. About six, Pierre had called Rirette and she had met him at the *Dôme*.

" But you," Pierre said, " weren't you supposed to see her this morning at nine ? "

" I saw her."

" She didn't look strange ? "

" No indeed," Rirette said, " I didn't notice anything. She was a little tired but she told me she hadn't slept after you left because she was so excited about seeing Nice and she was a little afraid of the Algerian bellboy. . . . Wait . . . she even asked me if I thought you'd bought first-class tickets on the train, she said it was the dream of her life to travel first class. No," Rirette decided, " I'm sure she didn't have anything like that in mind ; at least not while I was there. I stayed with her for two hours and I can tell those things, I'll be surprised if I missed anything. You tell me she's very close-mouthed but I've known her for four years and I've seen her in all sorts of situations. I know Lulu through and through."

" Then the Texiers made her mind up. It's funny . . ." He mused a few moments and suddenly began again. " I wonder who gave them Lulu's address. I picked out the hotel and she'd never heard of it before."

He toyed distractedly with Lulu's letter and Rirette was annoyed because she wanted to read it and he hadn't offered it to her.

" When did you get it ? " she asked finally.

" The letter . . . ? " He handed it to her with simplicity. " Here, you can read it. She must have given it to the concierge around one o'clock."

It was a thin, violet sheet, the kind sold in cigar stores :

46

Dearest Darling,

The Texiers came (I don't know who gave them the address) and I'm going to cause you a lot of sorrow, but I'm not going, dearest, darling Pierre ; I am staying with Henri because he is too unhappy. They went to see him this morning, he didn't want to open the door and Mme Texier said he didn't look human. They were very nice and they understood my reasons, they said all the wrong was on his side, that he was a bear but he wasn't bad at heart. She said he needed that to make him understand how much he needed me. I don't know who gave them the address, they didn't say, they must have happened to see me when I was leaving the hotel this morning with Rirette. Mme Texier said she knew she was asking me to make an enormous sacrifice but that she knew me well enough to know that I wouldn't sneak out. I'll miss our lovely trip to Nice very much, darling, but I thought you would be less unhappy because I am still yours. I am yours with all my heart and all my body and we shall see each other as often as before. But Henri would kill himself if he didn't have me any more. I am indispensable to him ; I assure you that it doesn't amuse me to feel such a responsibility. I hope you won't make your naughty little face which frightens me so, you wouldn't want me to be sorry, would you ? I am going back to Henri soon, I'm a little sick when I think that I'm going to see him in such a state but I will have the courage to name my own conditions. First, I want more freedom because I love you and I want him to leave Robert alone and not say anything bad about Mama any more, ever. Dearest, I am so sad, I wish you could be here, I want you, I press myself against you and I feel your caresses in all my body. I will be at the Dôme tomorrow at five.

LULU.

" Poor Pierre."

Rirette took his hand.

" I'll tell you," Pierre said, " I feel sorry for her.
She needed air and sunshine. But since she decided
that way . . . My mother made a frightful scene," he
went on. " The villa belongs to her, she didn't want
me to have a woman there."

" Ah ? " Rirette said, in a broken voice, " Ah ? So
everything's all right then, everybody's happy ! "

She dropped Pierre's hand : without knowing why,
she felt flooded with bitter regret.

The Wall

They pushed us into a big white room and I began to
blink because the light hurt my eyes. Then I saw a
table and four men behind the table, civilians, looking
over the papers. They had bunched another group of
prisoners in the back and we had to cross the whole
room to join them. There were several I knew and
some others who must have been foreigners. The two
in front of me were blond with round skulls; they
looked alike. I supposed they were French. The smaller
one kept hitching up his pants: nerves.

It lasted about three hours; I was dizzy and my head
felt empty; but the room was well heated and I found
that pleasant enough: for the past twenty-four hours
we hadn't stopped shivering. The guards brought the
prisoners up to the table, one after the other. The four
men asked each one his name and occupation. Most
of the time they didn't go any further—or they would
simply ask a question here and there: " Did you have
anything to do with the sabotage of munitions ? " Or,
" Where were you the morning of the 9th and what
were you doing ? " They didn't listen to the answers or
at least didn't seem to. They were quiet for a moment

looking straight in front of them, and then began to write. They asked Tom if it were true he was in the International Brigade ; Tom couldn't tell them otherwise because of the papers they found in his coat. They didn't ask Juan anything but they wrote for a long time after he told them his name.

" My brother José is the anarchist," Juan said, " you know he isn't here any more. I don't belong to any party, I never had anything to do with politics."

They didn't answer. Juan went on, " I haven't done anything. I don't want to pay for somebody else."

His lips trembled. A guard shut him up and took him away. It was my turn.

" Your name is Pablo Ibbieta ? "

" Yes."

The man looked at the papers and asked me, " Where is Ramon Gris ? "

" I don't know."

" You hid him in your house from the 6th to the 19th."

" No."

They wrote for a minute and then the guards took me out. In the corridor Tom and Juan were waiting between two guards. We started walking. Tom asked one of the guards, " So ? "

" So what ? " the guard said.

" Was that the cross-examination or the judgment ? "

" Judgment," the guard said.

" What are they going to do with us ? "

The guard answered dryly, " Sentence will be read in your cell."

As a matter of fact, our cell was one of the hospital cellars. It was terrifically cold there because of the draughts. We shivered all night and it wasn't much better during the day. I had spent the previous five days in a cell in a monastery, a sort of hole in the wall that must have dated from the Middle Ages : since there were a lot of prisoners and not much room, they locked us up anywhere. I didn't miss my cell ; I hadn't suffered too much from the cold but I was alone ; after a while it gets irritating. In the cellar I had company. Juan hardly ever spoke : he was afraid and he was too young to have anything to say. But Tom was a good talker and he knew Spanish very well.

There was a bench in the cellar and four mats. When they took us back we sat and waited in silence. After a long moment, Tom said, " We're screwed."

" I think so too," I said, " but I don't think they'll do anything to the kid."

" They don't have a thing against him," said Tom. " He's the brother of a militiaman and that's all."

I looked at Juan : he didn't seem to hear. Tom went on, " You know what they do in Saragossa ? They lay the men down on the road and run over them with trucks. A Moroccan deserter told us that. They said it was to save ammunition."

" It doesn't save petrol," I said.

I was annoyed at Tom : he shouldn't have said that.

" Then there's officers walking along the road," he went on, " supervising it all. They stick their hands in their pockets and smoke cigarettes. You think they finish off the guys ? Hell no. They let them scream. Sometimes for an hour. The Moroccan said he damned near puked the first time."

" I don't believe they'll do that here," I said. " Unless they're really short on ammunition."

51

The light came in through four airholes and a round opening they had made in the ceiling, on the left, and you could see the sky through it. Through this hole, usually closed by a trap, they unloaded coal into the cellar. Just below the hole there was a big pile of coal dust ; it had been used to heat the hospital but since the beginning of the war the patients were evacuated and the coal stayed there, unused ; sometimes it even got rained on because they had forgotten to close the trap.

Tom began to shiver. " Good Jesus Christ, I'm cold," he said. " Here it goes again."

He got up and began to do exercises. At each movement his shirt opened on his chest, white and hairy. He lay on his back, raised his legs in the air and bicycled. I saw his great rump trembling. Tom was husky but he had too much fat. I thought how rifle bullets or the sharp points of bayonets would soon be sunk into this mass of tender flesh as in a lump of butter. It wouldn't have made me feel like that if he'd been thin.

I wasn't exactly cold, but I couldn't feel my arms and shoulders any more. Sometimes I had the impression I was missing something and began to look around for my coat and then suddenly remembered they hadn't given me a coat. It was rather uncomfortable. They took our clothes and gave them to their soldiers, leaving us only our shirts—and those canvas pants that hospital patients wear in the middle of summer. After a while Tom got up and sat next to me, breathing heavily.

" Warmer ? "

" Good Christ, no. But I'm out of wind. "

Around eight o'clock in the evening a major came in with two *falangistas*. He had a sheet of paper in his hand. He asked the guard, " What are the names of those three ? "

" Steinbock, Ibbieta and Mirbal, " the guard said.

The Major put on his eyeglasses and scanned the list : " Steinbock . . . Steinbock . . . Oh yes . . . You are sentenced to death. You will be shot tomorrow morning. " He went on looking. " The other two as well. "

" That's not possible, " Juan said. " Not me. "

The major looked at him amazed. " What's your name ? "

" Juan Mirbal," he said.

" Well, your name is there," said the major. " You're sentenced. "

" I didn't do anything, " Juan said.

The major shrugged his shoulders and turned to Tom and me.

" You're Basque ? "

" Nobody is Basque. "

He looked annoyed. " They told me there were three Basques. I'm not going to waste my time running after them. Then naturally you don't want a priest ? "

We didn't even answer.

He said, " A Belgian doctor is coming shortly. He is authorized to spend the night with you. " He made a military salute and left.

" What did I tell you," Tom said. " We get it."

" Yes, " I said, " it's a rotten deal for the kid. "

I said that to be decent but I didn't like the kid. His face was too thin and fear and suffering had disfigured it, twisting all his features. Three days before he had been a smart sort of kid, not too bad ; but now he

53

looked like an old fairy and I thought how he'd never be young again, even if they were to let him go. It wouldn't have been too hard to have a little pity for him but pity disgusts me, or rather it horrifies me. He hadn't said anything more but he had turned grey; his face and hands were both grey. He sat down again and looked at the ground with round eyes. Tom was good hearted, he wanted to take his arm, but the kid tore himself away violently and made a face.

" Let him alone, " I said in a low voice, " you can see he's going to blubber. "

Tom obeyed regretfully; he would have liked to comfort the kid, it would have passed his time and he wouldn't have been tempted to think about himself. But it annoyed me: I'd never thought about death because I never had any reason to, but now the reason was here and there was nothing to do but think about it.

Tom began to talk. " Say, have you ever knocked any guys off ? " he asked me. I didn't answer. He began explaining to me that he had knocked off six since the beginning of August; he didn't realize the situation and I could tell he didn't *want* to realize it. I hadn't quite realized it myself, I wondered if it hurt much, I thought of bullets, I imagined their burning hail through my body. All that was beside the real question; but I was calm: we had all night to understand. After a while Tom stopped talking and I watched him out of the corner of my eye: I saw he too had turned grey and he looked rotten; I told myself " Now it starts. " It was almost dark, a dim glow filtered through the airholes and the pile of coal and made a big stain beneath the spot of sky; I could already see a star through the hole in the ceiling : the night would be pure and icy.

The door opened and two guards came in, followed by a blond man in a tan uniform. He saluted us. "I am the doctor," he said. "I have authorization to help you in these trying hours."

He had an agreeable and distinguished voice. I said, "What do you want here?"

"I am at your disposal. I shall do all I can to make your last moments less difficult."

"What did you come here for? There's others, the hospital's full of them."

"I was sent here," he answered with a vague look. "Ah! Would you like to smoke?" he added hurriedly, "I have cigarettes and even cigars."

He offered us English cigarettes and *puros*, but we refused. I looked him in the eyes and he seemed irritated. I said to him, "You aren't here on an errand of mercy. Besides, I know you. I saw you with the fascists in the barracks yard the day I was arrested."

I was going to continue, but something surprising suddenly happened to me ; the presence of this doctor no longer interested me. Generally when I'm on somebody I don't let go. But the desire to talk left me completely ; I shrugged and turned my eyes away. A little later I raised my head ; he was watching me curiously. The guards were sitting on a mat. Pedro, the tall thin one, was twiddling his thumbs, the other shook his head from time to time to keep from falling asleep.

"Do you want a light?" Pedro suddenly asked the doctor. The other nodded "Yes" : I think he was about as smart as a log, but he surely wasn't bad.

Looking in his cold blue eyes it seemed to me that his only sin was lack of imagination. Pedro went out and came back with an oil lamp which he set on the corner of the bench. It gave a bad light but it was better than nothing : they had left us in the dark the night before. For a long time I watched the circle of light the lamp made on the ceiling. I was fascinated. Then suddenly I woke up, the circle of light disappeared and I felt myself crushed under an enormous weight.

It was not the thought of death, or fear ; it was nameless. My cheeks burned and my head ached.

I shook myself and looked at my two friends. Tom had hidden his face in his hands. I could only see the fat white nape of his neck. Little Juan was the worst, his mouth was open and his nostrils trembled. The doctor went and put his hand on his shoulder as if to comfort him : but his eyes stayed cold. Then I saw the Belgian's hand drop stealthily along Juan's arm, down to the wrist. Juan paid no attention. The Belgian took his wrist between three fingers, distractedly, the same time drawing away a little and turning his back to me. But I leaned backward and saw him take a watch from his pocket and look at it for a moment, never letting go of the wrist. After a minute he let the hand fall inert and went and leaned his back against the wall, then, as if he suddenly remembered something very important which had to be jotted down on the spot, he took a notebook from his pocket and wrote a few lines. " Bastard, " I thought angrily, " let him come and take my pulse. I'll shove my fist in his rotten face. "

He didn't come but I felt him watching me. I raised my head and returned his look. Impersonally,

he said to me, "Doesn't it seem cold to you here?"
He looked cold, he was blue.

"I'm not cold," I told him.

He never took his hard eyes off me. Suddenly I
understood and my hands went to my face: I was
drenched in sweat. In this cellar, in the midst of
winter, in the midst of draughts, I was sweating. I ran
my hands through my hair, gummed together with
perspiration; at the same time I saw my shirt was
damp and sticking to my skin: I had been dripping
for an hour and hadn't felt it. But that swine of a
Belgian hadn't missed a thing; he had seen the drops
rolling down my cheeks and thought: this is the
manifestation of an almost pathological state of terror;
and he had felt normal and proud of being so because
he was cold. I wanted to stand up and smash his face
but no sooner had I made the slightest gesture than my
rage and shame were wiped out; I fell back on the
bench with indifference.

I satisfied myself by rubbing my neck with my
handkerchief because now I felt the sweat dropping
from my hair on to my neck and it was unpleasant.
I soon gave up rubbing, it was useless; my handkerchief was already soaked and I was still sweating. My
buttocks were sweating too and my damp trousers were
glued to the bench.

Suddenly Juan spoke. "You're a doctor?"

"Yes," the Belgian said.

"Does it hurt . . . very long?"

"Eh? When . . . Oh, no," the Belgian said paternally. "Not at all. It's over quickly." He acted as
though he were calming a cash customer.

" But I . . . they told me . . . sometimes they have to
fire twice. "

" Sometimes," the Belgian said, nodding. " It may
happen that the first volley reaches no vital organs. "

" Then they have to reload their rifles and aim all
over again ? " He thought for a moment and then
added hoarsely, " That takes time ! "

He had a terrible fear of suffering, it was all he
thought about : it was his age. I never thought much
about it and it wasn't fear of suffering that made me
sweat.

I got up and walked to the pile of coal dust. Tom
jumped up and threw me a hateful look : I had
annoyed him because my shoes squeaked. I wondered
if my face looked as earthy as his : I saw he was
sweating too. The sky was superb, no light filtered
into the dark corner and I had only to raise my head
to see the Big Dipper. But it wasn't like it had been :
the night before I could see a great piece of sky from
my monastery cell and each hour of the day brought
me a different memory. Morning, when the sky was
a hard, light blue, I thought of beaches on the Atlantic ;
at noon I saw the sun and I remembered a bar in
Seville where I drank *manzanilla* and ate olives and
anchovies ; afternoons I was in the shade and I thought
of the deep shadow which spreads over half a bull-ring
leaving the other half shimmering in sunlight ; it was
really hard to see the whole world reflected in the
sky like that. But now I could watch the sky as much
as I pleased, it no longer evoked anything in me. I
liked that better. I came back and sat near Tom. A
long moment passed.

Tom began speaking in a low voice. He had to

talk, without that he wouldn't have been able to recognize himself in his own mind. I thought he was talking to me but he wasn't looking at me. He was undoubtedly afraid to see me as I was, grey and sweating : we were alike and worse than mirrors of each other. He watched the Belgian, the living.

" Do you understand ? " he said. " I don't understand. "

I began to speak in a low voice too. I watched the Belgian. " Why ? What's the matter ? "

" Something is going to happen to us that I can't understand. "

There was a strange smell about Tom. It seemed to me I was more sensitive than usual to odours. I grinned. " You'll understand in a while. "

" It isn't clear, " he said obstinately. " I want to be brave but at least I have to know . . . Listen, they're going to take us into the courtyard. Good. They're going to stand up in front of us. How many ? "

" I don't know. Five or eight. Not more. "

" All right. There'll be eight. Someone'll holler ' aim ! ' and I'll see eight rifles looking at me. I'll think how I'd like to get inside the wall, I'll push against it with my back . . . with every ounce of strength I have, but the wall will stay, like in a nightmare. I can imagine all that. If you only knew how well I can imagine it. "

" All right, all right ! " I said, " I can imagine it too. "

" It must hurt like hell. You know, they aim at the eyes and the mouth to disfigure you, " he added maliciously. " I can feel the wounds already ; I've had pains in my head and in my neck for the past hour. Not real pains. Worse. This is what I'm going to feel tomorrow morning. And then what ? "

I well understood what he meant but I didn't want to act as if I did. I had pains too, pains in my body like a crowd of tiny scars. I couldn't get used to it. But I was like him, I attached no importance to it. " After," I said, " you'll be pushing up daisies."

He began to talk to himself : he never stopped watching the Belgian. The Belgian didn't seem to be listening. I knew what he had come to do ; he wasn't interested in what we thought ; he came to watch our bodies, bodies dying in agony while yet alive.

" It's like a nightmare, " Tom was saying. " You want to think something, you always have the impression that it's all right, that you're going to understand and then it slips, it escapes you and fades away. I tell myself there will be nothing afterwards. But I don't understand what it means. Sometimes I almost can . . . and then it fades away and I start thinking about the pains again, bullets, explosions. I'm a materialist, I swear it to you ; I'm not going crazy. But something's the matter. I see my corpse ; that's not hard but *I'm* the one who sees it, with *my* eyes. I've got to think . . . think that I won't see anything anymore and the world will go on for the others. We aren't made to think that, Pablo. Believe me : I've already stayed up a whole night waiting for something. But this isn't the same : this will creep up behind us, Pablo, and we won't be able to prepare for it. "

" Shut up, " I said, " Do you want me to call a priest ? "

He didn't answer. I had already noticed he had a tendency to act like a prophet and call me Pablo, speaking in a toneless voice. I didn't like that : but it seems all the Irish are that way. I had the vague impression he smelled of urine. Fundamentally, I hadn't much sympathy for Tom and I didn't see why, under the pretext of dying together, I should have any more. It would have been different with some others. With Ramon Gris, for example. But I felt alone between Tom and Juan. I liked that better, anyhow : with Ramon I might have been more deeply moved. But I was terribly hard just then and I wanted to stay hard.

He kept on chewing his words, with something like distraction. He certainly talked to keep himself from thinking. He smelled of urine like an old prostate case. Naturally, I agreed with him, I could have said everything he said : it isn't *natural* to die. And since I was going to die, nothing seemed natural to me, not this pile of coal dust, or the bench, or Pedro's ugly face. Only it didn't please me to think the same things as Tom. And I knew that, all through the night, every five minutes, we would keep on thinking things at the same time. I looked at him sideways and for the first time he seemed strange to me : he wore death on his face. My pride was wounded : for the past twenty-four hours I had lived next to Tom, I had listened to him, I had spoken to him and I knew we had nothing in common. And now we looked as much alike as twin brothers, simply because we were going to die together. Tom took my hand without looking at me.

"Pablo, I wonder . . . I wonder if it's really true that everything ends. "

61

I took my hand away and said, "Look between your feet, you pig."

There was a big puddle between his feet and drops fell from his pants-leg.

"What is it?" he asked, frightened.

"You're pissing in your pants," I told him.

"It isn't true," he said furiously. "I'm not pissing. I don't feel anything."

The Belgian approached us. He asked with false solicitude, "Do you feel ill?"

Tom did not answer. The Belgian looked at the puddle and said nothing.

"I don't know what it is," Tom said ferociously. "But I'm not afraid. I swear I'm not afraid."

The Belgian did not answer. Tom got up and went to piss in a corner. He came back buttoning his fly, and sat down without a word. The Belgian was taking notes.

All three of us watched him because he was alive. He had the motions of a living human being, the cares of a living human being; he shivered in the cellar the way the living are supposed to shiver; he had an obedient, well-fed body. The rest of us hardly felt ours—not in the same way anyhow. I wanted to feel my pants between my legs but I didn't dare; I watched the Belgian, balancing on his legs, master of his muscles, someone who could think about tomorrow. There we were, three bloodless shadows; we watched him and we sucked his life like vampires.

Finally he went over to little Juan. Did he want to feel his neck for some professional motive or was he obeying an impulse of charity? If he was acting by charity it was the only time during the whole night.

He caressed Juan's head and neck. The kid let himself be handled, his eyes never leaving him, then suddenly, he seized the hand and looked at it strangely. He held the Belgian's hand between his own two hands and there was nothing pleasant about them, two grey pincers gripping this fat and reddish hand. I suspected what was going to happen and Tom must have suspected it too : but the Belgian didn't see a thing, he smiled paternally. After a moment the kid brought the fat red hand to his mouth and tried to bite it. The Belgian pulled away quickly and stumbled back against the wall. For a second he looked at us with horror, he must have suddenly understood that we were not men like him. I began to laugh and one of the guards jumped up. The other was asleep, his wide-open eyes were blank.

I felt relaxed and over-excited at the same time. I didn't want to think any more about what would happen at dawn, or death. It made no sense. I only found words or emptiness. But as soon as I tried to think of anything else I saw rifle barrels pointing at me. I lived my execution twenty times perhaps ; once I even thought it was for good : I must have slept a minute. They were dragging me to the wall and I was struggling ; I was asking for mercy. I woke up with a start and looked at the Belgian : I was afraid I might have cried out in my sleep. But he was stroking his moustache, he hadn't noticed anything. If I had wanted to, I think I could have slept a while ; I had been awake for 48 hours. I was at the end of my tether.

But I didn't want to lose two hours of life : they would come to wake me up at dawn, I would follow them, stupefied with sleep and I would have croaked

without so much as an " Oof ! " ; I didn't want that,
I didn't want to die like an animal, I wanted to understand. Then I was afraid of having nightmares. I got
up, walked back and forth, and, to change my ideas,
I began to think about my past life. A crowd of
memories came back to me pell-mell. There were good
and bad ones—or at least I called them that *before*.
There were faces and incidents. I saw the face of a
little *novillero* who was gored in Valencia during the
Feria, the face of one of my uncles, the face of Ramon
Gris. I remembered my whole life : how I was out
of work for three months in 1926, how I almost starved
to death. I remembered a night I spent on a bench in
Granada : I hadn't eaten for three days. I was angry,
I didn't want to die. That made me smile. How madly
I ran after happiness, after women, after liberty. Why ?
I wanted to free Spain, I admired Pi y Margall, I
joined the anarchist movement, I spoke at public
meetings : I took everything as seriously as if I were
immortal.

At that moment I felt that I had my whole life in
front of me and I thought, " It's a damned lie." It
was worth nothing because it was finished. I wondered
how I'd been able to walk, to laugh with the girls :
I wouldn't have moved so much as my little finger if
I had only imagined I would die like this. My life was
in front of me, shut, closed, like a bag and yet everything inside of it was unfinished. For an instant I tried
to judge it. I wanted to tell myself, this is a beautiful
life. But I couldn't pass judgment on it ; it was only a
sketch ; I had spent my time counterfeiting eternity, I
had understood nothing. I had missed nothing : there
were so many things I could have missed, the taste of

manzanilla or the baths I took in summer in a little creek near Cadiz; but death had disenchanted everything.

The Belgian suddenly had a bright idea. " My friends," he told us, " I will undertake if the military administration will allow it—to send a message for you, a souvenir to those who love you . . ."

Tom mumbled, " I don't have anybody."

I said nothing. Tom waited an instant then looked at me with curiosity. " You don't have anything to say to Concha ? "

" No."

I hated this tender complicity : it was my own fault, I had talked about Concha the night before, I should have controlled myself. I was with her for a year. Last night I would have given an arm to see her again for five minutes. That was why I talked about her, it was stronger that I was. Now I had no more desire to see her, I had nothing more to say to her. I would not even have wanted to hold her in my arms : my body filled me with horror because it was grey and sweating —and I wasn't sure that her body didn't fill me with horror. Concha would cry when she found out I was dead, she would have no taste for life for months afterwards. But I was still the one who was going to die. I thought of her soft, beautiful eyes. When she looked at me something passed from her to me. But I knew it was over : if she looked at me *now* the look would stay in her eyes, it wouldn't reach me. I was alone.

Tom was alone too but not in the same way. Sitting cross-legged, he had begun to stare at the bench with a sort of smile, he looked amazed. He put out his hand and touched the wood cautiously as if he were afraid of breaking something, then drew back his hand quickly and shuddered. If I had been Tom I wouldn't have amused myself by touching the bench; this was some more Irish nonsense, but I too found that objects had a funny look : they were more obliterated, less dense than usual. It was enough for me to look at the bench, the lamp, the pile of coal dust, to feel that I was going to die. Naturally I couldn't think clearly about my death but I saw it everywhere, on things, in the way things fell back and kept their distance, discreetly, as people who speak quietly at the bedside of a dying man. It was *his* death which Tom had just touched on the bench.

In the state I was in, if someone had come and told me I could go home quietly, that they would leave me my life whole, it would have left me cold : several hours or several years of waiting is all the same when you have lost the illusion of being eternal. I clung to nothing, in a way I was calm. But it was a horrible calm—because of my body ; my body, I saw with its eyes, I heard with its ears, but it was no longer me ; it sweated and trembled by itself and I didn't recognise it any more. I had to touch it and look at it to find out what was happening, as if it were the body of someone else. At times I could still feel it, I felt sinkings and fallings, as when you're in a plane taking a nosedive, or I felt my heart beating. But that didn't reassure me. Everything that came from my body was all cockeyed. Most of the time it was quiet and I felt no more than a sort of weight, a filthy presence against me ; I had the impression of being tied to an enormous vermin. Once I felt my pants and I felt they were damp; I didn't know whether it was sweat or urine, but I went to piss on the coal pile as a precaution.

The Belgian took out his watch, looked at it. He said, " It is three thirty."

Bastard ! He must have done it on purpose. Tom jumped; we hadn't noticed time was running out; night surrounded us like a shapeless, sombre mass, I couldn't even remember that it had begun.

Little Juan began to cry. He wrung his hands, pleaded, " I don't want to die. I don't want to die."

He ran across the whole cellar waving his arms in the air then fell sobbing on one of the mats. Tom watched him with mournful eyes, without the slightest desire to console him. Because it wasn't worth the trouble : the kid made more noise than we did, but he was less touched : he was like a sick man who defends himself against his illness by fever. It's much more serious when there isn't any fever.

He wept : I could clearly see he was pitying himself ; he wasn't thinking about death. For one second, one single second, I wanted to weep myself, to weep with pity for myself. But the opposite happened : I glanced at the kid, I saw his thin sobbing shoulders and I felt inhuman : I could pity neither the others nor myself. I said to myself, " I want to die cleanly."

Tom had got up, he placed himself just under the round opening and began to watch for daylight. I was determined to die cleanly and I only thought of that. But ever since the doctor told us the hour, I felt time flying, flowing away drop by drop.

It was still dark when I heard Tom's voice : " Do you hear them ? "

" Yes."

Men were marching in the courtyard.

"What the hell are they doing? They can't shoot in the dark."

After a while we heard no more. I said to Tom, "It's day."

Pedro got up, yawning, and came to blow out the lamp. He said to his companion, "Cold as hell."

The cellar was all grey. We heard shots in the distance.

"It's starting," I told Tom. "They must do it in the court in the rear."

Tom asked the doctor for a cigarette. I didn't want one: I didn't want cigarettes or alcohol. From that moment on they never stopped firing.

"Do you realise what's happening?" Tom said.

He wanted to add something but kept quiet, watching the door. The door opened and a lieutenant came in with four soldiers. Tom dropped his cigarette.

"Steinbock?"

Tom didn't answer. Pedro pointed him out.

"Juan Mirbal?"

"On the mat."

"Get up," the lieutenant said.

Juan did not move. Two soldiers took him under the arms and set him on his feet. But he fell as soon as they released him.

The soldiers hesitated.

"He's not the first sick one," said the lieutenant. "You two carry him; they'll fix it up down there."

He turned to Tom. "Let's go."

Tom went out between two soldiers. Two others followed, carrying the kid by the armpits and legs. He hadn't fainted; his eyes were wide open and tears

68

ran down his cheeks. When I wanted to go out the lieutenant stopped me.

" You Ibbieta ? "

" Yes."

" You wait here ; they'll come for you later."

They left. The Belgian and the two jailers left too, I was alone. I did not understand what was happening to me but I would have liked it better if they had got it over with right away. I heard shots at almost regular intervals ; I shook with each one of them. I wanted to scream and tear out my hair. But I gritted my teeth and pushed my hands in my pockets because I wanted to stay clean.

After an hour they came to get me and led me to the first floor, to a small room that smelt of cigars and where the heat was stifling. There were two officers sitting smoking in the armchairs, papers on their knees.

" You're Ibbieta ? "

" Yes."

" Where is Ramon Gris ? "

" I don't know."

The one questioning me was short and fat. His eyes were hard behind his glasses. He said to me, " Come here."

I went to him. He got up and took my arms, staring at me with a look that should have pushed me into the earth. At the same time he pinched my biceps with all his might. It wasn't to hurt me, it was only a game ; he wanted to dominate me. He also thought he had to blow his stinking breath square in my face. We stayed for a moment like that, and I almost felt like laughing. It takes a lot to intimidate a man who is going to die ; it didn't work. He pushed me back violently and sat down again. He said, "It's his life against yours. You can have yours if you tell us where he is."

These men dolled up with their riding crops and boots were still going to die. A little later than I, but not too much. They busied themselves looking for names in their crumpled papers, they ran after other men to imprison or suppress them; they had opinions on the future of Spain and on other subjects. Their little activities seemed shocking and burlesqued to me; I couldn't put myself in their place, I thought they were insane.

The little man was still looking at me, whipping his boots with the riding crop. All his gestures were calculated to give him the look of a live and ferocious beast.

"So? You understand?"

"I don't know where Gris is," I answered. "I thought he was in Madrid."

The other officer raised his pale hand indolently. This indolence was also calculated. I saw through all their little schemes and I was stupefied to find there were men who amused themselves that way.

"You have a quarter of an hour to think it over," he said slowly. "Take him to the laundry, bring him back in fifteen minutes. If he still refuses he will be executed on the spot."

They knew what they were doing: I had passed the night in waiting; then they had made me wait an hour in the cellar while they shot Tom and Juan and now they were locking me up in the laundry; they must have prepared their game the night before. They told themselves that nerves eventually wear out and they hoped to get me that way.

They were badly mistaken. In the laundry I sat on a stool because I felt very weak and I began to think. But not about their proposition. Of course I knew where Gris was; he was hiding with his cousins, four kilometres from the city. I also knew that I would not reveal his hiding place unless they tortured me (but they didn't seem to be thinking about that). All that was perfectly regulated, definite and in no way interested me. Only I would have liked to understand the reasons for my conduct. I would rather die than give up Gris. Why? I didn't like Ramon Gris any more. My friendship for him had died a little while before dawn at the same time as my love for Concha, at the same time as my desire to live. Undoubtedly I thought highly of him : he was tough. But it was not for this reason that I consented to die in his place ; his life had no more value than mine ; no life had value. They were going to slap a man up against a wall and shoot at him till he died, whether it was me or Gris or somebody else made no difference. I knew he was more useful than I to the cause of Spain but I thought to hell with Spain and anarchy ; nothing was important. Yet I was there, I could save my skin and give up Gris and I refused to do it.

I found that somehow comic ; it was obstinacy. I thought, " I must be stubborn ! " And a droll sort of gaiety spread over me.

They came for me and brought me back to the two officers. A rat ran out from under my feet and that amused me. I turned to one of the *falangistas* and said, " Did you see the rat ? "

He didn't answer. He was very sober, he took himself seriously. I wanted to laugh but I held myself back because I was afraid that once I got started I wouldn't be able to stop. The *falangista* had a moustache. I said to him again, " You ought to shave off your moustache, idiot." I thought it funny that he would let the hairs of his living being invade his face. He kicked me without great conviction and I kept quiet.

" Well," said the fat officer, " have you thought about it ? "

I looked at them with curiosity, as insects of a very rare species. I told them, " I know where he is. He is hidden in the cemetery. In a vault or in the grave-diggers' shack."

It was a farce. I wanted to see them stand up, buckle their belts and give orders busily.

They jumped to their feet. " Let's go, Molés. Get fifteen men from Lieutenant Lopez. You," the little fat man said, " I'll let you off if you're telling the truth, but it'll cost you plenty if you're making monkeys out of us."

They left in a great clatter and I waited peacefully under the guard of *falangistas*. From time to time I smiled, thinking about the spectacle they would make. I felt stunned and malicious. I imagined them lifting up tombstones, opening the doors of the vaults one by one. I represented this situation to myself as if I had been someone else : this prisoner obstinately playing the hero, these grim *falangistas* with their moustaches and their men in uniform running among the graves ; it was irresistibly funny.

After half an hour the little fat man came back alone. I thought he came to give the orders to execute me. The others must have stayed in the cemetery.

The officer looked at me. He didn't look at all sheepish. "Take him into the big courtyard with the others," he said, "After the military operations a regular court will decide what happens to him."

I didn't think I had understood. I asked :

"Then they're not . . . not going to shoot me ? "

"Not now, anyway. What happens afterwards is none of my business."

I still didn't understand. I asked, "But why . . . ? "

He shrugged his shoulders without answering and the soldiers took me away. In the big courtyard there were about a hundred prisoners, women, children and a few old men. I began walking around the central grass-plot, I was stupefied. At noon they let us eat in the mess hall. Two or three people questioned me. I must have known them, but I didn't answer : I didn't even know where I was.

Around evening they pushed about ten new prisoners into the court. I recognized Garcia, the baker. He said, "What damned luck you have ! I didn't think I'd see you alive."

"They sentenced me to death," I said, "and then they changed their minds. I don't know why."

"They arrested me at two o'clock," Garcia said.

"Why ? " Garcia had nothing to do with politics.

"I don't know," he said. "They arrest everybody who doesn't think the way they do." He lowered his voice. "They got Gris."

I began to tremble. "When ? "

"This morning. He balled it up. He left his cousin's on Tuesday because they had an argument. There were plenty of people to hide him but he didn't want to owe anything to anybody. He said, 'I'd go and hide in

Ibbieta's place, but they got him, so I'll hide in the cemetery.' "

" In the cemetery ? "

" Yes. What a fool. Of course they went by there this morning, that was sure to happen. They found him in the gravediggers' shack. He shot at them and they got him."

" In the cemetery ! "

Everything began to spin and I found myself sitting on the ground : I laughed so hard I cried.

The Room

Mme Darbédat held a *rahat-loukoum* between her fingers. She brought it carefully to her lips and held her breath, afraid that the fine dust of sugar that powdered it would blow away. " Just right," she told herself. She bit quickly into its glassy flesh and a scent of stagnation filled her mouth. "Odd how illness sharpens the sensations." She began to think of mosques, of obsequious Orientals (she had been to Algeria for her honeymoon) and her pale lips started in a smile : the *rahat-loukoum* was obsequious too.

Several times she had to pass the palm of her hand over the pages of her book, for in spite of the precautions she had taken they were covered with a thin coat of white powder. Her hand made the little grains of sugar slide and roll, grating on the smooth paper : "That makes me think of Arcachon, when I used to read on the beach." She had spent the summer of 1907 at the seashore. Then she wore a big straw hat with a green ribbon ; she sat close to the jetty, with a novel by Gyp or Colette Yver. The wind made eddies of sand rain down upon her knees, and from time to time she had to shake the book, holding it by the corners. It was the same sensation : only the grains of sand were dry while the small bits of sugar stuck a little to the ends of her fingers. Again she saw a band of pearl grey sky above a black sea. " Eve wasn't born yet." She felt herself all weighted down with memories as precious as a coffer of sandalwood. The name of the book she used to read suddenly came back to mind : it was called *Petite Madame,* not at all boring. But ever since an unknown illness had confined her to her room she preferred memoirs and historical works.

She hoped that suffering, heavy readings, a vigilant attention to her memories and the most exquisite sensations would ripen her as a lovely hothouse fruit.

She thought, with some annoyance, that her husband would soon be knocking at her door. On other days of the week he came only in the evening, kissed her brow in silence and read *Le Temps,* sitting in the armchair across from her. But Thursday was M. Darbédat's *day* : he spent an hour with his daughter, generally from three to four. Before going he stopped in to see his wife and both discussed their son-in-law with bitterness. These Thursday conversations, predictable to their slightest detail, exhausted Mme Darbédat. M. Darbédat filled the quiet room with his presence. He never sat, but walked in circles about the room. Each of his outbursts wounded Mme Darbédat like a glass splintering. This particular Thursday was worse than usual : at the thought that it would soon be necessary to repeat Eve's confessions to her husband, and to see his great terrifying body convulse with fury, Mme Darbédat broke out in a sweat. She picked up a *loukoum* from the saucer, studied it for a while with

76

hesitation, then sadly set it down : she did not like her husband to see her eating *loukoums*.

She heard a knock and started up. " Come in," she said weakly.

M. Darbédat entered on tiptoe. " I'm going to see Eve," he said, as he did every Thursday. Mme Darbédat smiled at him. " Give her a kiss for me."

M. Darbédat did not answer and his forehead wrinkled worriedly : every Thursday at the same time, a muffled irritation mingled with the load of his digestion. " I'll stop in and see Franchot after leaving her, I wish he'd talk to her seriously and try to convince her."

He made frequent visits to Dr. Franchot. But in vain. Mme Darbédat raised her eyebrows. Before, when she was well, she shrugged her shoulders. But since sickness had weighted down her body, she replaced the gestures which would have tired her by plays of emotion in the face : she said *yes* with her eyes, *no* with the corners of her mouth : she raised her eyebrows instead of her shoulders.

" There should be some way to take him away from her by force."

" I told you already it was impossible. And besides, the law is very poorly drawn up. Only the other day Franchot was telling me that they have a tremendous amount of trouble with the families : people who can't make up their mind, who want to keep the patient at home ; the doctor's hand are tied. They can give their advice periodically. That's all. He would," he went on, " have to make a public scandal or else she would have to ask to have him put away herself."

" And that," said Mme Darbédat, " isn't going to happen tomorrow."

" No." He turned to the mirror and began to comb his fingers through his beard. Mme Darbédat looked at the powerful red neck of her husband without affection.

" If she keeps on," said M. Darbédat, " she'll be crazier than he is. It's terribly unhealthy. She doesn't leave his side, she only goes out to see you. She has no visitors. The air in their room is simply unbreathable. She never opens the window because Pierre doesn't want it open. As if you should ask a sick man. I believe they burn incense, some rubbish in a little pan, you'd think it was a church. Really, sometimes I wonder . . . she's got a funny look in her eyes, you know."

" I haven't noticed," Mme Darbédat said. " I find her quite normal. She looks sad, obviously."

" She has a face like an unburied corpse. Does she sleep ? Does she eat ? But we aren't supposed to ask her about those things. But I should think that with a fellow like Pierre next to her, she wouldn't sleep a wink all night." He shrugged his shoulders. " What I find amazing is that we, her parents, don't have the right to protect her against herself. Understand that Pierre would be much better cared for by Franchot. There's a big park. And besides, I think," he added, smiling a little, " he'd get along much better with people of his own type. People like that are children, you have to leave them alone with each other ; they form a sort of freemasonry. That's where he should have been put the first day and for his own good, I'd say. Of course it's in his own best interest."

After a moment, he added, "I tell you I don't like to know she's alone with Pierre, especially at night. Suppose something happened. Pierre has a very sly way about him."

"I don't know," Mme Darbédat said, "if there's any reason to worry. He always looked like that. He always seemed to be making fun of the world. Poor boy," she sighed, "to have had his pride and then come to that. He thought he was cleverer than all of us. He had a way of saying 'You're right' simply to end the argument . . . It's a blessing for him that he can't see the state he's in."

She recalled with displeasure the long, ironic face, always turned a little to the side. During the first days of Eve's marriage, Mme Darbédat asked nothing more than a little intimacy with her son-in-law. But he had discouraged her : he almost never spoke, he always agreed quickly and absent-mindedly.

M. Darbédat pursued his idea. "Franchot let me visit his place," he said. "It was magnificent. The patients have private rooms with leather armchairs, if you please, and day-beds. You know, they have a tennis court and they're going to build a swimming pool."

He was planted before the window, looking out, rocking a little on his bent legs. Suddenly he turned lithely on his heel, shoulders lowered, hands in his pockets. Mme Darbédat felt she was going to start perspiring : it was the same thing every time : now he was pacing back and forth like a bear in a cage and his shoes squeaked at every step.

"Please, please won't you sit down. You're tiring

79

me." Hesitating, she added, " I have something important to tell you."

M. Darbédat sat in the armchair and put his hands on his knees ; a slight chill ran up Mme Darbédat's spine : the time had come, she had to speak.

" You know," she said with an embarrassed cough, " I saw Eve on Tuesday."

" Yes."

" We talked about a lot of things, she was very nice, she hasn't been so confiding for a long time. Then I questioned her a little, I got her to talk about Pierre. Well, I found out," she added, again embarrassed, " that she is *very* attached to him."

" I know that too damned well," said M. Darbédat.

He irritated Mme Darbédat a little : she always had to explain things in such detail. Mme Darbédat dreamed of living in the company of fine and sensitive people who would understand her slightest word.

" But I mean," she went on, " that she is attached to him *differently* than we imagined."

M. Darbédat rolled furious, anxious eyes, as he always did when he never completely grasped the sense of an allusion or something new.

" What does that all mean ? "

" Charles," said Mme Darbédat, " don't tire me. You should understand a mother has difficulty in telling certain things."

" I don't understand a damned word of anything you say," M. Darbédat said with irritation. " You can't mean . . ."

" Yes," she said.

" They're still . . . now, still . . . ? "

80

" Yes ! Yes ! Yes ! " she said, in three annoyed and dry little jolts.

M. Darbédat spread his arms, lowered his head and was silent.

" Charles," his wife said worriedly, " I shouldn't have told you. But I couldn't keep it to myself."

" Our child," he said slowly. " With this madman ! He doesn't even recognise her any more. He calls her Agatha. She must have lost all sense of her own dignity."

He raised his head and looked at his wife severely. " You're sure you aren't mistaken ? "

" No possible doubt. Like you," she added quickly, " I couldn't believe her and still can't. Nothing but the idea of being touched by that wretch . . . So . . . " she sighed, " I suppose that's how he holds on to her."

" Do you remember what I told you," M. Darbédat said, " when he came to ask for her hand ? I told you I thought he pleased Eve *too much*. You wouldn't believe me." He struck the table suddenly, blushing violently. " It's perversity ! He takes her in his arms, kisses her and calls her Agatha, selling her on a lot of nonsense about flying statues and God knows what else ! Without a word from her ! But what in heaven's name's between those two ? Let her be sorry for him, let her put him in a sanitorium and see him every day—fine. But I never thought . . . I considered her a widow. Listen, Jeanette," he said gravely, " I'm going to speak frankly to you ; if she has any sense, I'd rather see her take a lover ! "

" Be quiet, Charles ! " Mme Darbédat cried.

M. Darbédat wearily took his hat and the cane he left on the stool. " After what you've just told me," he concluded, " I don't have much hope left. In any case, I'll have a talk with her because it's my duty."

Mme Darbédat wished he would go quickly.

" You know " she said to encourage him, " I think Eve is more headstrong than . . . than anything. She know's he's incurable but she's obstinate, she doesn't want to be in the wrong."

M. Darbédat stroked his beard absently. " Headstrong? Maybe so. If you're right, she'll finally get tired of it. He's not agreeable all the time and he doesn't have much to say. When I say hello to him he gives me a flabby handshake and doesn't say a word. As soon as they're alone, I think they go back to his obsessions : she tells me sometimes he screams as though his throat were being cut because of his hallucinations. He sees statues. They frighten him because they buzz. He says they fly around and make fishy eyes at him."

He put on his gloves and continued, " She'll get tired of it, I'm not saying she won't. But suppose she goes crazy before that ? I wish she'd go out a little, see people : she'd meet some nice young man—well, someone like Schroeder, an engineer with Simplon, somebody with a future, she could see him a little here and there and she'd get used to the idea of making a new life for herself."

Mme Darbédat did not answer, afraid of starting the conversation up again. Her husband bent over her.

" So," he said, " I've got to be on my way."

" Goodbye, Papa," Mme Darbédat said, lifting her forehead up to him. " Kiss her for me and tell her for me she's a poor dear."

Once her husband had gone, Mme Darbédat let herself sink to the bottom of her armchair and closed her eyes, exhausted. " What vitality," she thought reproachfully. As soon as she got a little strength back, she quietly stretched out her pale hand and took a *loukoum* from the saucer, groping for it without opening her eyes.

Eve lived with her husband on the sixth floor of an old building on the Rue du Bac. M. Darbédat slowly climbed the 112 steps of the stairway. He was not even out of breath when he pushed the bell. He remembered with satisfaction the words of Mlle Dormoy : " Charles, for your age, you're simply marvellous." Never did he feel himself stronger and healthier than on Thursday, especially after these invigorating climbs.

Eve opened the door : that's right, she doesn't have a maid. No girls *can* stay with her. I can put myself in their place. He kissed her. " Hello, poor darling."

Eve greeted him with a certain coldness.

" You look a little pale," M. Darbédat said, touching her cheek. " You don't get enough exercise."

There was a moment of silence.

" Is Mamma well ? " Eve asked.

" Not good, not too bad. You saw her Tuesday ? Well, she's just the same. Your Aunt Louise came to see her yesterday, that pleased her. She likes to have visitors, but they can't stay too long. Aunt Louise came to Paris for that mortgage business. I think I told you about it, a very odd sort of affair. She stopped in at the office to ask my advice. I told her there was only one thing to do : sell. She found a taker, by the way : Bretonnel. You remember Bretonnel. He retired from business."

He stopped suddenly : Eve was hardly listening. He thought sadly that nothing interested her any more. It's like the books. Before, you had to tear them away from her. Now she doesn't even read any more.

" How is Pierre ? "

" Well," Eve said. " Do you want to see him ? "

" Of course," M. Darbédat said ·gaily, " I'd like to pay him a little call."

He was full of compassion for this poor young man, but he could not see him without repugnance. *I detest unhealthy people*. Obviously, it was not Pierre's fault : his heredity was terribly loaded down. M. Darbédat sighed : *All the precautions are taken in vain, you find out those things too late*. No, Pierre was not responsible. But still he had always carried that fault in him ; it formed the base of his character ; it wasn't like cancer or tuberculosis, something you could always put aside when you wanted to judge a man as he is. His nervous grace, this subtlety which pleased Eve so much when he was courting her were the flowers of madness. He was already mad when he married her only you couldn't tell.

It makes you wonder, thought M. Darbédat, *where responsibility begins, or rather, where it ends*. In any case, he was always analysing himself too much, always turned in on himself. But was it the cause or effect of his sickness ? He followed his daughter through a long, dim corridor.

" This apartment is too big for you," he said. " You ought to move out."

" You say that every time, Papa," Eve answered, " but I've already told you Pierre doesn't want to leave his room."

Eve was amazing. Enough to make you wonder if she realized her husband's state. He was insane enough to be in a strait-jacket and she respected his decisions and advice as if he still had good sense.

"What I'm saying is for your own good." M. Darbédat went on, somewhat annoyed, "it seems to me that if I were a woman I'd be afraid of these badly lighted old rooms. I'd like to see you in a bright apartment, the kind they've put up near Auteuil, three airy little rooms. They lowered the rents because they couldn't find any tenants; this would be just the time."

Eve quietly turned the doorknob and they entered the room. M. Darbédat's throat tightened at the heavy odour of incense. The curtains were drawn. In the shadows he made out a thin neck above the back of an armchair: Pierre's back was turned. He was eating.

"Hello, Pierre," M. Darbédat said, raising his voice. "How are we today?" He drew near him: the sick man was seated in front of a small table; he looked sly.

"I see we had soft boiled eggs," M. Darbédat said, raising his voice higher. "That's good!"

"I'm not deaf," Pierre said quietly.

Irritated, M. Darbédat turned his eyes towards Eve as his witness. But Eve gave him a hard glance and was silent. M. Darbédat realized he had hurt her. Too bad for her. It was impossible to find just the right tone for this boy. He had less sense than a child of four and Eve wanted him treated like a man. M. Darbédat could not keep himself from waiting with impatience for the moment when all this ridiculous business would be finished. Sick people always annoyed him a little—especially madmen because they were wrong. Poor Pierre, for example, was wrong all along the line, he couldn't speak a reasonable word and yet it would be useless to expect the least humility from him, or even occasional recognition of his errors.

Eve cleared away the eggshells and the cup. She put a knife and fork in front of Pierre.

" What's he going to eat now ? " M. Darbédat said jovially.

" A steak."

Pierre had taken the fork and held it in the ends of his long, pale fingers. He inspected it minutely and then gave a slight laugh.

" They won't get me this time," he murmured, setting it down, " I was warned."

Eve came and looked at the fork with passionate interest.

" Agatha," Pierre said, " give me another one."

Eve obeyed and Pierre began to eat. She had taken the suspect fork and held it tightly in her hands, her eyes never leaving it ; she seemed to make a violent effort. How suspicious all their gestures and relationships are ! thought M. Darbédat. He was uneasy.

" Be careful," Pierre said, " take it by the middle because of the claws."

Eve sighed and laid the fork on the serving table. M. Darbédat felt his gall rising. He did not think it well to give in to all this poor man's whims—even from Pierre's viewpoint it was pernicious. Franchot had said : " One must never enter the delirium of a madman." Instead of giving him another fork, it would have been better to have reasoned quietly and made him understand that the first was like all the others.

He went to the serving table, took the fork ostenta-
tiously and tested the prongs with a light finger. Then
he turned to Pierre. But the latter was cutting his meat
peacefully : he gave his father-in-law a gentle, inexpressive glance.

" I'd like to have a little talk with you," M. Darbédat
said to Eve.

She followed him docilely into the salon. Sitting on
the couch, M. Darbédat realized he had kept the fork
in his hand. He threw it on the table.

" It's much better here," he said.

" I never come here."

" All right to smoke ? ".

" Of course, Papa," Eve said hurriedly. " Do you
want a cigar ? "

M. Darbédat preferred to roll a cigarette. He thought
eagerly of the discussion he was about to begin. Speaking of Pierre he felt as embarrassed of his reason as a
giant of his strength when playing with a child. All
his qualities of clarity, sharpness, precision, turned
against him ; *I must confess it's somewhat the same
with my poor Jeanette.* Surely Mme Darbédat was not
insane, but this illness had . . . stultified her. Eve, on
the other hand, took after her father . . . a straight,
logical nature ; discussion with her was a pleasure ;
that's why I don't want her to be spoiled. M. Darbédat
raised his eyes. Once again he wanted to see the fine
intelligent features of his daughter. He was disappointed with this face ; once so reasonable and trans-
parent, there was now something clouded and opaque
in it. Eve had always been beautiful. M. Darbédat
noticed she was made up with great care, almost with
pomp. She had blued her eyelids and put mascara on

her long lashes. This violent and perfect make-up made a poor impression on her father.

" You're green beneath your rouge," he told her. " I'm afraid you're getting sick. And the way you make yourself up now ! You used to be so discreet." Eve did not answer and for an embarrassed moment M. Darbédat considered this brilliant, worn out face beneath the heavy mass of black hair. He thought she looked like a tragedian. *I even know who she looks like. That woman . . . that Roumanian who played* Phèdre *in French at the Mur d'Orange.* He regretted having made this disagreeable remark : *It escaped me ! Better not worry her with little things.*

" Excuse me," he said, smiling, " you know I'm an old purist. I don't like all these creams and paints women stick on their face today. But I'm in the wrong. You must live in your time."

Eve smiled amiably at him. M. Darbédat lit his cigarette and drew several puffs.

" My child," he began, " I wanted to talk with you : the two of us are going to talk the way we used to. Come, sit down and listen to me nicely ; you must have confidence in your old Papa."

" I'd rather stand," Eve said. " What did you want to tell me ? "

" I am going to ask you a single question," M. Darbédat said a little more dryly. " Where will all this lead you ? "

" All this ? " Eve asked, astonished.

" Yes . . . this whole life you've made for yourself. Listen," he went on, " don't think I don't understand you (he had a sudden illumination) but what you want to do is beyond human strength. You want to live solely by imagination, isn't that it ? You don't want to admit he's sick. You don't want to see the Pierre of today, do you ? You have eyes only for the Pierre of before. My dear, my darling little girl, it's an impossible bet to win," M. Darbédat continued. "Now I'm going to tell you a story which perhaps you don't know. When we were at Sables-d'Olonne, you were three years old, your mother made the acquaintance of a charming young woman with a superb little boy. You played on the beach with this little boy, you were thick as thieves, you were engaged to marry him. A while later, in Paris, your mother wanted to see this young woman again ; she was told she had a terrible accident.

" That fine little boy's head was cut off by a car. They told your mother, ' Go and see her, but above all don't talk to her about the death of her child, she *will not* believe he is dead.' Your mother went, she found a half-mad creature : she lived as though her boy were still alive ; she spoke to him, she set his place at the table. She lived in such a state of nervous tension that after six months they had to take her away by force to a sanatorium where she was obliged to stay three years. No, my child," M. Darbédat said, shaking his head, " these things are impossible. It would have been better if she had recognized the truth courageously. She would have suffered once, then time would have erased the past. There is nothing like looking things in the face, believe me."

" You're wrong," Eve said with effort. " I know very well that Pierre is . . ."

The word did not escape. She held herself very straight and put her hands on the back of the armchair : there was something dry and ugly in the lower part of her face.

" So . . . ? " asked M. Darbédat, astonished.

" So . . . ? "

" You . . . ? "

" I love him as he is," said Eve rapidly and with an irritated look.

" Not true," M. Darbédat said forcefully. " It isn't true : you don't love him, you can't love him. You can only feel that way about a healthy, normal person. You pity Pierre, I don't doubt it, surely you have the memory of three years of happiness he gave you. But don't tell me you love him. I won't believe you."

Eve remained wordless, staring at the carpet absently.

" You could at least answer me," M. Darbédat said coldly. " Don't think this conversation has been any less painful for me than it has for you."

" More than you think."

" Well then, if you love him," he cried, exasperated, " it is a great misfortune for you, for me and for your poor mother because I'm going to tell you something I would rather have hidden from you : before three years are passed Pierre will be sunk in complete dementia, he'll be like a beast."

He watched his daughter with hard eyes : he was angry at her for having compelled him, by stubbornness, to make this painful revelation.

Eve was motionless ; she did not so much as raise her eyes.

" I knew."

" Who told you ? " he asked, stupified.

" Franchot. I knew six months ago."

" And I told him to be careful with you," said M.

Darbédat with bitterness. " Maybe it's better. But
under those circumstances you must understand that
it would be unpardonable to keep Pierre with you. The
struggle you have undertaken is doomed to failure,
his illness won't spare him. If there were something
to be done, if we could save him by care, I'd say
yes. But look : you're pretty, intelligent, gay, you're
destroying yourself willingly and without profit. I know
you've been admirable, but now it's over . . . done,
you've done your duty and more ; now it would be
immoral to continue. We also have duties to ourselves,
child. And then you aren't thinking about us. You
must," he repeated, hammering the words, " send
Pierre to Franchot's clinic. Leave this apartment where
you've had nothing but sorrow and come home to us.
If you want to be useful and ease the sufferings of
someone else, you have your mother. The poor woman
is cared for by nurses, she needs someone closer to
her, and *she*," he added, " can appreciate what you do
for her and be grateful."

There was a long silence. M. Darbédat heard Pierre
singing in the next room. It was hardly a song, rather
a sort of sharp, hasty recitative. M. Darbédat raised
his eyes to his daughter.

" It's no, then ? "

" Pierre will stay with me," she said quietly. " I
get along well with him."

" By living like an animal all day long ? "

Eve smiled and shot a glance at her father, strange,
mocking and almost gay. *It's true,* M. Darbédat
thought furiously, *that's not all they do; they sleep
together.*

" You are completely mad," he said, rising.

Eve smiled sadly and murmured, as if to herself, " Not enough so."

" Not enough ? I can only tell you one thing, my child. You frighten me."

He kissed her hastily and left. Going down the stairs he thought : *we should send out two strong-arm men who'd take the poor imbecile away and stick him under a shower without asking his advice on the matter.*

It was a fine autumn day, calm and without mystery ; the sunlight gilded the faces of the passers-by. M. Darbédat was struck with the simplicity of the faces ; some weather beaten, others smooth, but they reflected all the happiness and care with which he was so familiar.

I *know exactly what I resent in Eve,* he told himself, entering the Boulevard St. Germain. *I resent her living outside the limits of human nature. Pierre is no longer a human being : in all the care and all the love she gives him she deprives human beings of a little. We don't have the right to refuse ourselves to the world ; no matter what, we live in society.*

He watched the faces of the passers-by with sympathy ; he loved their clear, serious looks. In these sunlit streets, in the midst of mankind, one felt secure, as in the midst of a large family.

A woman stopped in front of an open air display counter. She was holding a little girl by the hand.

" What's that ? " the little girl asked, pointing to a radio set.

" Mustn't touch," her mother said. " It's a radio ; it plays music."

They stood for a moment without speaking, in

ecstasy. Touched, M. Darbédat bent down to the little girl and smiled.

II

"He's gone." The door closed with a dry snap. Eve was alone in the salon. *I wish he'd die.*

She clenched her hands upon the back of the armchair; she had just remembered her father's eyes. M. Darbédat was bent over Pierre with a competent air; he had said "That's good!" the way someone says when they speak to invalids. He had looked and Pierre's face had been painted in the depths of his sharp, bulging eyes. *I hate him when he looks at him, when I think he sees him.*

Eve's hands slid along the armchair and she turned to the window. She was dazzled. The room was filled with sunlight, it was everywhere, in pale splotches on the rug, in the air like a blinding dust. Eve was not accustomed to this diligent, indiscreet light which darted from everywhere, scouring all the corners, rubbing the furniture like a busy housewife and making it glisten. However, she went to the window and raised the muslin curtain which hung against the pane. Just at that moment M. Darbédat left the building; Eve suddenly caught sight of his broad shoulders. He raised his head and looked at the sky, blinking, then with the stride of a young man he walked away. *He's straining himself*, thought Eve, *soon he'll have a stitch in the side*. She hardly hated him any longer; there was so little in that head; only the tiny worry of appearing young. Yet rage took her again when she saw him

turn the corner of the Boulevard St. Germain and disappear. *He's thinking about Pierre.* A little of their
life had escaped from the closed room and was being
dragged through the streets, in the sun, among the
people. *Can they never forget about us?*

The Rue du Bac was almost deserted. An old lady
crossed the street with mincing steps; three girls
passed, laughing. Then men, strong, serious men
carrying briefcases and talking among themselves.
Normal people, thought Eve, astonished at finding such
a powerful hatred in herself. A handsome, fleshy
woman ran heavily toward an elegant gentleman. He
took her in his arms and kissed her on the mouth. Eve
gave a hard laugh and let the curtain fall.

Pierre sang no more but the woman on the fourth
floor was playing the piano; she played a Chopin
Etude. Eve felt calmer; she took a step toward Pierre's
room but stopped almost immediately and leaned
against the wall in anguish; each time she left the
room, she was panic-stricken at the thought of going
back. Yet she knew she could live nowhere else:
she loved the room. She looked around it with cold
curiosity as if to gain a little time: this shadowless,
odourless room where she waited for her courage to
return. *You'd think it was a dentist's waiting room.*
Armchairs of pink silk, the divan, the tabourets were
sombre and discreet, a little fatherly; man's best
friends. Eve imagined those grave gentlemen dressed
in light suits. All like the ones she saw at the window,
entering the room, continuing a conversation already
begun. They did not even take time to reconnoitre,
but advanced with firm step to the middle of the room;
one of them, letting his hand drag behind him like a

94

wake in passing, knocked over cushions, objects on the table and was never disturbed by their contact. And when a piece of furniture was in their way, these poised men, far from making a detour to avoid it, quietly changed its place. Finally they sat down, still plunged in their conversation, without even glancing behind them. *A living-room for normal people,* thought Eve. She stared at the knob of the closed door and anguish clutched her throat : *I must go back. I never leave him alone so long.* She would have to open the door, then stand for a moment on the threshold, trying to accustom her eyes to the shadow and the room would push her back with all its strength. Eve would have to triumph over this resistance and enter all the way into the heart of the room. Suddenly she wanted violently to see Pierre ; he would have liked to make fun of M. Darbédat with him. But Pierre had no need of her ; Eve could not foresee the welcome he had in store for her. Suddenly she thought with a sort of pride that she had no place anywhere. *Normal people think I belong with them. But I couldn't stay an hour among them. I need to live out there, on the other side of the wall. But they don't want me out there.*

A profound change was taking place around her. The light had grown old and greying : it was heavy, like the water in a vase of flowers that hasn't been changed since the day before. In this aged light Eve found a melancholy she had long forgotten : the melancholy of an autumn afternoon that was ending. She looked around her, hesitant, almost timid : all that was so far away : there was neither day nor night nor season nor melancholy in the room. She vaguely recalled autumns long past, autumns of her childhood, then suddenly she stiffened : she was afraid of memories.

She heard Pierre's voice. " Agatha ! Where are you ? "

" Coming ! " she cried.

She opened the door and penetrated the room.

The heavy odour of incense filled her mouth and nostrils as she opened her eyes and stretched out her hands—for a long time the perfume and shadow had meant nothing more to her than a single element, acrid and heavy, as simple, as familiar as water, air or fire—and she prudently advanced toward a pale stain which seemed to float in the fog. It was Pierre's face : Pierre's clothing (he dressed in black ever since he had been sick) melted in obscurity. Pierre had thrown back his head and closed his eyes. He was handsome. Eve looked at his long, curved lashes, then sat close to him on the low chair. *He seems to be suffering*, she thought. Little by little her eyes grew used to the shadow. The bureau emerged first, then the bed, then Pierre's personal things : scissors, the pot of glue, books, the herbarium which shed its leaves onto the rug near the armchair.

" Agatha ? "

Pierre had opened his eyes. He was watching her, smiling.

" You know, that fork ? " he said. " I did it to frighten that fellow. There was *almost* nothing the matter with it."

Eve's apprehensions faded and she gave a light laugh.

" You succeeded," she said, " You drove him completely out of his mind."

Pierre smiled. " Did you see ? He played with it a long time, he held it right in his hands. The trouble is," he said, " they don't know how to take things ; they grab them."

" That's right," Eve said.

Pierre tapped the palm of his left hand lightly with the index of his right.

" They take with that. They reach out their fingers and when they catch hold of something they crack down on it to knock it out."

He spoke rapidly and hardly moving his lips ; he looked puzzled.

" I wonder what they want," he said at last. " That fellow has already been here. Why did they send him to me ? If they want to know what I'm doing all they have to do is read it on the screen, they don't even need to leave the house. They make mistakes. They have the power but they make mistakes. I never make any, that's my trump card. *Hoffka !*" he said. He shook his long hands before his forehead. " The bitch ! Hoffka ! Paffka ! Suffka ! Do you want any more ? "

" Is it the bell ? " asked Eve.

" Yes. It's gone." He went on severely. " This fellow, he's just a subordinate. You know him, you went into the living room with him."

Eve did not answer.

" What did he want ? " asked Pierre. " He must have told you."

She hesitated an instant, then answered brutally. " He wanted you locked up."

When the truth was told quietly to Pierre he distrusted it. He had to be dealt with violently in order to daze and paralyse his suspicions. Eve preferred to

brutalize him rather than lie : when she lied and he
acted as if he believed it she could not avoid a very
slight feeling of superiority which made her horrified at
herself.

" Lock me up ! " Pierre repeated ironically,
" They're crazy. What can walls do to me ? Maybe
they think that's going to stop me. I sometimes wonder
if there aren't two groups. The real one, the negro—
and then a bunch of fools trying to stick their noses
in and making mistake after mistake."

He made his hand jump up from the arms of the
chair and looked at it happily.

" I can get through walls. What did you tell
them ? " he asked, turning to Eve with curiosity.

" Not to lock you up."

He shrugged. " You shouldn't have said that. You
made a mistake too . . . unless you did it on purpose.
You've got to call their bluff."

He was silent. Eve lowered her head sadly : " *They
grab things.*" *How scornfully he said that—and he
was right. Do I grab things, too ? It doesn't do any
good to watch myself, I think most of my movements
annoy him. But he doesn't say anything.* Suddenly
she felt as miserable as when she was fourteen and
Mme Darbédat told her " You don't know what to do
with your hands." She didn't dare make a move and
just at that time she had an irresistible desire to change
her position. Quietly she put her feet under the chair,
barely touching the rug. She watched the lamp on the
table—the lamp whose base Pierre had painted black
—and the chess set. Pierre had left only the black
pawns on the board. Sometimes he would get up, go
to the table and take the pawns in his hands one by

one. He spoke to them, called them Robots and they seemed to stir with a mute life under his fingers. When he set them down, Eve went and touched them in her turn (she always felt somewhat ridiculous about it). They had become little bits of dead wood again but something vague and incomprehensible stayed in them, something like understanding. *These are* his *things,* she thought. *There is nothing of mine in the room.* She had had a few pieces of furniture before; the mirror and the little inlaid dresser handed down from her grandmother and which Pierre jokingly called "*your* dresser". Pierre had carried them away with him; things showed their true face to Pierre alone. Eve could watch them for hours: they were unflaggingly stubborn and determined to deceive her, offering her nothing but their appearance—as they did to Dr. Franchot and M. Darbédat. *Yet,* she told herself with anguish, *I don't see them quite like my father. It isn't possible for me to see them exactly like him.*

She moved her knees a little : her legs felt as though they were crawling with ants. Her body was stiff and taut and hurt her ; she felt it too alive, too demanding. *I would like to be invisible and stay here seeing him without him seeing me. He doesn't need me ; I am useless in this room.* She turned her head slightly and looked at the wall above Pierre. Threats were written on the wall. Eve knew it but she could not read them. She often watched the big red roses on the wallpaper until they began to dance before her eyes. The roses flamed in shadow. Most of the time the threat was written near the ceiling, a little to the left of the bed ; but sometimes it moved. *I must get up. I can't . . . I can't sit down any longer.* There were also white

99

discs on the wall that looked like slices of onion. The discs spun and Eve's hands began to tremble: *Sometimes I think I'm going mad. But no*, she thought, *I can't go mad. I get nervous, that's all.*

Suddenly she felt Pierre's hand on hers.

"Agatha," Pierre said tenderly.

He smiled at her but he held her hand by the ends of his fingers with a sort of revulsion, as though he had picked up a crab by the back and wanted to avoid its claws.

"Agatha," he said, "I would so much like to have confidence in you."

She closed her eyes and her breast heaved. *I mustn't answer anything, if I do he'll get angry, he won't say anything more.*

Pierre had dropped her hand. "I like you, Agatha," he said, "but I can't understand you. Why do you stay in the room all the time?"

Eve did not answer.

"Tell me why."

"You know I love you," she said dryly.

"I don't believe you," Pierre said. "Why should you love me? I must frighten you: I'm haunted." He smiled but suddenly became serious. "There is a wall between you and me. I see you, I speak to you, but you're on the other side. What keeps us from loving? I think it was easier before. In Hamburg."

"Yes," Eve said sadly. Always Hamburg. He never spoke of their real past. Neither Eve nor he had ever been to Hamburg.

"We used to walk along the canal. There was a barge, remember? The barge was black; there was a dog on the deck."

He made it up as he went along ; it sounded false.

" I held your hand. You had another skin. I believed all you told me. Be quiet ! " he shouted.

He listened for a moment. " They're coming," he said mournfully.

Eve jumped up. " They're coming ? I thought they wouldn't ever come again."

Pierre had been calmer for the past three days ; the statues did not come. Pierre was terribly afraid of the statues even though he would never admit it. Eve was not afraid : but when they began to fly, buzzing, around the room, she was afraid of Pierre.

" Give me the ziuthre," Pierre said.

Eve got up and took the ziuthre : it was a collection of pieces of cardboard Pierre had glued together ; he used it to conjure the statues. The ziuthre looked like a spider. On one of the cardboards Pierre had written " Power over ambush " and on the other " Black ". On a third he had drawn a laughing face with wrinkled eyes : it was Voltaire.

Pierre seized the ziuthre by one end and looked at it darkly.

" I can't use it any more," he said.

" Why ? "

" They turned it upside down."

" Will you make another ? "

He looked at her for a while. " You'd like me to, wouldn't you ? " he said between his teeth.

Eve was angry at Pierre. *He's warned every time they come : how does he do it ? He's never wrong.*

The ziuthre dangled pitifully from the ends of Pierre's fingers. *He always finds a good reason not to use it. Sunday when they came he pretended he'd lost*

*it but I saw it behind the paste pot and he couldn't fail
to see it. I wonder if he isn't the one who brings them.*
One could never tell if he were completely sincere.
Sometimes Eve had the impression that despite himself Pierre was surrounded by a swarm of unhealthy
thoughts and visions. But at other times Pierre seemed
to invent them. *He suffers. But how much does he*
believe *in the statues and the negro. Anyhow, I know
he doesn't see the statues, he only hears them : when
they pass he turns his head away ; but he still says he
sees them ; he describes them.* She remembered the
red face of Dr. Franchot : " But my dear madame, all
mentally unbalanced persons are liars ; you're wasting
your time if you're trying to distinguish between what
they really feel and what they pretend to feel." She
gave a start. *What is Franchot doing here? I don't
want to start thinking like him.*

Pierre had risen. He went to throw the ziuthre into
the wastebasket : I *want to think like you,* she murmured. He walked with tiny steps, on tiptoe, pressing
his elbows against his hips so as to take up the least
possible space. He came back and sat down and looked
at Eve with a closed expression.

" We'll have to put up black wallpaper," he said.
" There isn't enough black in this room."

He was crouched in the armchair. Sadly Eve
watched his meagre body, always ready to withdraw,
to shrink ; the arms, legs and head looked like retract-
able organs. The clock struck six. The piano downstairs was silent. Eve sighed ; the statues would not
come right away ; they had to wait for them.

" Do you want me to turn on the light ? "

She would rather not wait for them in darkness.

"Do as you please," Pierre said.

Eve lit the small lamp on the bureau and a red mist filled the room. Pierre was waiting too.

He did not speak but his lips were moving, making two dark stains in the red mist. Eve loved Pierre's lips. Before, they had been moving and sensual; but they had lost their sensuality. They were wide apart, trembling a little, coming together incessantly, crushing against each other only to separate again. They were the only living things in this black face; they looked like two frightened animals. Pierre could mutter like that for hours without a sound leaving his mouth and Eve often let herself be fascinated by this tiny, obstinate movement. *I love his mouth.* He never kissed her any more; he was horrified at contacts: at night they touched him—the hands of men, hard and dry, pinched him all over; the long-nailed hands of women caressed him. Often he went to bed with his clothes on but the hands slipped under the clothes and tugged at his shirt. Once he heard laughter and puffy lips were placed on his mouth. He never kissed Eve after that night.

"Agatha," Pierre said, "don't look at my mouth."

Eve lowered her eyes.

"I am not unaware that people can learn to read lips," he went on insolently.

His hand trembled on the arm of the chair. The index finger stretched out, tapped three times on the thumb and the other fingers curled: this was a spell. *It's going to start,* she thought. She wanted to take Pierre in her arms.

Pierre began to speak at the top of his voice in a very sophisticated tone.

"Do you remember San Pauli?"

103

No answer. Perhaps it was a trap.

" I met you there," he said, satisfied. " I took you away from a Danish sailor. We almost fought but I paid for a round of drinks and he let me take you away. All that was only a joke."

He's lying, he doesn't believe a word of what he says. He knows my name isn't Agatha. I hate him when he lies. But she saw his staring eyes and her rage melted. *He isn't lying,* she thought, *he can't stand it any more. He feels them coming ; he's talking to keep from hearing them.* Pierre dug both hands into the arm of the chair. His face was pale ; he was smiling.

" These meetings are often strange," he said, " but I don't believe it's by chance. I'm not asking who sent you. I know you wouldn't answer. Anyhow, you've been smart enough to bluff me."

He spoke with great difficulty, in a sharp, hurried voice. There were words he could not pronounce and which left his mouth like some soft and shapeless substance.

" You dragged me away right in the middle of the party, between the rows of black automobiles, but behind the cars there was an army with red eyes which glowed as soon as I turned my back. I think you made signs to them, all the time hanging on my arm, but I didn't see a thing. I was too absorbed by the great ceremonies of the Coronation."

He looked straight ahead, his eyes wide open. He passed his hand over his forehead very rapidly, in one spare gesture, without stopping his talking. He did not want to stop talking.

" It was the Coronation of the Republic," he said stridently, " an impressive spectacle of its kind because

104

of all the species of animals that the colonies sent for
the ceremony. You were afraid to get lost among the
monkeys. I said among the monkeys," he repeated
arrogantly, looking around him, " I could say *among
the negroes!*

" The abortions sliding under the tables, trying to
pass unseen, are discovered and nailed to the spot by
my Look. The password is silence. To be silent.
Everything in place and attention for the entrance of
the statues, that's the countersign. Tralala . . ." he
shrieked and cupped his hands to his mouth. " Tralalala, tralalala ! "

He was silent and Eve knew that the statues had
come into the room. He was stiff, pale and distrustful.
Eve stiffened too and both waited in silence. Someone
was walking in the corridor : it was Marie the house-
cleaner ; she had undoubtedly just arrived. Eve thought,
I have to give her money for the gas. And then the
statues began to fly ; they passed between Eve and
Pierre.

Pierre went " Ah ! " and slunk down in the armchair,
folding his legs beneath him. He turned his face away ;
sometimes he grinned, but drops of sweat pearled his
forehead. Eve could stand the sight no longer—this
pale cheek, this mouth deformed by a trembling
grimace ; she closed her eyes. Gold threads began to
dance on the red background of her eyelids ; she felt
old and heavy. Not far from her Pierre was breathing
violently. *They're flying, they're buzzing, they're bending over him.* She felt a slight tickling, a pain in the
shoulder and right side. Instinctively her body bent to
the left as if to avoid some disagreeable contact, as if
to let a heavy, awkward object pass. Suddenly the floor

creaked and she had an insane desire to open her eyes, to look to her right, sweeping the air with her hand.

She did nothing; she kept her eyes closed and a bitter joy made her tremble: *I am afraid too*, she thought. Her entire life had taken refuge in her right side. She leaned towards Pierre without opening her eyes. The slightest effort would be enough and she would enter this tragic world for the first time. *I'm afraid of the statues*, she thought. It was a violent, blind affirmation, an incantation. She wanted to believe in their presence with all her strength. She tried to make a new sense, a sense of touch out of the anguish which paralysed her right side. She *felt* their passage in her arm, in her side and shoulder.

The statues flew low and gently; they buzzed. Eve knew that they had an evil look and that eyelashes stuck out from the stone around their eyes; but she pictured them badly. She knew, too, that they were not quite alive but that slabs of flesh, warm scales appeared on their great bodies; they stone peeled from the ends of their fingers and their palms were eaten away. Eve could not *see* all that: she simply thought of enormous women sliding against her, solemn and grotesque, with a human look and compact heads of stone. *They are bending over Pierre*—Eve made such a violent effort that her hands began trembling—*they are bending over me*. A horrible cry suddenly chilled her. They had touched him. She opened her eyes: Pierre's head was in his hands, he was breathing heavily. Eve felt exhausted: *a game*, she thought with remorse; *it was only a game. I didn't sincerely believe it for an instant. And all that time he suffered as if it were real.*

Pierre relaxed and breathed freely. But his pupils were strangely dilated and he was perspiring.

" Did you see them ? " he asked.

" I can't see them."

" Better for you. They'd frighten you," he said. " I am used to them."

Eve's hands were still shaking and the blood had rushed to her head. Pierre took a cigarette from his pocket and brought it up to his mouth. But he did not light it.

" I don't care whether I see them or not," he said, " but I don't want them to touch me : I'm afraid they'll give me pimples."

He thought for an instant, then asked, " Did you hear them ? "

" Yes," Eve said, " it's like an airplane engine." (Pierre had told her this the previous Sunday.)

Pierre smiled with condescension. " You exaggerate," he said. But he was still pale. He looked at Eve's hands. " Your hands are trembling. That made quite an impression on you, my poor Agatha. But don't worry. They won't come back again before tomorrow." Eve could not speak. Her teeth were chattering and she was afraid Pierre would notice it. Pierre watched her for a long time.

" You're tremendously beautiful," he said, nodding his head. " It's too bad, too bad."

He put out his hand quickly and toyed with her ear. " My lovely devil-woman. You disturb me a little, you are too beautiful : that distracts me. If it weren't a question of recapitulation . . ."

He stopped and looked at Eve with surprise.

"That's not the word . . . it came . . . it came," he said, smiling vaguely. "I had another on the tip of my tongue . . . but this one . . . came in its place. I forget what I was telling you."

He thought for a moment, then shook his head.

"Come," he said, "I want to sleep." He added in a childish voice, "You know, Agatha, I'm tired. I can't collect my thoughts any more."

He threw away his cigarette and watched the rug anxiously. Eve slipped a pillow under his head.

"You can sleep too," he told her, "they won't be back."

. . . *Recapitulation* . . .

Pierre was asleep, a candid, half smile on his face; his head was turned to one side: one might have thought he wanted to caress his cheek with his shoulders. Eve was not sleepy, she was thoughtful: *Recapitulation*. Pierre had suddenly looked stupid and the word had slipped out of his mouth, long and whitish. Pierre had stared ahead of him in astonishment, as if he had seen the word and didn't recognize it; his mouth was open, soft: something seemed broken in it. *He stammered. That's the first time it ever happened to him: he noticed it, too. He said he couldn't collect his thoughts any more*. Pierre gave a voluptuous little whimper and his hand made a vague movement. Eve watched him harshly: *How is he going to wake up?* It gnawed at her. As soon as Pierre was asleep she had to think about it. She was afraid he would wake up wild-eyed and stammering. *I'm stupid*, she thought, *it can't start before a year; Franchot said so*. But the anguish did not leave her; a year: a winter, a springtime, a summer, the beginning of another autumn. One day his features would grow confused, his jaw would hang loose, he would half open his weeping eyes. Eve bent over Pierre's hand and pressed her lips against it : *I'll kill you before that.*

Erostratus

You really have to see men from above. I'd put out
the light and stand at the window : they never suspected
for a moment you could watch them from up there.
They're careful of their fronts, sometimes of their backs,
but their whole effect is calculated for spectators of
about five feet eight. Who ever thought about the
shape of a derby hat seen from the seventh floor ? They
neglect protecting their heads and shoulders with bright
colours and garish clothes, they don't know how to
fight this great enemy of Humanity, the downward
perspective. I'd lean on the window sill and begin to
laugh : where was this wonderful upright stance they're
so proud of : they were crushed against the sidewalk
and two long legs jumped out from under their
shoulders.

On a seventh floor balcony : that's where I should
have spent my whole life. You have to prop up moral
superiorities with material symbols or else they'll
tumble. But exactly what is my superiority over men ?
Superiority of position, nothing more : I have placed
myself above the human within me and I study it.
That's why I always liked the towers of Notre-Dame,
the platforms in the Eiffel Tower, the Sacré-Coeur, my
seventh floor on the Rue Delambre. These are excellent
symbols.

Sometimes I had to go down into the street. To the office, for example. I stifled. It's much harder to consider people as ants when you're on the same plane as they are : they *touch* you. Once I saw a dead man in the street. He had fallen on his face. They turned him over, he was bleeding. I saw his open eyes and his cockeyed look and all the blood. I said to myself, " It's nothing, it's no more touching than wet paint. They painted his nose red, that's all." But I felt a nasty softness in my legs and neck and I fainted. They took me into a drugstore, gave me a few slaps on the face and a drink. I could have killed them.

I knew they were my enemies but they didn't know it. They liked each other, they rubbed elbows ; they would even have given me a hand, here and there, because they thought I was like them. But if they could have guessed the least bit of the truth, they would have beaten me. They did later, anyhow. When they got me and knew *who* I was, they gave me the works ; they beat me up for two hours in the station house, they slapped me and punched me and twisted my arms, they ripped off my trousers and to finish they threw my glasses on the floor and while I looked for them, on all fours, they laughed and kicked me. I always knew they'd end up beating me ; I'm not strong and I can't defend myself. Some of them had been on the lookout for me for a long time : the big ones. In the street they'd bump into me to see what I'd do. I said nothing. I acted as if I didn't understand. But they still got me. I was afraid of them : it was a foreboding. But don't think I didn't have more serious reasons for hating them.

As far as that was concerned, everything went along

111

much better starting from the day I bought a revolver. You feel strong when you assiduously carry on your person something that can explode and make a noise. I took it every Sunday, I simply put it in my trousers pocket and then went out for a walk—generally along the boulevards. I felt it pulling at my trousers like a crab, I felt it cold against my thigh. But little by little it got warmer with the contact of my body. I walked with a certain stiffness. I slipped my hand in my pocket and felt the *object*. From time to time I went into a *urinoir* —even in there I had to be careful because I often had neighbours—I took out my revolver, I felt the weight of it, I looked at its black checkered butt and its trigger that looked like a half-closed eyelid. The others, the ones who saw me from the outside, thought I was pissing. But I never piss in the *urinoirs*.

One night I got the idea of shooting people. It was a Saturday evening, I had gone out to pick up Lea, a blonde who works out in front of an hotel on the Rue Montparnasse. I never had intercourse with a woman : I would have felt robbed. You get on top of them, of course, but from what I hear, they're the ones—by a long shot—who gain on the deal. I don't ask anybody for anything, but I don't give anything, either. Or else I'd have to have a cold, pious woman who would give in to me with disgust. The first Saturday of every month I went to one of the rooms in the Hotel Duquesne with Lea. She undressed and I watched her without touching her. That night I didn't find her. I waited for a little while and, as I didn't see her coming, I supposed she had a cold. It was the beginning of January and it was very cold. I was desolated : I'm the imaginative kind and I had pictured to myself all the pleasure I would have got from the evening. On the Rue Odessa there was a brunette I had often noticed, a little ripe but firm and plump. I don't exactly despise ripe women : when they're undressed they look more naked than the others. But she didn't know anything of my wants and I was a little scared to ask her right off the bat. And then I don't care too much for new acquaintances : these women can be hiding some thug behind a door, and after, the man suddenly jumps out and takes your money. You're lucky if you get off without a beating. Still, that evening I had nerve. I decided to go back to my place, pick up the revolver and try my luck.

So when I went up to this woman, fifteen minutes later, my gun was in my pocket and I wasn't afraid of anything. Looking at her closely, she seemed rather miserable. She looked like my neighbour across the way, the wife of the police sergeant, and I was very pleased because I'd been wanting to see her naked for a long time. She dressed with the window open when the sergeant wasn't there, and I often stayed behind' my curtain to catch a glimpse of her. But she always dressed in the back of the room.

There was only one free room in the Hotel Stella, on the fifth floor. We went up. The woman was fairly heavy and stopped to catch her breath after each step. I felt good : I have a wiry body, in spite of my belly, and it takes more than five floors to wind me. On the fifth floor landing, she stopped and put her right hand to her heart and breathed heavily. She had the key to the room in her left hand.

" It's a long way up," she said, trying to smile at me. Without answering, I took the key from her and opened the door. I held my revolver in my left hand, pointing straight ahead through the pocket, and I didn't let go of it until I switched the light on. The room was empty. They had put a little square of green soap on the washbasin, enough for one customer. I smiled: I don't have much to do with bidets and little squares of soap. The woman was still breathing heavily behind me and that excited me. I turned; she put out her lips towards me. I pushed her away.

" Undress," I told her.

There was an upholstered armchair; I sat down and made myself comfortable. It's times like this I wish I smoked. The woman took off her dress and stopped, looking at me distrustfully.

" What's your name ? " I asked, leaning back.

" Renée."

" All right, Renée, hurry up. I'm waiting."

" You aren't going to undress ? "

" Go on," I said, " don't worry about me."

She dropped her panties, then picked them up and put them carefully on top of her dress along with her brassière.

" So you're a little lazybones, honey ? " she asked me. " You want your little girl to do all the work ? "

At the same time she took a step towards me, and, leaning her hands on the arm of the chair, tried heavily to kneel in front of me. I got up brusquely.

" None of that," I told her.

She looked at me with surprise.

" Well, what do you want me to do ? "

" Nothing. Just walk. Walk around. I don't want any more from you."

She began to walk back and forth awkwardly.

Nothing annoys women more than walking when they're naked. They don't have the habit of putting their heels down flat. The whore arched her back and let her arms hang. I was in heaven : there I was calmly sitting in an armchair, dressed up to my neck, I had even kept my gloves on, and this ripe woman had stripped herself naked at my command and was turning back and forth in front of me. She turned her head towards me, and, for appearance, smiled coquettishly.

" You think I'm pretty ? You like what you see ? "

" Don't worry about that."

" Look," she asked with sudden indignation, " do you think you're going to make me walk up and down like this very long ? "

" Sit down."

She sat on the bed and we watched each other in silence. She had gooseflesh. I could hear the ticking of an alarm clock from the other side of the wall. Suddenly I told her something.

" Bastard," she said between her teeth, blushing.

But I laughed louder, then she jumped up and took her brassière from the chair.

" Hey ! " I said, " it isn't over. I'm going to give you fifty francs after a while, but I want my money's worth."

She picked up her panties nervously.

" I've had enough, get it ? I don't know what you want. And if you had me come up here to make a fool out of me . . ."

Then I took out my revolver and showed it to her. She looked at me seriously and dropped the panties without a word.

" Walk," I told her, " walk around."

115

She walked around for another five minutes. Then
I gave her my cane and made her do exercises. Afterwards I got up and gave her a fifty-franc note. She
took it.

"So long," I added. "I don't think I tired you out
very much for the money."

I went out, I left her naked in the middle of the
room, the brassière in one hand and the fifty-franc note
in the other. I didn't regret the money I'd spent: I
had dumbfounded her and it isn't easy to surprise a
whore. Going down the stairs I thought, "That's what
I want. To surprise them all." I was happy as a child.
I had brought along the green soap and after I reached
home I rubbed it under the hot water for a long time
until there was nothing left of it but a thin film between
my fingers and it looked like a mint candy someone
had sucked on for a long time.

But that night I woke up with a start and I saw her
face again, her eyes when I showed her my gun, and
her fat belly that bounced up and down at every step.

What a fool, I thought. And I felt bitter remorse: I
should have shot her while I was at it, shot that belly
full of holes. That night and three nights afterwards,
I dreamed of six little red holes grouped in a circle
about the navel.

As a result I never went out without my revolver.
I looked at people's backs, and I imagined, from their
walk, the way they would fall if I shot them. I was in
the habit of hanging around the Châtelet every Sunday
when the classical concerts ended. About six o'clock
I heard a bell ring and the ushers came to fasten back
the plate-glass doors with hooks. This was the beginning: the crowd came out slowly; the people walked

with floating steps, their eyes still full of dreams, their hearts still full of pretty sentiments. There were a lot of them who looked around in amazement : the street must have looked quite strange to them. Then they smiled mysteriously : they were passing from one world to another. I was waiting for them in this other world. I slid my right hand into my pocket and gripped the gun butt with all my strength. After a while, I *saw* myself shooting them. I knocked them off like clay pipes, they fell, one after the other, and the panic-stricken survivors streamed back into the theatre, breaking the glass in the doors. It was an exciting game : when it was over, my hands were trembling and I had to go to Dreher's and drink a cognac to get myself in shape.

I wouldn't have killed the women. I would have shot them in the kidneys. Or in the calves, to make them dance.

I still hadn't decided anything. But I did everything just as though my power of decision had stopped. I began with minor details. I went to practise in a shooting gallery at Denfert-Rochereau. My scores weren't tremendous, but men are bigger targets, especially when you shoot point blank. Then I arranged my publicity. I chose a day when all my colleagues would be together in the office. On Monday morning. I was always very friendly with them, even though I had a horror of shaking their hands. They took off their gloves to greet you ; they had an obscene way of undressing their hand, pulling the glove back and sliding it slowly along the fingers, unveiling the fat, wrinkled nakedness of the palm. I always kept my gloves on.

We never did much on Mondays. The typist from

the commercial service came to bring us receipts. Lemercier joked pleasantly with her and when she had gone, they described her charms with a blasé competence. Then they talked about Lindbergh. They liked Lindbergh. I told them :

" I like the black heroes."

" Negroes ? " Massé asked.

" No, black as in black magic. Lindbergh is a white hero. He doesn't interest me."

" Go see if it's easy to cross the Atlantic," Bouxin said sourly.

I told them my conception of a black hero.

" An anarchist," Lemercier said.

" No," I said quietly, " in their way, the anarchists love people."

" Then it must be a crazy man."

But Massé, who had some education, intervened just then.

" I know your character," he said to me. " His name is Erostratus. He wanted to become famous and he couldn't find anything better to do than to burn down the temple of Ephesus, one of the seven wonders of the world."

" And what was the name of the man who built the temple ? "

" I don't remember," he confessed, " I don't believe anybody knows his name."

" Really ? But you remember the name of Erostratus ? You see, he didn't figure things out too badly."

The conversation ended on these words, but I was quite calm. They would remember it when the time came. For myself, who, until then, had never heard of

Erostratus, his story was encouraging. He had been dead for more than two thousand years and his act was still shining like a black diamond. I began to think that my destiny would be short and tragic. First it frightened me but I got used to it. If you look at it a certain way, it's terrible, but, on the other hand, it gives the passing moment considerable force and beauty. I felt a strange power in my body when I went down into the street. I had my revolver on me, the thing that explodes and makes noise. But I no longer drew my assurance from that, it was from myself. I was a being like a revolver, a torpedo or a bomb. I too, one day at the end of my sombre life, would explode and light the world with a flash as short and violent as magnesium. At that time I had the same dream several nights in a row. I was an anarchist. I had put myself in the path of the Tsar and I carried an infernal machine on me. At the appointed hour, the cortège passed, the bomb exploded and we were thrown in the air, myself, the Tsar, and three gold-braided officers, before the eyes of the crowd.

I now went for weeks on end without showing up at the office. I walked the boulevards in the midst of my future victims or locked myself in my room and made my plans. They fired me at the beginning of October. Then I spent my leisure working on the following letter, of which I made 102 copies :

Monsieur,
   You are a famous man and your works sell by the thousands. I am going to tell you why: because you love men. You have humanism in your blood: you are lucky. You expand when you are with people ; as soon as you see one of your fellows, even without

knowing him, you feel sympathy for him. You have a taste for his body, for the way he is jointed, for his legs which open and close at will, and above all for his hands: it pleases you because he has five fingers on each hand and he can set his thumb against the other fingers. You are delighted when your neighbour takes a cup from the table because there is a way of taking it which is strictly human and which you have often described in your works; less supple, less rapid than that of a monkey, but is it not so much more intelligent? You also love the flesh of man, his look of being heavily wounded with re-education, seeming to re-invent walking at every step, and his famous look which even wild beasts cannot bear. So it has been easy for you to find the proper accent for speaking to man about himself: a modest, yet frenzied accent. People throw themselves greedily upon your books, they read them in a good armchair, they think of a great love, discreet and unhappy, which you bring them and that makes up for many things, for being ugly, for being cowardly, for being cuckolded, for not getting a rise on the first of January. And they say willingly of your latest book: it's a good deed.

I suppose you might be curious to know what a man can be like who does not love men. Very well, I am such a man, and I love them so little that soon I am going out and kill half a dozen of them; perhaps you might wonder why *only* half a dozen? Because my revolver has only six cartridges. A monstrosity, isn't it? And moreover, an act strictly impolitic? But I tell you I *cannot* love them. I understand very well the way you feel. But what attracts you to them disgusts me. I have seen, as you, men chewing slowly, all the while keeping an eye on everything, the left hand leafing through an economic review. Is it my fault I prefer to watch the sea-lions feeding? Man can do nothing with his face without its turning into a game of physiognomy. When he chews, keeping his mouth shut, the corners of his mouth go up and down, he looks as though he were passing incessantly from serenity to tearful surprise. You love this, I know, you call it the watchfulness of the Spirit. But it makes me sick; I don't know why; I was born like that.

If there were only a difference of taste between us I would not trouble you. But everything happens as if you had grace and I had none. I am free to like or dislike lobster newberg, but if I do not like men I am a wretch and can find no place in the sun. They have monopolized the sense of life. I hope you will understand what I mean. For the past 33 years I have been beating against closed doors on which is written "No entrance if not a humanist." I had to abandon all I have undertaken; I had to choose: either it was an absurd and ill-fated attempt, or sooner or later it had to turn to their profit. I could not succeed in detaching from myself thoughts I did not expressly destine for them, in formulating them: they remained in me as slight organic movements. Even the tools I used I felt belonged to them; words, for example: I wanted my own words. But the ones I use have dragged through I don't know how many consciences; they arrange themselves in my head by virtue of the habits I have picked up from the others and it is not without repugnance that I use them in writing to you. But this is the last time. I say to you: love men or it is only right for them to let you sneak out of it. Well, I do not want to sneak out. Soon I am going to take my revolver, I am going down into the street and see if anybody can do anything to *them*. Goodbye, perhaps it will be you I shall meet. You will never know then with what pleasure I shall blow your brains out. If not,—and this is more likely—read tomorrow's papers.

There you will see that an individual named Paul
Hilbert has killed, in a moment of fury, six passers-by
on the Boulevard Edgar-Quinet. You know better than
anyone the value of newspaper prose. You understand
then that I am not " furious." I am, on the contrary,
quite calm and I pray you to accept, Monsieur, the
assurance of my distinguished sentiments.

PAUL HILBERT.

I slipped the 102 letters in 102 envelopes and on the
envelopes I wrote the addresses of 102 French writers.
Then I put the whole business in my table drawer along
with six books of stamps.

I went out very little during the two weeks that
followed. I let myself become slowly occupied by my
crime. In the mirror, to which I often went to look at
myself, I noticed the changes in my face with pleasure.
The eyes had grown larger, they seemed to be eating
up the whole face. They were black and tender behind
the glasses and I rolled them like planets. The fine
eyes of an artist or assassin. But I counted on changing
ever more profoundly after the massacre. I have seen
photographs of two beautiful girls—those servants who
killed and plundered their mistresses. I saw their
photos *before* and *after*. *Before*, their faces poised like
shy flowers above piqué collars. They smelled of
hygiene and appetizing honesty. A discreet curling iron
had waved their hair exactly alike. And even more
reassuring than their curled hair, their collars and their
look of being at the photographer's, there was their
resemblance as sisters, their well-considered resemblance which immediately put the bonds of blood and
natural roots of the family circle to the fore. *After*,
their faces were resplendent as fire. They had the bare

necks of prisoners about to be beheaded. Everywhere wrinkles, horrible wrinkles of fear and hatred, folds, holes in the flesh as though a beast with claws had walked over their faces. And those eyes, always those black, depthless eyes—like mine. Yet they did not resemble one another. Each one, in her own way, bore the memory of the common crime. "If it is enough," I told myself, "for a crime which was mostly chance, to transform these orphans' faces, what can I not hope for from a crime entirely conceived and organized by myself." It would possess me, overturning my all-too-human ugliness . . . a crime, cutting the life of him who commits it in two. There must be times when one would like to turn back, but this shining object is there behind you, barring the way. I asked only an hour to enjoy mine, to feel its crushing weight. This time, I would arrange to have everything my way ; I decided to carry out the execution at the top of the Rue Odessa. I would profit by the confusion to escape, leaving them to pick up their dead. I would run, I would cross the Boulevard Edgar-Quinet and turn quickly into the Rue Delambre. I would need only 30 seconds to reach the door of my building. My pursuers would still be on the Boulevard Edgar-Quinet, they would lose my trail and it would surely take them more than an hour to find it again. I would wait for them in my room and when I would hear them beating on the door I would re-load my revolver and shoot myself in the mouth.

I began to live more expensively ; I made an arrangement with the proprietor of a restaurant on the Rue Vavin who had a tray sent up every morning and evening. The boy rang, but I didn't open, I waited a few minutes, then opened the door halfway and saw full plates steaming in a long basket set on the floor.

On October 27, at six in the evening, I had only 17 francs 50 centimes left. I took my revolver and the packet of letters and went downstairs. I took care not to close the door, so as to re-enter more rapidly once I had finished. I didn't feel well, my hands were cold and blood was rushing to my head, my eyes tickled me. I looked at the stores, the Hotel des Ecoles, the stationer's where I buy my pencils and I didn't recognize them. I wondered, " What street is this ? " The Boulevard du Montparnasse was full of people. They jostled me, pushed me, bumped me with their elbows or shoulders. I let myself be shoved around, I didn't have the strength to slip in between them. Suddenly I saw myself in the heart of this mob, horribly alone and little. How they could have hurt me if they wanted ! I was afraid because of the gun in my pocket. It seemed to me they could guess it was there. They would look at me with their hard eyes and would say : " Hey there . . . hey . . ." with happy indignation, harpooning me with their men's paws. Lynched ! They would throw me above their heads and I would fall back in their arms like a marionette. I thought it wiser to put off the execution of my plan until the next day. I went to eat at the *Coupole* for 16 francs 80. I had 70 centimes left and I threw them in the gutter.

I stayed three days in my room, without eating, without sleeping. I had drawn the blinds and I didn't dare go near the window or make a light. On Monday, someone rang at my door. I held my breath and waited. After a minute they rang again. I went on tiptoe and glued my eye to the keyhole. I could only see a piece of black cloth and a button. The man rang again and then went away. I don't know who it was. At night I had refreshing visions, palm trees, running water, a purple sky above a dome. I wasn't thirsty because hour after hour I went and drank at the spigot. But I was hungry. I saw the whore again. It was in a castle I had built at Causses Noires, about 60 miles from any town. She was naked and alone with me. Threatening her with my revolver I forced her to kneel and then run on all fours; then I tied her to a pillar and after I explained at great length what I was going to do, I riddled her with bullets. These images troubled me so much that I had to satisfy myself. Afterwards, I lay motionless in the darkness, my head absolutely empty. The furniture began to creak. It was five in the morning. I would have given anything to leave the room, but I couldn't go out because of the people walking in the streets.

Day came, I didn't feel hungry any more, but I began to sweat: my shirt was soaked. Outside there was sunlight. Then I thought: "He is crouched in blackness, in a closed room. For three days he has neither eaten nor slept. They rang and he didn't open. Soon, He is going into the street and He will kill."

I frightened myself. At six o'clock in the evening hunger struck me again. I was mad with rage. I bumped into the furniture, then I turned lights on in the rooms, the kitchen, the bathroom. I began to sing at the top of my voice. I washed my hands and I went out. It took me a good two minutes to put all the letters in the box. I shoved them in by tens. I must have crumpled a few envelopes. Then I followed the Boulevard du Montparnasse as far as the Rue Odessa.

I stopped in front of a haberdasher's window and when I saw my face I thought, " Tonight."

I posted myself at the top of the Rue Odessa, not far from the street lamp, and waited. Two women passed, arm in arm.

I was cold but I was sweating freely. After a while I saw three men come up ; I let them by : I needed six. The one on the left looked at me and clicked his tongue. I turned my eyes away.

At seven-five, two groups, following each other closely, came out on to the Boulevard Edgar-Quinet. There were a man and a woman with two children. Behind them came three old women. I took a step forward. The woman looked angry and was shaking the little boy's arm. The man drawled :

" What a little bastard he is."

My heart was beating so hard it hurt my arms. I advanced and stood in front of them, motionless. My fingers, in my pocket, were all soft around the trigger.

" Pardon," the man said, bumping into me.

I remembered I had closed the door of the apartment and that provoked me. I would have to lose precious time opening it. The people were getting farther away. I turned around and followed them mechanically. But I didn't feel like shooting them any more. They were lost in the crowd on the Boulevard. I leaned against the wall. I heard eight and nine o'clock strike. I repeated to myself, " Why must I kill all these people who are dead *already*," and I wanted to laugh. A dog came and sniffed at my feet.

When the big man passed me, I jumped and followed him. I could see the fold of his red neck between his derby and the collar of his overcoat. He bounced a little in walking and breathed heavily, he looked husky. I took out my revolver : it was cold and bright, it disgusted me, I couldn't remember very well what I was supposed to do with it. Sometimes I looked at it and sometimes I looked at his neck. The fold in the neck smiled at me like a smiling, bitter mouth. I wondered if I wasn't going to throw my revolver into the sewer.

Suddenly the man turned around the looked at me, irritated. I stepped back.

" I wanted to ask you . . ."

He didn't seem to be listening, he was looking at my hands. I went on with difficulty : ". . . how to get to the Rue de la Gaîté ? "

His face was thick and his lips trembled. He said nothing. He stretched out his hand. I drew back farther and said :

" I'd like . . ."

Then I *knew* I was going to start screaming. I didn't want to : I shot him three times in the belly. He fell with an idiotic look on his face, dropped to his knees and his hand rolled on his left shoulder.

" Bastard," I said, " rotten bastard ! "

I ran. I heard him coughing. I also heard shouts and feet clattering behind me. Somebody asked, " Is it a fight ? " then right after that someone shouted " Murder ! Murder ! " I didn't think these shouts concerned me. But they seemed sinister, like the sirens of the fire engines when I was a child. Sinister and slightly ridiculous. I ran as fast as my legs could carry me.

Only I had committed an unpardonable error :

instead of going up the Rue Odessa to the Boulevard Edgar-Quinet, *I was running down it toward the Boulevard du Montparnasse*. When I realized it, it was too late : I was already in the midst of the crowd, astonished faces turned toward me (I remember the face of a heavily rouged woman wearing a green hat with an aigrette) and I heard the fools in the Rue Odessa shouting " Murder " after me. A hand took me by the shoulder. I lost my head then : I didn't want to die stifled by this mob. I shot twice. People began to scream and scatter. I ran into a café. The drinkers jumped up as I ran through but made no attempt to stop me. I crossed the whole length of the café and locked myself in the lavatory. There was still one bullet in my revolver.

A moment went by. I was out of breath and gasping. Everything was extraordinarily silent, as though the people were keeping quiet on purpose. I raised the gun to my eyes and I saw its small hole, round and black : the bullet would come out there ; the powder would burn my face. I dropped my arm and waited. After a while they came ; there must have been a crowd of them, judging by the scuffling of feet on the floor. They whispered a little and then were quiet. I was still breathing heavily and I thought they must hear me breathing from the other side of the partition. Someone advanced quietly and rattled the door knob. He must have been flattened beside the door to avoid my bullets. I still wanted to shoot—but the last bullet was for me.

" What are they waiting for ? " I wondered. " If they pushed against the door and broke it down *right away* I wouldn't have time to kill myself and they would take me alive." But they were in no hurry ; they gave me all the time in the world to die. The bastards, they were afraid.

After a while, a voice said, " All right, open up. We won't hurt you."

There was silence and the same voice went on, " You know you can't get away."

I didn't answer, I was still gasping for breath. To encourage myself to shoot, I told myself, " If they get me, they're going to beat me, break my teeth, maybe put an eye out." I wanted to know if the big man was dead. Maybe I only wounded him . . . and perhaps the other two bullets hadn't hit anyone. . . . They were getting something ready, they were dragging something heavy across the floor. I hurriedly put the barrel of the gun in my mouth, and I bit hard on it. But I couldn't shoot, I couldn't even put my finger on the trigger. Everything was dead silent.

I threw away the revolver and opened the door.

The Childhood of a Leader

" I look adorable in my little angel's costume." Mme
Portier told mamma : " Your little boy looks good
enough to eat. He's simply adorable in his little angel's
costume." M. Bouffardier drew Lucien between his
knees and stroked his arms : " A real little girl," he
said, smiling. " What's your name ? Jacqueline,
Lucienne, Margot ? " Lucien turned red and said,
" My name is Lucien." He was no longer quite sure
about not being a little girl : a lot of people had kissed
him and called him mademoiselle, everybody thought
he was so charming with his gauze wings, his long blue
robe, small bare arms and blond curls : he was afraid
that the people would suddenly decide he wasn't a little
boy any more ; he would have protested in vain, no one
would listen to him, they wouldn't let him take off his
dress any more except to sleep and every morning when
he woke up he would find it at the foot of his bed and
when he wanted to wee-wee during the day, he'd have
to lift it up like Nenette and sit on his heels. Everybody would say : my sweet little darling ; maybe it's

happened already and I *am* a little girl; he felt so soft
inside that it made him a little sick and his voice came
out of his mouth like a flute and he offered flowers to
everybody in rounded, curved gestures; he wanted to
kiss his soft upper arm. He thought: it isn't real. He
liked things that weren't real, but he had a better time
on Mardi Gras: they dressed him up as Pierrot, he ran
and jumped and shouted with Riri and they hid under
the tables. His mother gave him a light tap with her
lorgnette. "I'm proud of my little boy." She was
impressive and beautiful, the fattest and biggest of all
these ladies. When he passed in front of the long buffet
covered with a white tablecloth, his papa, who was
drinking a glass of champagne, lifted him up and said,
"Little man!" Lucien felt like crying and saying
"Nah!" He asked for orangeade because it was cold
and they had forbidden him to drink it. But they
poured him some in a tiny glass. It had a pitchy taste
and wasn't as cold as they said: Lucien began to think
about the orangeade with castor oil he swallowed when
he was sick. He burst out sobbing and found it com-
forting to sit between papa and mamma in the car.
Mamma pressed Lucien against her, she was hot and
perfumed and all in silk. From time to time the inside
of the car grew white as chalk, Lucien blinked his eyes,
the violets Mamma was wearing on her corsage came
out of the shadows and Lucien suddenly smelled their
perfume. He was still sobbing a little but he felt moist
and itchy, somewhat pitchy like the orangeade; he
would have liked to splash in his little bathtub and have
Mamma wash him with the rubber sponge. They let
him sleep in papa and mamma's room because he was
a little baby; he laughed and made the springs of his

little bed jingle and papa said, "The child is over-excited." He drank a little orange-blossom water and saw papa in shirtsleeves.

The next day Lucien was sure he had forgotten something. He remembered the dream he had very clearly : papa and mamma were wearing angel's robes, Lucien was sitting all naked on his pot beating a drum, papa and mamma flew around him ; it was a nightmare. But there had been something before the dream, Lucien must have wakened. When he tried to remember, he saw a long black tunnel lit by a small blue lamp like the night-light they turned on in his parents' room every evening. At the very bottom of this dark blue night something went past, something white. He sat on the ground at mamma's feet and took his drum. Mamma asked him, "Why are you looking at me like that, darling ? " He lowered his eyes and beat on his drum, crying "Boom, boom, taraboom." But when she turned her head he began to scrutinize her minutely as if he were seeing her for the first time. He recognized the blue robe with the pink stuff and the face too. Yet it wasn't the same. Suddenly he thought he had it ; if he thought about it a tiny bit more, he would find what he was looking for. The tunnel lit up with a pale grey light and he could see something moving. Lucien was afraid and cried out. The tunnel disappeared. "What's the matter, little darling ? " Mamma asked. She was kneeling close to him and looked worried. " I'm having fun," Lucien said. Mamma smelled good but he was afraid she would touch him : she looked funny to him, papa too. He decided he would never sleep in their room any more.

Mamma noticed nothing the following day. Lucien

was always under her feet, as usual, and he gossiped with her like a real little man. He asked her to tell him Little Red Riding Hood and Mamma took him on her knees. She talked about the wolf and little Red Riding Hood's grandmother, with a finger raised, smiling and grave; Lucien looked at her and said, "And then what?" And sometimes he touched the little hairs on the back of her neck; but he wasn't listening, he was wondering if she were his real mother. When she finished, he said, "Mamma, tell me about when you were a little girl." And mamma told him; but maybe she was lying. Maybe she was a little boy before and they put dresses on her—like Lucien, the other night—and she kept on wearing them to act like a little girl. Gently he felt her beautiful fat arms which were soft as butter under the silk. What would happen if they took off mamma's dress and she put on papa's pants? Maybe right away she'd grow a black moustache. He clasped mamma's arms with all his might; he had a feeling she was going to be transformed into a horrible beast before his eyes—or maybe turned into a bearded lady like the one in the carnival. She laughed, opening her mouth wide, and Lucien saw her pink tongue and the back of her throat: it was dirty, he wanted to spit in it. "Hahaha!" Mamma said. "How you hug me, little man. Hug me tight. As tight as you love me." Lucien took one of her lovely hands with the silver rings on it and covered it with kisses. But the next day when she was sitting near him holding his hands while he was on the pot and said to him "Push, Lucien, push, little darling . . . please," he suddenly stopped pushing and asked her, a little breathlessly, "But you're my real mother, aren't you ? " She said, " Silly," and asked him if it wasn't going to come soon. From that day Lucien was sure she was playing a joke on him and he never again told her he would marry her when he grew up. But he was not quite sure what the joke was : maybe one night in the tunnel, robbers came and took papa and mamma and put those two in their place. Or maybe it was really papa and mamma but during the day they played one part and at night they were all different. Lucien was hardly surprised on Christmas Eve when he suddenly woke up and saw them putting toys in front of the fireplace. The next day they talked about Father Christmas and Lucien pretended he believed them : he thought it was their rôle, they must have stolen the toys. He had scarlatina in February and had a lot of fun.

After he was cured, he developed the habit of playing orphan. He sat under the chestnut tree in the middle of the lawn, filling his hands with earth, and thought : I'm an orphan. I'm going to call myself Louis. I haven't eaten for six days. Germaine, the maid, called him to lunch and at table he kept on playing ; papa and mamma noticed nothing. He had been picked up by robbers who wanted to make a pickpocket out of him. After he had eaten he would run away and denounce them. He ate and drank very little ; he had read in *L'Auberge de l'Ange Gardien* that the first meal of a starving man should be light. It was amusing because everybody was playing. Papa and mamma were playing papa and mamma ; mamma was playing worried because her little darling wasn't eating, papa was playing at reading the paper and sometimes shaking his finger in Lucien's face, saying " Badaboom, little man!" And Lucien was playing too, but finally he didn't know at what. Orphan? Or Lucien? He looked at the water bottle. There was a little red light dancing in the bottom of the water and he would have sworn papa's hand was in the water bottle, enormous, luminous, with little black hairs on the fingers. Lucien suddenly felt that the water bottle was playing at being a water bottle. He barely touched his food and he was so hungry in the afternoon that he stole a dozen plums and almost had indigestion. He thought he had enough of playing Lucien.

Still, he could not stop himself and it seemed to him that he was always playing. He wanted to be like M. Bouffardier who was so ugly and serious. When M. Bouffardier came to dinner, he bent over mamma's hand and said "Your servant, dear madame" and Lucien planted himself in the middle of the salon and watched him with admiration. But nothing serious happened to Lucien. When he fell down and bumped himself, he sometimes stopped crying and wondered "Do I really hurt?" Then he felt even sadder and his tears flowed more than ever. When he kissed mamma's hand and said "Your servant, dear madame," she rumpled his hair and said, "It isn't nice, little mouse, you mustn't make fun of grown-ups," and he felt all discouraged. The only important things he could find were the first and third Fridays of the month. Those days a lot of ladies came to see mamma and two or three were always in mourning; Lucien loved ladies in mourning, especially when they had big feet. Generally, he liked grown-ups because they were so respectable —and you could never imagine they forgot themselves in bed or did all the other things little boys do, because

they have so many dark clothes on their bodies and
you can't imagine what's underneath. When they're
all together they eat everything and talk and even their
laughs are serious. It's beautiful, like at mass. They
treated Lucien like a grown-up person. Mme Couffin
took Lucien on her lap and felt his calves, declaring,
" He's the prettiest, cutest one I've seen." Then she
questioned him about his likes and dislikes, kissed him
and asked him what he would do when he was big.
And sometimes he answered he'd be a great general
like Joan of Arc and he'd take back Alsace-Lorraine
from the Germans, or sometimes he wanted to be a
missionary. As he spoke, he believed what he said.
Mme Besse was a large strong woman with a slight
moustache. She romped with Lucien, tickled him and
called him " my little doll." Lucien was overjoyed, he
laughed easily and squirmed under the ticklings ; he
thought he was a little doll, a charming little doll for
the grown-ups, and he would have liked Mme Besse to
undress him and wash him like a rubber doll and send
him bye-bye in a tiny little cradle. And sometimes
Mme Besse asked, " And does my little doll talk ? "
and she squeezed his stomach suddenly. Then Lucien
pretended to be a mechanical doll and said " Crick ! "
in a muffled voice and they both laughed.

The curé who came to the house every Saturday
asked him if he loved his mother. Lucien adored his
pretty mamma and his papa who was so strong and
good. He answered " Yes," looking the curé straight
in the eyes with a little air of boldness that made
everybody laugh. The curé had a face like a raspberry,
red and lumpy with a hair on each lump. He told
Lucien it was very nice and that he should always love

his mamma; then he asked who Lucien preferred, his mother or God. Lucien could not guess the answer on the spot and he began to shake his curls and stamp his feet, shouting, " Baroom, taratamaboom ! " and the grown-ups continued their conversation as though he did not exist. He ran to the garden and slipped out by the back door; he had brought his little reed cane with him. Naturally, Lucien was never supposed to leave the garden; it was forbidden; usually Lucien was a good little boy but that day he felt like disobeying. He looked defiantly at the big nettle patch; you could see it was a forbidden place; the wall was black, the nettles were naughty, harmful plants, a dog had done his business just at the foot of the nettles; it smelled of plants, dog dirt and hot wine. Lucien lashed at the nettles with his cane, crying " I love my mamma, I love my mamma." He saw the broken nettles hanging sadly, oozing a white juice, their whitish, downy necks had unravelled in breaking; he heard a small solitary voice which cried " I love my mamma, I love my mamma " ; a big blue fly was buzzing around : a horsefly, Lucien was afraid of it—and a forbidden, powerful odour, putrid and peaceful, filled his nostrils. He repeated " I love my mamma," but his voice seemed strange, he felt deep terror and ran back into the salon like a flash. From that day on, Lucien understood that he did not love his mamma. He did not feel guilty but redoubled his niceties because he thought he should pretend to love his parents all his life, or else he was a naughty little boy. Mme Fleurier found Lucien more and more tender and just then there was the war and papa went off to fight and mamma was glad, in her sorrow, that Lucien was so full of attention ; in the afternoons, when she rested on her beach chair in the garden because she was so full of sorrow, he ran to get her a cushion and slipped it beneath her head and put a blanket over her legs and she protested, laughing, " But I'll be too hot, my little man, how sweet you are ! " He kissed her furiously, all out of breath, saying, " My own mamma," and sat down at the foot of the chestnut tree.

He said " Chestnut tree " and waited. But nothing happened. Mamma was stretched out on the verandah, all tiny at the bottom of a heavily stifling silence. There was a smell of hot grass, you could play explorer in the jungle ; but Lucien did not feel like playing. The air trembled about the red crest of the wall and the sunlight made burning spots on the earth and on Lucien's hands. " Chestnut tree ! " It was shocking : when Lucien told mamma " My pretty little mamma," she smiled and when he called Germaine " Stinkweed " she cried and went complaining to mamma. But when he said chestnut tree nothing at all happened. He muttered between his teeth " Nasty old tree " and was not reassured, but since the tree did not move he repeated, louder, " Nasty old tree, nasty old chestnut tree, you wait, just you wait and see ! " and he kicked it. But the tree stayed still—just as though it were made of wood. That evening at dinner Lucien told Mamma, " You know, mamma, the trees, well . . . they're made out of wood," making a surprised little face which mamma liked. But Mme Fleurier had received no mail at noon. She said dryly, " Don't act like a fool." Lucien became a little roughneck. He broke his toys to see how they were made, he whittled the arm of a chair with one of papa's old razors, he knocked down a tanagra figure in the living room to see if it were hollow and if there were anything inside: when he walked he struck the heads from plants and flowers with his cane: each time he was deeply disappointed, things were stupid, nothing really and truly existed. Often mamma showed him flowers and asked him " What's the name of this ? " But Lucien shook his head and answered, " That isn't anything, that doesn't have any name." All that wasn't worth bothering with. It was much more fun to pull the legs off a grasshopper because they throbbed between your fingers like a top and a yellow cream came out when you pressed its stomach. But even so, the grasshoppers didn't make a noise. Lucien would have liked to torture an animal that cried when it was hurt, a chicken for instance, but he didn't dare go near them. M. Fleurier came back in March because he was a manager and the general told him he would be much more useful at the head of his factory than in the trenches like just anybody. He thought Lucien had changed very much and said he didn't recognize his little man any more. Lucien had fallen into a sort of somnolence ; he answered quickly, he always had a finger in his nose or else he breathed on his fingers and smelled them and he had to be begged to do his little business. Now he went alone to the bathroom ; he had only to leave the door half open and from time to time, mamma or Germaine came to encourage him. He stayed whole hours on the throne and once he was so bored he went to sleep. The doctor said he was growing too quickly and prescribed a tonic. Mamma wanted to teach Lucien new games but Lucien thought he played enough as it was and anyhow all games were the

same; it was always the same thing. He often pouted;
it was also a game and rather amusing. It hurt mamma,
you felt all sad and resentful, you got a little deaf and
your mouth was pursed up and your eyes misty; inside
it was warm and soft like when you're under the sheets
at night and smell your own odour; you were alone in
the world. Lucien could no longer leave his broodings
and when papa put on his mocking voice to tell him
" You're going to hatch chickens," Lucien rolled on
the ground and sobbed. He still went to the salon
when mamma was having visitors, but since they had
cut off his curls, the grown-ups paid less attention to
him unless it was to point out a moral for him and
tell him instructive stories. When his cousin Riri and
Aunt Bertha, his pretty mamma, came to Férolles
because of the bombings, Lucien was very glad and
tried to teach him how to play. But Riri was too busy
hating the Boches and he still smelled like a baby even
though he was six months older than Lucien; he had
freckles and didn't always understand things very well.
However, Lucien confided to him that he walked in
his sleep. Some people get up at night and talk and
walk around still sleeping: Lucien had read that in the
Petit Explorateur and he thought there must be a real
Lucien who talked, walked, and really loved his parents
at night, only as soon as morning came, he forgot
everything and began to pretend to be Lucien. In the
beginning Lucien only half believed this story, but one
day they went near the nettles and they compared
organs and Lucien's was smaller but Riri cheated: he
pulled his to make it longer. " I have the biggest,"
Riri said. " Yes, but I'm a sleepwalker," Lucien said
calmly. Riri didn't know what a sleepwalker was and

Lucien had to explain it to him. When he finished, he thought, " Then it's true I'm a sleepwalker " and he had a terrible desire to cry. Since they slept in the same bed they agreed that Riri would stay up the next night and watch Lucien when Lucien got up and remember all he said. " You wake me up after a while," Lucien said, " to see if I remember anything I did." That night, Lucien, unable to sleep, heard sharp snores and had to wake up Riri. " Zanzibar ! " Riri said. " Wake up, Riri, you have to watch me when I get up." " Let me sleep," Riri said in a thick, pasty voice. Lucien shook him and pinched him under his shirt and Riri began to jump around and he stayed awake, his eyes open and a funny smile on his lips. Lucien thought about a bicycle his father was to buy him, he heard a train whistle and suddenly the maid came in and opened the curtains ; it was eight o'clock in the morning. Lucien never knew what he did during the night. But God knew because God saw everything. Lucien knelt on the prie-dieu and forced himself to behave so that his mamma would congratulate him after mass, but he hated God : God knew more about Lucien than Lucien himself. God knew that Lucien didn't love his mamma or papa and that he pretended to be good and touched himself in bed at night.

Luckily, God couldn't remember everything because there were so many little boys in the world. When Lucien tapped his forehead and said " Picotin " right away God forgot everything He had seen. Lucien also undertook to persuade God that he loved his mamma. From time to time he said in his head, " How I love my dear mamma ! " There was always a little corner in him which wasn't quite persuaded and of course

God saw that corner. In that case, He won. But
sometimes you could absorb yourself so completely in
what you were saying. You said very quickly, " Oh
how I love my mamma," pronouncing it carefully and
you saw mamma's face and felt all tender, you thought
vaguely, vaguely, that God was watching you and
afterwards you didn't think about it any more, you
were all creamy with tenderness and then there were
words dancing in your ears : mamma, MAMMA,
MAMMA. That only lasted an instant, of course ; it
was like Lucien trying to balance a chair on his feet.
But if, just at that moment, you said, " Pacota," God
had lost : He had only seen Good and what He saw
engraved itself in His memory forever. But Lucien
tired of this game because he had to make too much
effort and besides you never knew whether God had
won or lost. Lucien had nothing more to do with God.
When he made his first communion, the curé said he
was the best behaved little boy and the most pious of
all the catechism class. Lucien grasped things quickly
and he had a good memory but his head was full of
fog.

Sundays were a bright spot. The fog lifted when
Lucien went walking with his father on the Paris road.
He had on his handsome sailor suit and they met
workers who saluted papa and Lucien. Papa went up
to them and they said " Good morning, M. Fleurier,"
and also " Good morning, Master Fleurier." Lucien
liked the workers because they were grown-ups but not
like the others. First, they called him master. And
they wore caps and had short nails and big hands
which always looked chapped and hurt. They were
responsible and respectful. You mustn't pull old

Bouligaud's moustache: papa would have scolded Lucien. But when he spoke to papa, old Bouligaud took off his cap and papa and Lucien kept their hats on and papa spoke in a loud voice, smiling and somewhat testy. "So, we're waiting for our boy, are we, Bouligaud? When does he get leave?" "At the end of the month, M. Fleurier, thank you, Monsieur Fleurier." Old Bouligaud looked happy and he wasn't allowed to slap Lucien on the rear and call him Toad, like M. Bouffardier. Lucien hated M. Bouffardier because he was so ugly. But when he saw old Bouligaud he felt all tender and wanted to be good. Once, coming back from the walk, papa took Lucien on his knees and explained to him what it was to be a boss. Lucien wanted to know how papa talked to the workers when he was at the factory and papa showed him how you had to do it and his voice was all changed. "Will I be a boss too?" Lucien asked. "Yes indeed, my little man, that's what I made you for." "And who will I command?" "Well, when I'm dead you'll be the boss of my factory and you'll command my workers." "But they'll be dead too." "Well, you'll command their children and you must know how to make yourself be obeyed and liked." "And how will I make myself be liked, papa?" Papa thought a little and said, "First, you must know them all by name." Lucien was deeply touched and when the foreman Morel's son came to the house to announce that his father had two fingers cut off, Lucien spoke seriously and gently with him, looking him straight in the eye and calling him Morel. Mamma said she was proud to have such a good, sensitive little boy. After that came the armistice; papa read the papers aloud every evening, everybody was talking about the Russians and the German government and reparations and papa showed Lucien the countries on the map : Lucien spent the most boring year of his life ; he liked it better when the war was still going on ; now everybody looked lost and the lights you saw in Mme Coffin's eyes went out. In October 1919 Mme Fleurier made him attend the Ecole Saint-Joseph as a day student.

It was hot in Abbé Geromet's office. Lucien was standing near the abbé's armchair ; he had his hands clasped behind him and was deeply bored. " Isn't mamma going to go soon ? " But Mme Fleurier had not yet thought of leaving. She was seated on the very edge of a green armchair and stretched out her ample bosom to the abbé ; she spoke quickly and she had her musical voice she used when she was angry and didn't want to show it. The abbé spoke slowly and the words seemed much longer in his mouth than in other people's ; you might think he was sucking them the way you suck barley sugar before swallowing it. He explained to mamma that Lucien was a good little boy and polite and a good worker but so terribly indifferent to everything and Mme Fleurier said that she was very disappointed because she thought a change would do him good. She asked if he played, at least, during recess. " Alas, madame," the old priest answered, " even games do not seem to interest him. He is sometimes turbulent and even violent but he tires quickly ; I believe he lacks perseverance." Lucien thought : they're talking about me. They were two grown-ups and he was the subject of their conversation, just like the war, the German government or M. Poincaré ; they looked serious and they reasoned out his case. But even this thought did not please him. His ears were full of his mother's little singing words; the sucked and sticky words of the abbé, he wanted to cry. Luckily the bell rang and they let him go. But during the geography class he felt enervated and asked Abbé Jacquin permission to leave the room because he needed to move around.

First, the coolness, the solitude and the good smell of the toilet calmed him. He squatted down simply to clear his conscience but he didn't feel like it; he raised his head and began reading the inscriptions which covered the door. Someone had written in blue pencil *Barataud is a louse*. Lucien smiled: it was true, Barataud was a louse, he was small and they said he'd grow a little but not much because his father was little, almost a dwarf. Lucien wondered if Barataud had read this inscription and he thought not: otherwise it would be rubbed out. Barataud would have wet his finger and rubbed the letters until they disappeared. Lucien rejoiced a little, imagining that Barataud would go to the toilet around four o'clock and that he would take down his velvet pants and read *Barataud is a louse*. Maybe he had never thought he was so small. . . . Lucien promised himself to call him a louse, starting the next day at recess. He got up and on the right-hand wall, read another inscription written in the same blue pencil: *Lucien Fleurier is a big beanpole*. He wiped it out carefully and went back to class. It's true, he thought, looking around at his schoolmates, they're all smaller than I am. He felt uncomfortable. Big beanpole. He was sitting at his little desk of holy wood. Germaine was in the kitchen, mamma hadn't come home yet. He wrote " big beanpole " on a sheet of white paper to re-establish the spelling. But the words seemed too well known and made no effect on him. He called, "Germaine! Germaine!" "What do you want now?" Germaine asked. "Germaine, I'd like you to write on this paper: 'Lucien Fleurier is a big bean-pole.'" "Have you gone out of your mind, Monsieur Lucien?" He put his arms around her neck. "Be nice, Germaine." Germaine began to laugh and wiped her fat fingers on her apron. He did not look while she was writing, but afterwards he carried the paper to his room and studied it for a long time. Germaine's writing was pointed. Lucien thought he heard a dry voice saying in his ear: big beanpole. He thought "I'm big." He was crushed with shame: big as Bara-taud was small and the others laughed behind his back. It was as if someone had cast a spell over him; until then it had seemed natural to see his friends from above. But now it seemed he had been suddenly con-demned to be big for the rest of his life. That evening he asked his father if a person could shrink if he wanted to with all his might. M. Fleurier said no: all the Fleuriers had been big and strong and Lucien would grow still bigger. Lucien was without hope. After his mother tucked him in, he got up and went to look at himself in the mirror. "I'm big." But he looked in vain, he could not see it, he seemed neither big nor little. He lifted up his nightshirt a little and saw his legs; then he imagined Costil saying to Hébrard: Say, look at those long beanpoles, and it made him feel funny. He was cold, he shivered and someone said, "The beanpole has gooseflesh!" Lucien lifted his shirt-tail very high and they all saw his navel and his whole business and then he ran and slipped into bed. When he put his hand under his shirt he thought that Costil saw him and was saying, Look what the big beanpole's doing! He squirmed and turned in bed, breathing heavily.

The following days, he wanted to ask the abbé's permission to sit in the rear of the class. It was because of Boisset, Winckelmann and Costil who were behind him and could look at the back of his neck. Lucien felt the back of his neck but he could not see it and often even forgot about it. But while he was answering the abbé as well as he could and was reciting the tirade from *Don Diego,* the others were behind him watching the back of his neck and they could be laughing and thinking, " How thin he is, he has two cords to his neck." Lucien forced himself to make his voice swell and express the humiliation of Don Diego. He could do what he wanted with his voice ; but the back of his neck was always there, peaceful, inexpressive, like someone resting, and Boisset saw it. He dared not change his seat because the last row was reserved for the dunces, but the back of his neck and his shoulder blades were constantly itching and he was obliged to scratch unceasingly. Lucien invented a new game : in the morning, when he took his bath, he imagined someone was watching him through the keyhole, sometimes Costil, sometimes old Bouligaud, sometimes Germaine. Then he turned all around for them to see him from all sides and sometimes he turned his rear towards the door, going down on all fours so that it would look all plump and ridiculous ; M. Bouffardier was coming on tiptoe to give him an enema. One day when he was in the bathroom he heard sounds ; it was Germaine rubbing polish on the buffet in the hall. His heart stopped beating, he opened the door quietly and went out, his trousers round his heels, his shirt rolled up around his back. He was obliged to make little hops in order to go forward without losing his balance. Germaine looked at him calmly: "What are you doing, running a sack race?" she asked. Enraged, he pulled up his trousers and ran and threw himself on his bed. Mme Fleurier was heartbroken. She often told her husband, "He was so graceful when he was little and now look how awkward he is; if that isn't a shame." M. Fleurier glanced carelessly at Lucien and answered, "It's his age." Lucien did not know what to do with his body; no matter what he did, he felt this body existed on all sides at once, without consulting him. Lucien indulged himself by imagining he was invisible and then he took the habit of looking through keyholes to see how the others were made without their knowing it. He saw his mother while she was washing. She was seated on the *bidet*, she seemed asleep and she had surely quite forgotten her body and her face, because she thought that no one saw her. The sponge went back and forth by itself over this abandoned flesh; she moved lazily and he felt she was going to stop somewhere along the way. Mamma rubbed a washcloth with a piece of soap and her hand disappeared. Her face was restful, almost sad; surely she was thinking of something else, about Lucien's education or M. Poincaré. But during this time she *was* this gross pink mass, this voluminous body hanging over the porcelain *bidet*. Another time, Lucien removed his shoes and climbed all the way up to the eaves. He saw Germaine. She had on a long green chemise which fell to her feet; she was combing her hair before a small round mirror and she smiled softly at her image. Lucien began to laugh uncontrolledly and had to climb down hurriedly. After that he smiled and made faces at himself in front of the mirror in the salon and after a moment was seized with terrible fears.

Lucien finally went completely asleep but no one noticed except Mme Coffin who called him her sleeping beauty; a great air bubble he could neither swallow nor spit out was always in his half open mouth: it was his *yawning*; when he was alone the bubble grew larger, caressing his palate and tongue; his mouth opened wide and tears ran down his cheeks: these were the very pleasant moments. He did not amuse himself as much in the bathroom but to make up for it he liked very much to sneeze; it woke him up and for an instant he looked around him, exhilarated, then dozed off again. He learned to recognize different sorts of sleep: in winter, he sat before the fireplace and stretched his head toward the blaze; when it was quite red and roasted it suddenly emptied; he called that "head sleeping." Sunday morning, on the other hand, he went to sleep by the feet: he got into his bath, slowly lowered himself and sleep climbed in ripples all along his legs and thighs. Above the sleeping body, all white and swollen like a stewed chicken at the bottom of the water, a little blonde head was enthroned, full of wise words, templum, templi, templo, iconoclasts. In class, sleep was white and riddled with flashes: First: Lucien Fleurier. " What was the third estate ? Nothing." First, Lucien Fleurier, second, Winckelmann; Pellereau was first in algebra; he had only one testicle; he made them pay two sous to see and ten to touch. Lucien gave the ten sous, hesitated, stretched out his hand and left without touching, but afterwards his regrets were so great that sometimes they kept him awake for more than an hour. He was less good in geology than in history. First, Winckelmann, second, Fleurier. On Sundays he went bicycling with Costil and Winckelmann. Through russet, heat-crushed countrysides, the bicycles skidded in the marrowy dust ; Lucien's legs were active and muscular but the sleepy odour of the roads went to his head ; he bent over the handlebars ; his eyes grew pink and half closed. He had the honour prize three times in a row. They gave him *Fabiola, or The Church in the Catacombs,* the *Gènie du Christianisme* and the *Life of Cardinal Lavigerie.* Costil, back from the long vacation, taught them all *De Profondis Morpionibus* and the *Artilleur de Metz.* Lucien decided to do better and consulted his father's *Larousse Médical* on the article " Uterus ; " then he explained to them how women were made ; he even made a sketch on the board and Costil declared it disgusting ; but after that they could hear no mention of " tubes " without bursting out laughing and Lucien thought with satisfaction that in all of France you couldn't find a second class student and perhaps even a rhetoric student who knew female organs as well as he.

It was like a flash of magnesium when the Fleuriers moved to Paris. Lucien could no longer sleep because of the movies, cars and streets. He learned to distinguish a Voisin from a Packard, a Hispano-Suiza from a Rolls and he spoke frequently of them. He had been wearing long trousers for more than a year. His father sent him to England as a reward for his success in the first part of the baccalaureat ; Lucien saw plains swollen with water and white cliffs, he boxed with John Latimer and learned the over-arm stroke, but, one fine day, he woke up to find himself asleep; it had come back; he went somnolently back to Paris. The elementary mathematics class in the Lycée Condorcet had 37 pupils. Eight of these pupils said they knew all about women and called the others virgins. The Enlightened scorned Lucien until the first of November, but on All Saints' Day, Lucien went walking with Garry, the most experienced of them all and negligently showed him proof of such anatomical knowledge that Garry was astonished. Lucien did not enter the group of the enlightened because his parents did not allow him out at night, but he had powerful relations among them.

On Thursday, Aunt Berthe and Riri came to lunch at Rue Raynouard. She had grown enormous and sad and spent her time sighing; but since her skin had remained very fine and white, Lucien would have liked to see her naked. He thought about it in bed at night; it would be a winter day, in the Bois de Boulogne; he would come upon her naked in a copse, her arms crossed on her breast, shivering with gooseflesh. He imagined that a near-sighted passer-by touched her with his cane and said "Well, what can that be?" Lucien did not get along too well with his cousin: Riri had become a very handsome young man, a little too elegant. He was taking philosophy at Lakanal and understood nothing of mathematics. Lucien could not keep himself from thinking that Riri, seven years ago, still did number two in his pants and after that walked with his legs wide apart like a duck and looked at his mother with candid eyes saying, "No, mamma, I didn't do it, I promise." And he had

some repugnance about touching Riri's hand. Yet he
was very nice to him and explained his mathematics
courses ; sometimes he had to make a great effort not
to lose patience because Riri was not very intelligent.
But he never let himself be carried away and kept
always a calm, poised voice. Mme Fleurier thought
Lucien had much tact but Aunt Berthe showed him no
gratitude. When Lucien proposed to give Riri a lesson
she blushed a little, moved about on her chair, saying,
" No, you're very kind, my little Lucien, but Riri is
too big a boy. He can if he wants ; but he must not
get in the habit of counting on others." One night Mme
Fleurier told Lucien brusquely, " You think Riri's
grateful for what you're doing for him ? Well, don't
kid yourself, my boy : he thinks you're stuck up, your
Aunt Berthe told me so." She had assumed her musical
voice and familiar air ; Lucien realized she was mad
with rage. He felt vaguely intrigued but could find
nothing to answer. The next day and the day after
that he had a lot of work and the whole episode left
his mind.

Sunday morning he set his pen down brusquely and
wondered " Am I stuck up ? " It was eleven o'clock ;
sitting in his study Lucien watched the pink cretonne
designs which lined the walls ; on his left cheek he felt
the dry and dusty warmth of the first April sunlight,
on his right cheek he felt the heavy, stifling heat of the
radiator. " Am I stuck up ? " It was hard to answer.
Lucien first tried to remember his last conversation with
Riri and to judge his own attitude impartially. He had
bent over Riri and smiled at him, saying, " You get
it ? If you don't catch on, don't be afraid to say so,
and we'll start again." A little later he had made an

error in a delicate problem and said, gaily, "That's one on me." It was an expression he had taken from M. Fleurier which amused him: "But was I stuck up when I said that?" By dint of searching, he suddenly made something round and white appear, soft as a bit of cloud: it was his thought of the other day: he had said "Do you get it?" and it was in his head but it couldn't be described. Lucien made desperate efforts to *look* at this bit of cloud and he suddenly felt as though he were falling into it head first; he found himself in the mist and became mist himself, he was no more than a damp white warmth which smelled of linen. He wanted to tear himself from this mist and come back but it came with him. He thought "I'm Lucien Fleurier, I'm in my room, I'm doing a problem in physics, it's Sunday." But his thoughts melted into banks of white fog. He shook himself and began counting the cretonne characters, two shepherdesses, two shepherds and Cupid. Then suddenly he told himself, "I am . . ." and there was a slight click: he had awakened from his long somnolence.

It was not pleasant. The shepherds had jumped back; it seemed to Lucien that he was looking at them from the wrong end of a telescope. In place of this stupor so sweet to him and which lost itself in its own folds, there was now a small, wide awake perplexity which wondered "Who am I?"

"Who am I?" I look at the bureau, I look at the notebook. My name is Lucien Fleurier but that's only a name. I'm stuck up. I'm not stuck up. I don't know, it doesn't make sense."

"I'm a good student. No. That's a lie: a good student likes to work—not me. I have good marks but

153

I don't like to work. I don't hate it either, I don't give a damn. I don't give a damn about anything. I'll never be a boss." He thought with anguish " But what will I be ? " A moment passed : he scratched his cheek and shut his left eye because the sun was in it : " What am I, *I* . . . ? " There was this fog rolling back on itself, indefinite. " I ! " He looked into the distance ; the word rang in his head and then perhaps it was possible to make out something, like the top of a pyramid whose sides vanished, far off, into the fog. Lucien shuddered and his hands trembled. " Now I have it ! " he thought, " Now I have it ! I was sure of it : *I don't exist !* "

During the months that followed, Lucien often tried to go back to sleep but did not succeed : he slept well and regularly nine hours a night and the rest of the time was more lively and more and more perplexed : his parents said he had never been so healthy. When he happened to think he did not have the stuff to make a boss he felt romantic and wanted to walk for hours under the moon ; but his parents still did not allow him out at night. Often, then, he would stretch out on his bed and take his temperature : the thermometer showed 98.6 or 98.7 and Lucien thought with bitter pleasure that his parents found him looking fine. " I don't exist." He closed his eyes and let himself drift : " existence is an illusion because I *know* I don't exist ; all I have to do is plug my ears and not think about anything and I'll become nothingness." But the illusion was tenacious. Over other people, at least, he had the malicious superiority of possessing a secret : Garry, for instance, didn't exist any more than Lucien. But it was enough to see him snorting tempestuously in the midst of his admirers; you could see right away he thought his own existence as solid as iron. Neither did M. Fleurier exist—nor Riri—nor anyone—the world was a comedy without actors. Lucien, who had been given an " A " for his dissertation on " Morality and Science " dreamed of writing a " Treatise on Nothingness " and he imagined that people, reading it, would disappear one after the other like vampires at cockcrow. Before beginning this treatise, he wanted the advice of the Baboon, his philosophy prof. " Excuse me, Sir," he said at the end of the class, " could anyone claim that we don't exist ? " The Baboon said no. " Goghito," he said, " ergo zum. You exist because you doubt your existence." Lucien was not convinced but he gave up his work. In July, he was given, without fanfare, his baccalaureat in mathematics and left for Férolles with his parents. The perplexity still did not leave him : it was like wanting to sneeze.

Old Bouligaud had died and the mentality of M. Fleurier's workers had changed a lot. Now they were drawing large salaries and their wives bought silk stockings. Mme Bouffardier cited frightful examples to Mme Fleurier : " My maid tells me she saw that little Ansiaume girl in the cook-shop. She's the daughter of one of your husband's best workers, the one we took care of when she lost her mother. She married a fitter from Beaupertuis. Well, she ordered a 20 franc chicken. And so arrogant ! Nothing's good enough for them : they want to have everything we have." Now, when Lucien took short Sunday walks with his father, the workers barely touched their caps on seeing them and there were even some who crossed over so as not to salute them. One day Lucien met Bouligaud's son who did not even seem to recognize him. Lucien was a little excited about it : here was a chance to prove himself a boss. He threw an eagle eye on Jules Bouligaud and went toward him, his hands behind his back. But Bouligaud did not seem intimidated : he turned vacant eyes to Lucien and passed by him, whistling. " He didn't recognize me," Lucien told himself. But he was deeply disappointed and, in the following days, thought more than ever that the world did not exist.

Mme Fleurier's little revolver was put away in the left hand drawer of her dressing table. Her husband made her a present of it in September 1914 before he left for the front. Lucien took it and turned it around in his hand for a long while : it was a little jewel, with a gilded barrel and a butt inlaid with mother of pearl. He could not rely on a philosophical treatise to persuade people they did not exist. Action was needed, a really desperate act which would dissolve appearances and show the nothingness of the world in full light. A shot, a young body bleeding on the carpet, a few words scribbled on a piece of paper : " I kill myself because I do not exist. And you too, my brothers, you are nothingness ! " People would read the newspaper in the morning and would see " An adolescent has dared ! " And each would feel himself terribly troubled and would wonder. " And what about me ? Do I exist ? " There had been similar epidemics of suicide in history, among others after the publication of *Werther*. Lucien thought how " martyr " in Greek meant " witness." He was too sensitive for a boss but not for a martyr. As a result, he often entered his mother's room and looked at the revolver ; he was filled with agony. Once he even bit the gilded barrel, gripping his fingers tightly around the butt. The rest of the time he was very gay for he thought that all true leaders had know the temptation of suicide. Napoleon, for example. Lucien did not hide from himself the fact that he was touching the depths of despair but he hoped to leave this crisis with a tempered soul and he read the *Memorial de Saint-Hélène* with interest. Yet he had to make a decision : Lucien set the 30th of September as the end of his hesitations. The last days were extremely difficult : surely the crisis was salutary, but it required of Lucien a tension so strong that he thought he would break, one day, like a glass. He no longer dared to touch the revolver ; he contented himself with opening the drawer, lifting up his mother's slips a little and studying at great lengths the icy, headstrong little monster which rested in a hollow of pink silk. Yet he felt a sharp disappointment when he decided to live and found himself completely un-occupied. Fortunately, the multiple cares of going back to school absorbed him : his parents sent him to the Lycée Saint-Louis to take preparatory courses for the Ecole Centrale. He wore a fine red-bordered cap with an insignia and sang :

> C'est le piston qui fait marcher les machines
> C'est le piston qui fait marcher les wagons . . .

This new dignity of *piston* filled Lucien with pride ; and then his class was not like the others : it had traditions and a ceremonial ; it was a force. For instance, it was the usual thing at the end of the French class for a voice to ask " What's a *cyrard* ? " and

everybody answered softly " A *con* ! " After which the
voice repeated " What's an *agro* ? " and they answered
a little louder " A *con* ! " Then M. Béthune, who was
almost blind and wore dark glasses, said wearily,
" Please, gentlemen ! " There were a few moments of
absolute silence and the students looked at each other
with smiles of intelligence, then someone shouted,
" What's a *piston* ? " and they all roared " A great
man ! " At those times Lucien felt galvanized. In the
evening he told his parents the various incidents of the
day in great detail and when he said " Then the whole
class started laughing . . ." or " the whole class decided
to put Meyrinez in quarantine " the words, in passing,
warmed his mouth like a drink of liquor. Yet the first
months were very hard : Lucien missed his maths and
physics and then, individually, his schoolmates were
not too sympathetic : they were on scholarships, mostly
grinds, untidy and ill-mannered. " There isn't one,"
he told his father, " I could make a friend of." " Young
men on scholarships," M. Fleurier said dreamily,
" represent an intellectual élite and yet they're poor
leaders : they have missed one thing." Hearing him
talk about " poor leaders," Lucien felt a disagreeable
pinching in his heart and again thought of killing himself during the weeks that followed, but he had not the
same enthusiasm as he had during vacation. In
January, a new student named Berliac scandalized the
whole class : he wore coats ringed in green or purple,
in the latest styles, little round collars and trousers that
are seen in tailor's engravings, so narrow that one
wondered how he could even get into them. From the
beginning he was classed last in mathematics. " I don't
give a damn," he said, " I'm literary, I take maths to

mortify myself." After a month he had won everyone's heart : he distributed contraband cigarettes and told them he had women and showed letters they sent him. The whole class decided he was all right and it would be best to let him alone. Lucien greatly admired his elegance and manners, but Berliac treated Lucien with condescension and called him a " rich kid." " After all," Lucien said one day, " it's better than being a poor kid." Berliac smiled. " You're a little cynic ! " he told him and the next day he let him read one of his poems : " Caruso gobbled raw eyes every evening, otherwise he was sober as a camel. A lady made a bouquet with the eyes of her family and threw it on the stage. Everyone bows before this exemplary gesture. But do not forget that her hour of glory lasts only 27 minutes : precisely from the first bravo to the extinction of the great chandelier in the opera (after that she must keep her husband on a leash, winner of several contests, who filled the pink cavities of his orbits with two croix-de-guerre). And note well : all those among us who eat too much canned human flesh shall perish with scurvy." " It's very good," Lucien said, taken aback—" I get them by a new technique called automatic writing." Some time later Lucien had a violent desire to kill himself and decided to ask Berliac's advice. " What must I do ? " he asked after he had explained the case. Berliac listened attentively ; he was in the habit of sucking his fingers and then coating the pimples on his face with saliva, so that his skin glistened in spots like a road after a rainstorm. " Do what you want," he said, " it makes absolutely no difference." Lucien was a little disappointed but he realised Berliac had been profoundly touched when he asked Lucien to have tea with his mother the next Thursday. Mme Berliac was very friendly : she had warts and a wine-coloured birthmark on her left cheek : " You see," Berliac told Lucien, " we are the real victims of the war." That was also the opinion of Lucien and they agreed that they both belonged to the same sacrificed generation. Night fell ; Berliac was lying on his bed, his hands knotted behind his head. They smoked English cigarettes, played gramophone records and Lucien heard the voice of Sophie Tucker and Al Jolson. They grew melancholy and Lucien thought Berliac was his best friend. Berliac asked him if he knew psychoanalysis ; his voice was serious and he looked at Lucien with gravity. " I desired my mother until I was fifteen," he confided. Lucien felt uncomfortable ; he was afraid of blushing and remembered Mme Berliac's moles and could not understand how anyone could desire her. Yet when she came to bring them toast, he was vaguely troubled and tried to imagine her breasts through the yellow sweater she wore. When she left, Berliac said in a positive voice, " Naturally, you've wanted to sleep with your mother too." He did not question, he affirmed. Lucien shrugged. " Naturally," he said. Then next day he was worried, he was afraid Berliac would repeat their conversation. But he reassured himself quickly : After all, he thought, he's compromised himself more than I. He was enthralled by the scientific turn their confidences had taken and on the following Thursday he read a book on dreams by Freud he found in the Sainte-Geneviève Library. It was a revelation. " So that's it," Lucien repeated, roaming the streets, " so that's it." Next he bought *Introduction to Psycho-*

Analysis and *Psychopathology of Everyday Life*, and everything became clear to him. This strange feeling of not existing, this long emptiness in his conscience, his somnolence, his perplexities, his vain efforts to know himself which met only a curtain of fog . . . "My God," he thought, "I have a complex." He told Berliac how he was when he was a child, imagining he was a sleepwalker and how objects never seemed quite real to him. "I must have," he concluded, "a very extraordinary complex." "Just like me," said Berliac, "we both have terrific complexes!" They got the habit of interpreting their dreams and their slightest gestures; Berliac always had so many stories to tell that Lucien suspected him of inventing them, or at least enlarging them. But they got along well and approached the most delicate subjects with objectivity; they confessed to each other that they wore a mask of gaiety to deceive their associates but at heart were terribly tormented. Lucien was freed from his worries. He threw himself greedily into psychoanalysis because he realized it was something that agreed with him and now he felt reassured; he no longer needed to worry or to be always searching his conscience for palpable manifestations of his character. The true Lucien was deeply buried in his subconscious; he had to dream of him without ever seeing him, as an absent friend. All day Lucien thought of his complexes and with a certain pride he imagined the obscure world, cruel and violent, that rumbled beneath the mists of his consciousness. "You understand," he told Berliac, "in appearance I was a sleepy kid, indifferent to everything, somebody not too interesting. And even inside, you know, it seemed to be so much like that that I almost let myself

be caught. But I knew there was something else."
" There's *always* something else," Berliac answered.
They smiled proudly at each other ; Lucien wrote a
poem called *When the Fog Lifts* and Berliac found it
excellent, but he reproached Lucien for having written
it in regular verse. Still, they learned it by heart and
when they wished to speak of their libidos they said
willingly :

" The great crabs wrapped in the mantle of fog,"
then, simply, " crabs," winking an eye. But after a
while, Lucien, when he was alone at night, began to
find all that a little terrifying. He no longer dared look
his mother in the face and when he kissed her before
going to bed he was afraid some shadowy power would
deviate his kiss and drop it on Mme Fleurier's mouth ;
it was as if he carried a volcano within himself. Lucien
treated himself with caution in order not to violate the
sumptuous, sinister soul he had discovered. Now he
knew the price of everything and dreaded the terrible
awakenings. " I'm afraid of myself," he said. For six
months he had renounced solitary practices because
they annoyed him and he had too much work but
he returned to them : everyone had to follow their
bent ; the books of Freud were filled with stories of
unfortunate young people who became neurotic because
they broke too quickly with their habits. " Are we
going to go crazy ? " he asked Berliac. And in fact, on
certain Thursdays they felt strange ; shadows had cun-
ningly slipped into Berliac's room ; they smoked whole
packets of scented cigarettes, and their hands trembled.
Then one of them would rise without a word, tiptoe to
the door and turn the switch. A yellow light flooded
the room and they looked at each other with defiance.

Lucien was not long in noticing that his friendship with Berliac was based on a misunderstanding; surely no one was more sensitive than he to the pathetic beauty of the Oedipus complex but in it he saw especially the sign of a power for passion which later he would like to use toward different ends. On the other hand, Berliac seemed to be content with his state and had no desire to leave it. " We're screwed," he said proudly, " we're flops. We'll never do anything." " Never anything," Lucien answered in echo. But he was furious. After the Easter vacation, Berliac told him he had shared his mother's room in an hotel in Dijon : he had risen very early in the morning, went to the bed on which his mother still was sleeping and gently lifted up the covers. " Her nightgown was up," he grinned. Hearing these words, Lucien could not keep himself from scorning Berliac a little and he felt quite alone. It was fine to have complexes but you had to know how to get rid of them eventually. How would a man be able to assume responsibilities and take command if he still had an infantile sexuality ? Lucien began to worry seriously : he would have liked to take the advice of some competent person but he did not know whom to see. Berliac often spoke to him about a surrealist named Bergère who was well versed in psychoanalysis and who seemed to have a great ascendancy over him ; but he had never offered to introduce him to Lucien. Lucien was also very disappointed because he had counted on Berliac to get women for him ; he thought that the possession of a pretty mistress would naturally change the course of his ideas. But Berliac spoke no more of his lady friends. Sometimes they went along the boulevards and followed women, never daring to speak to them : " What do you expect, old man ? " Berliac said, " we aren't the kind that pleases. Women feel something frightening in us." Lucien did not answer ; Berliac began to annoy him. He often made jokes in very bad taste about Lucien's parents ; he called them M. and Mme Dumollet. Lucien understood very well that a surrealist scorned the bourgeoisie in general, but Berliac had been invited several times by Mme Fleurier who had treated him with confidence and friendship : lacking gratitude, a simple attention to decency would have kept him from speaking of her in that manner. And then Berliac was terrible with his mania for borrowing money and never returning it ; in a café he only proposed to pay the round once out of five. Lucien told him plainly one day that he didn't understand, and that between friends, they should share all expenses. Berliac looked at him deeply and said, " I thought so," and he explained the Freudian relation to him ; faeces equal gold and the Freudian theory of guilt. They nearly fought.

From the beginning of May, Berliac began to cut school : Lucien went to meet him after class, in a bar on Rue des Petits-Champs where they drank Crucifix Vermouths. One Tuesday afternoon Lucien found Berliac sitting in front of an empty glass. " Oh, there you are," Berliac said, " Listen, I've got to beat it, I have an appointment with the dentist at five. Wait for me, he lives near here and it'll only take half an hour." " O.K." Lucien answered, dropping into a chair. " Francois, give me a white vermouth." Just then a man came into the bar and smiled surprisedly at seeing them. Berliac blushed and got up hurriedly. " Who can that be ? " Lucien wondered. Berliac, shak-

ing hands with the stranger, stood so as to hide Lucien;
he spoke in a low, rapid voice; the other answered
clearly, "Indeed not, my friend, you'll always be a
fool." At the same time he raised himself on tiptoe
and looked at Lucien over Berliac's head with calm
assurance. He could have been 35; he had a pale face
and magnificent white hair: "It's surely Bergère,"
Lucien thought, his heart pounding, "how handsome
he is."

Berliac had taken the man with white hair by the
elbow with an air of timid authority.

"Come with me," he said, "I'm going to the dentist,
just across the way."

"But you were with a friend, weren't you?" the
other answered, his eyes not leaving Lucien's face,
"You should introduce us."

Lucien got up, smiling, "Caught!" he thought; his
cheeks were burning. Berliac's neck disappeared into
his shoulders and for a second Lucien thought he was
going to refuse. "So introduce me," he said gaily. But
as soon as he had spoken the blood rushed to his
temples and he wished the ground would swallow him.
Berliac turned around and without looking at anyone,
muttered, "Lucien Fleurier, a friend from the lycée,
Monsieur Achille Bergère."

"I admire your works," Lucien said feebly. Bergère
took his hand in his own long, delicate fingers and
motioned him to sit down. Bergère enveloped Lucien
with a tender, warm look; he was still holding his
hand. "Are you worried?" he asked gently.

"I am worried," he answered distinctly. It seemed
he had just undergone the trials of an initiation.
Berliac hesitated an instant then angrily sat down again,

throwing his hat on the table. Lucien burned with a desire to tell Bergère of his attempted suicide ; this was someone to whom one had to speak of things abruptly and without preparation. He dared not say anything because of Berliac ; he hated Berliac.

" Do you have any *raki* ? " Bergère asked the waiter.

" No, they don't," Berliac said quickly ; " It's a nice little place but all they have to drink is vermouth."

" What's that yellow stuff you have in the bottle ? " Bergère asked with an ease full of softness.

" White Crucifix," the waiter answered.

" All right, I'll have some of that."

Berliac squirmed on his chair ; he seemed caught between a desire to show off his friends and the fear of making Lucien shine at his expense. Finally, he said, in a proud and dismal voice, " He wanted to kill himself."

" My God ! " Bergère said, " I should hope so ! "

There was another silence : Lucien had lowered his eyes modestly but he wondered if Berliac wasn't soon going to clear out : Bergère suddenly looked at his watch. " What about your dentist ? " he asked.

Berliac rose ungraciously. " Come with me, Bergère," he begged, " it isn't far."

" No, you'll be back. I'll keep your friend company."

Berliac stayed for another moment, shifting from one foot to the other.

" Go on," Bergère said imperiously, " You'll meet us here."

When Berliac had gone, Bergère got up and sat next to Lucien. Lucien told him of his suicide at great length ; he also explained to him that he had desired

his mother and that fundamentally he didn't love anything and that everything in him was a comedy.
Bergère listened without a word, watching him closely
and Lucien found it delicious to be understood. When
he finished, Bergère passed his arm familiarly around
his shoulders and Lucien smelled a scent of eau-de-
cologne and English tobacco.

" Do you know, Lucien, how I would describe your
condition ? " Lucien looked at Bergère hopefully ; he
was not disappointed.

" I call it," Bergère said, " Disorder."

Disorder : the word had begun tender and white as
moonlight but the final " order " had the coppered
flash of a trumpet.

" Disorder," Lucien said.

He felt grave and inquiet as the time he told Riri he
was a sleepwalker. The bar was dark but the door
opened wide on the street, on the luminous springtime
mist ; under the discreet perfume Bergère gave off,
Lucien perceived the heavy odour of the obscure room,
an odour of red wine and damp wood. " Disorder," he
thought ; " what good will that do me ? " He did not
know whether a dignity or new sickness had been discovered in him ; near his eyes he saw the quick lips
of Bergère veiling and unveiling incessantly the sparkle
of a gold tooth.

" I like people in disorder," Bergère said, " and I
think you are extraordinarily lucky. For after all, that
has been given you. You see all these swine ? They're
pedestrians. You'd have to give them to the red ants
to stir them up a little. Do you know they have the
consciousnesses of beasts ? "

" They eat men," Lucien said.

"Yes, they strip skeletons of their human meat."

"I see," Lucien said. He added, "And I? What must I do?"

"Nothing, for God's sake," Bergère said with a look of comic fear. "Above all, don't sit down. Unless," he said, laughing, "it's on a tack. Have you read Rimbaud?"

"N-no," Lucien said.

"I'll lend you *The Illuminations*. Listen, we must see each other again. If you're free Thursday, stop in and see me around 3, I live in Montparnasse, 9 Rue Campagne-Première."

The next Thursday Lucien went to see Bergère and he went back almost every day throughout May. They agreed to tell Berliac that they saw each other once a week, because they wanted to be frank with him and yet avoid hurting his feelings. Berliac showed himself to be completely out of sorts; he asked Lucien, grinning, "So, are you going steady? He gave you the worry business and you gave him the suicide business: a great game, what?" Lucien protested, "I'd like to have you know that it was you who talked about my suicide first." "Oh," Berliac said, "it was only to spare you the shame of telling it yourself." Their meetings became more infrequent. "Everything I liked about him," Lucien told Bergère one day, "he borrowed from you, I realize it now." "Berliac is a monkey," Bergère said, laughing, "that's what always attracted me. Did you know his maternal grandmother was a Jewess? That explains a lot of things." "Rather," Lucien answered. After an instant he added, "Besides, he's very charming." Bergère's apartment was filled with strange and comical objects:

hassocks whose red velvet seats rested on the legs of painted wooden women, negro statuettes, a studded chastity belt of forged iron, plaster breasts in which little spoons had been planted ; on the desk a gigantic bronze louse and a monk's skull stolen from the Mistra Ossuary served as paper weights. The walls were papered with notices announcing the death of the surrealist Bergère. In spite of all this, the apartment gave the impression of intelligent comfort and Lucien liked to stretch out on the deep divan in the den. What particularly surprised Lucien was the enormous quantity of practical jokes Bergère had accumulated on a shelf ; solid liquids, sneezing powder, itching powder, floating sugar, and a bride's garter. " These jokes," Bergère said, " have a revolutionary value. They disturb. There is more destructive power in them than in all the works of Lenin." Lucien, surprised and charmed, looked by turns at this handsome tormented face with hollow eyes and those long delicate fingers. Bergère spoke often of Rimbaud and the " systematic disordering of all the senses." " When you will be able, in crossing the Place de la Concorde, to see distinctly and at will a kneeling negress sucking the obelisk, you will be able to tell yourself that you have torn down the scenery and you are saved." He lent him *The Illuminations*, the *Chants de Maldoror* and the works of the Marquis de Sade. Lucien tried conscientiously to understand them, but many things escaped him and he was shocked because Rimbaud was a pederast. He told Bergère who began to laugh. " But why, my little friend ? " Lucien was very embarrassed. He blushed and for a minute began to hate Bergère with all his might, but he mastered it, raised his head and said with simple frankness, "I'm talking nonsense." Bergère stroked his hair; he seemed moved; "These great eyes full of trouble," he said, "these doe's eyes. . . . Yes, Lucien, you talked nonsense. Rimbaud's pederasty is the primary and genial disordering of his sensitivity. We owe his poems to it. To think that there are specific objects of sexual desire and that these objects are women, is the hideous and wilful error of the pedestrian. Look!" He took from his desk a dozen yellowing photos and threw them on Lucien's knees. Lucien gazed on horrible naked whores, laughing with toothless mouths. "I got the collection for 3 francs at Bou-Saada," Bergère said. "If you kiss the behind of one of those women, you are the son of the family and everybody will say you're a he-man. Because they're women, do you understand? I tell you the first thing to convince yourself of is that *everything* can be an object of sexual desire, a sewing machine, a measuring glass, a horse or a shoe." Bergère pinched Lucien's ear distractedly. Lucien emerged from these conversations with his face on fire; he thought Bergère was a genius but sometimes he woke up at night, drenched in sweat, his head filled with monstrous obscene visions and he wondered if Bergère was a good influence on him. "To be alone," he cried, wringing his hands, "to have no one to advise me, to tell me if I'm on the right path." If he went to the very end, if he really practised the disordering of the senses, would he lose his footing and drown? One day Bergère had spoken to him of André Breton: Lucien murmured, as if in a dream, "Yes, but afterwards, if I could never come back." Bergère started. "Come back? Who's talking about coming back? If

you go insane, so much the better. After that, as
Rimbaud says, ' *viendront d'autres horribles travail-
leurs* '." "That's what I thought," Lucien said sadly.
He had noticed that these long chats had the effect
opposite from the one wished for by Bergère : as soon
as Lucien caught himself showing the beginnings of a
fine sensation or an original impression, he began to
tremble : " Now it's starting," he thought. He would
willingly have wished to have only the most banal,
stupid perceptions ; he only felt comfortable in the
evenings with his parents : that was his refuge. They
talked about Briand, the bad faith of the Germans, of
cousin Jeanne's confinements and the cost of living ;
Lucien voluptuously exchanged good common sense
with them. One day after leaving Bergère, he was
entering his room and mechanically locked the door
and slid the bolt. When he noticed this gesture he
forced himself to laugh at it but that night he could
not sleep : he had just understood he was afraid.

However, nothing in the world would have stopped
him from seeing Bergère. " He fascinates me," he told
himself. And then he had a lively appreciation of the
fellowship so delicate and so particular which Bergère
had been able to establish between them. Without
dropping a virile, almost rude tone of voice, Bergère
had the artistry to make Lucien feel, and, in a way of
speaking, touch his tenderness : for instance he re-
knotted his tie and scolded him for being so untidy ;
he combed his hair with a gold comb from Cambodia.
He made Lucien discover his own body and explained
to him the harsh and pathetic beauty of youth : " You
are Rimbaud," he told him, " he had your big hands
when he came to Paris to see Verlaine. He had this

pink face of a young healthy peasant and this long slim body of a fair-haired girl." He made Lucien unbutton his collar and open his shirt, then led him, confused, before a mirror and made him admire the charming harmony of his red cheeks and white throat ; then he caressed Lucien's hips with a light hand and added, sadly, " We should kill ourselves at twenty." Often now, Lucien looked at himself in mirrors and he learned to enjoy his young awkward grace. " I am Rimbaud," he thought, in the evenings, removing his clothing with gestures full of gentleness and he began to believe that he would have the short and tragic life of a too-beautiful flower. At these times, it seemed to him that he had known, long before, similar impressions and an absurd image came to his mind : he saw himself again, small, with a long blue robe and angel's wings, distributing flowers at a charity sale. He looked at his long legs. " Is it true I have such a soft skin ? " he thought with amusement. And once he ran his lips over his forearm from the wrist to the elbow, along a charming blue vein.

One day, he had an unpleasant surprise going to Bergère's : Berliac was there, busy cutting with a knife fragments of a blackish substance that looked like a clod of earth. The two young people had not seen each other for ten days : they shook hands coldly. " See that ? " Berliac said, "that's hasheesh. We're going to put it in these pipes, between two layers of light tobacco ; it gives a surprising effect. There's some for you," he added. " No thanks," Lucien said, " I don't care for it." The other two laughed and Berliac insisted, looking ugly : " But you're crazy, old man, you've got to take some. You can't imagine how pleasant it is." "I told you no," Lucien said. Berliac said no more, merely smiled with a superior air and Lucien saw Bergère was smiling too. He tapped his foot and said, "I don't want any, I don't want to knock myself out. I think it's crazy to stupify yourself with that stuff." He had let that go in spite of himself, but when he realized the range of what he had just said and imagined what Bergère must think of him, he wanted to kill Berliac and tears came to his eyes. "You're a bourgeois," said Berliac, shrugging his shoulders, "you pretend to swim but you're much too afraid of going out of your depth." "I don't want to get in the drug habit," Lucien said in a calmer voice; "one slavery is like another and I want to stay clear." "Say you're afraid to get into it," Berliac answered violently. Lucien was going to slap him when he heard the imperious voice of Bergère. "Let him alone, Charles," he told Berliac, "he's right. His fear of being involved is *also* disorder." They both smoked, stretched out on the divan and an odour of Armenian paper filled the room. Lucien sat on a red velvet hassock and watched them in silence. After a time, Berliac let his head fall back and fluttered his eyelids with moist smile. Lucien watched him with rancour and felt humiliated. At last Berliac got up and walked unsteadily out of the room: to the end he had the funny, sleeping and voluptuous smile on his lips. "Give me a pipe," Lucien said hoarsely. Bergère began to laugh. "Don't bother," he said, "Don't worry about Berliac. Do you know what he's doing now?" "I don't give a damn," Lucien said. "Well, I'll tell you anyhow. He's vomiting," Bergère said calmly. "That's the only effect hasheesh ever had on him.

The rest is a joke, but I make him smoke it sometimes because he wants to show off and it amuses me." The next day Berliac came to the lycée and wanted to show off in front of Lucien. " You don't exactly go out on a limb, do you ? " he said. But he found out to whom he was talking. " You're a little show off," Lucien answered, " maybe you think I don't know what you were doing in the bathroom yesterday ? You were puking, old man ! " Berliac grew livid. " Bergère told you ? " " Who do you think ? " " All right," Berliac stammered, " but I wouldn't have thought Bergère would screw his old friends with new ones." Lucien was a little worried. He had promised Bergère not to repeat anything. " All right, all right," he said, " he didn't screw you, he just wanted to show me it didn't work." But Berliac turned his back and left without shaking hands. Lucien was not too glad when he met Bergère. " What did you say to Berliac," Bergère asked him neutrally. Lucien lowered his head without answering : he felt overwhelmed. But suddenly he felt Bergère's hand on his neck : " It doesn't make any difference. In any case it had to end : comedians don't amuse me very long." Lucien took heart ; he raised his head and smiled : " But I'm a comedian too," he said, blinking his eyes. " Yes, but you're pretty," Bergère answered, drawing him close. Lucien let himself go ; he felt soft as a girl and tears were in his eyes. Bergère kissed his cheeks and bit his ear, sometimes calling him " my lovely little scoundrel " and sometimes " my little brother " and Lucien thought it was quite pleasant to have a big brother who was so indulgent and understanding.

M. and Mme Fleurier wanted to meet this Bergère

of whom Lucien spoke so much and they invited him to dinner. Everyone found him charming, including Germaine who had never seen such a handsome man ; M. Fleurier had known General Nizan who was Bergère's uncle and he spoke of him at great length. Also, Mme Fleurier was only too glad to confide Lucien to Bergère for the spring vacation. They went to Rouen by car ; Lucien wanted to see the cathedral and the hotel-de-ville, but Bergère flatly refused. " That rubbish ? " he asked insolently. Finally, they spent two hours in a brothel on Rue des Cordeliers and Bergère was a scream : he called all the chippies " mademoiselle," nudging Lucien under the table ; then he agreed to go up with one of them but came back after five minutes : " Get the hell out," he gasped, " it's going to be rough." They paid quickly and left. In the street Bergère told what happened ; while the woman had her back turned he threw a handful of itching powder on the bed, then told her he was impotent and came down again. Lucien had drunk two whiskies and was a little tight ; he sang the *Artilleur de Metz* and *De Profondis Morpionibus* ; he thought it wonderful that Bergère was at the same time so profound and childish.

" I only reserved one room," Bergère said when they arrived at the hotel, " but there's a big bathroom." Lucien was not surprised : he had vaguely thought during the trip that he would share the room with Bergère without dwelling too much on the idea. Now that he could no longer retreat he found the thing a little disagreeable, especially because his feet were not clean. As the bags were being brought up, he imagined that Bergère would tell him, " How dirty you are, you'll make the sheets black," and he would answer

175

insolently, "Your ideas of cleanliness are really bourgeois." But Bergère shoved him into the bathroom with his bag, saying, "Get yourself ready in there, I'm going to undress in the room." Lucien took a footbath and a sitz bath. He wanted to go to the toilet but he did not dare and contented himself with urinating in the washbasin; then he put on his nightshirt and the slippers his mother lent him (his own were full of holes) and knocked. "Are you ready?" he asked. "Yes, yes, come in." Bergère had slipped a black dressing gown over sky blue pyjamas. The room smelled of eau-de-cologne. "Only one bed?" Lucien asked. Bergère did not answer: he looked at Lucien with a stupor that ended in a great burst of laughter. "Look at that shirt!" he said, laughing, "what did you do with your nightcap? Oh no, that's really too funny. I do wish you could see yourself." "For two years," Lucien said, angrily, "I've been asking my mother to buy me pyjamas." Bergère came toward him. "That's all right. Take it off," he said in a voice to which there was no answer, "I'll give you one of mine. It'll be a little big but it'll be better than that." Lucien stayed rooted in the middle of the room, his eyes riveted on the red and green lozenges of the wallpaper. He would have preferred to go back into the bathroom but he was afraid to act like a fool and with a crisp motion tossed the shirt over his head. There was a moment of silence: Bergère looked at Lucien, smiling, and Lucien suddenly realized he was naked in the middle of the room, wearing his mother's pom-pommed slippers. He looked at his hands—the big hands of Rimbaud—he wanted to clutch them to his stomach and cover that at least, but he pulled himself together and put them bravely behind his back. On the walls, between two rows of lozenges, there was a small violet square going back farther and farther. " My word," said Bergère, " he's as chaste as a virgin : look at yourself in the mirror, Lucien, you're blushing as far as your chest. But you're still better like that than in a nightshirt." " Yes," Lucien said with effort, " but you never look good when you're naked. Quick, give me the pyjamas." Bergère threw him silk pyjamas that smelled of lavender and they went to the bed. There was a heavy silence : " I'm sick," Lucien said, " I want to puke." Bergère did not answer and Lucien smelled whiskey in his throat. " He's going to sleep with me," he thought. And the lozenges on the wall-paper began to spin while the stifling smell of eau-de-cologne gagged him. " I shouldn't have said I'd take the trip." He had no luck ; twenty times, these last few days, he had almost discovered what Bergère wanted of him and each time, as if on purpose, something happened to turn away his thought. And now he was there, in this man's bed, waiting his good pleasure. I'll take my pillow and go and sleep in the bathroom. But he did not dare ; he thought of Bergère's ironic look. He began to laugh. " I'm thinking about the whore a while ago," he said, " she must be scratching now.". Bergère still did not answer him : Lucien looked at him out of the corner of his eye : he was stretched out innocently on his back, his hands under his head. Then a violent fury seized Lucien ; he raised himself on one elbow and asked him, " Well, what are you waiting for ? You didn't bring me here to string beads ! "

It was too late to regret his words : Bergère turned

to him and studied him with an amused eye. " Look
at that angel-faced little tart. Well, baby, I didn't
make you say it ! I'm the one you're counting on
to disorder your little senses." He looked at him an
instant longer, their faces almost touching, then he took
Lucien in his arms and caressed his breast beneath the
pyjama shirt. It was not unpleasant, it tickled a little,
only Bergère was frightening : he looked foolish and
repeated with effort, " You aren't ashamed, little pig,
you aren't ashamed, little pig ! " like the gramophone
records in a train station announcing the arrivals and
departures. On the contrary, Bergère's hand was swift
and light and seemed to be an entire person. It gently
grazed Lucien's breast as a caress of warm water in a
bath. Lucien wanted to catch this hand, tear it from
him and twist it, but Bergère would have laughed :
look at that virgin. The hand slid slowly to untie the
knot of the drawstring which held the trousers. Lucien
belched twice in a row and he was afraid of vomiting
on the handsome, silver hair so full of dignity. Tears
of rage came to Lucien's eyes and he pushed Bergère
away with all his might. He hissed, " You made me
drink too much, I want to puke." " All right, go !
Go ! " Bergère said, " and take your time." Between
his teeth he added, " Charming evening." Lucien
pulled up his trousers, slipped on the black dressing
gown and left. When he had closed the bathroom door
he felt so alone and abandoned that he burst out
sobbing. There were no handkerchiefs in the pocket
of the dressing gown so he wiped his eyes and nose
with toilet paper. In vain he pushed his fingers down
his throat ; he could not vomit. Then he dropped
his trousers mechanically and sat down on the toilet,

shivering. " The bastard," he thought, " the bastard."
He was atrociously humiliated but he did not know
whether he was ashamed for having submitted to
Bergère's caresses or for not getting excited. The
corridor on the other side of the door cracked and
Lucien started at each sound but could not decide to
go back into the room. " I have to go back," he
thought, " I must, or else he'll laugh at me—with
Berliac ! " and he rose halfway, but as soon as he
pictured the face of Bergère and his stupid look, and
heard him saying, " You aren't ashamed, little pig ? "
he fell back on the seat in despair. After a while he
was seized with violent diarrhoea which soothed him
a little : " It's going out by the back," he thought, " I
like that better." In fact, he had no further desire to
vomit. " He's going to hurt me," he thought suddenly
and thought he was going to faint. Finally, he got so
cold his teeth began to chatter : he thought he was
going to be sick and stood up brusquely. Bergère
watched him constrainedly when he went back ; he
was smoking a cigarette and his pyjamas were open,
showing his thin torso. Lucien slowly removed his
slippers and dressing gown and slipped under the covers
without a word. He thought of Mme Besse who pressed
her hand against his stomach and called him " my
little doll " and Hébrard who called him " big beanpole " and the baths he took in the morning imagining
that M. Bouffardier was going to come in and give
him an enema and he told himself, " I'm his little
doll ! "

The next day they awoke at noon. The bellboy
brought them breakfast in bed and Lucien thought he
looked haughty. " He thinks I'm a fairy," he thought

with a shudder of discomfort. Bergère was very nice,
he dressed first and went and smoked a cigarette in
the old market place while Lucien took his bath. " The
thing is," he thought, rubbing himself carefully with
a stiff brush, " that it's boring. I've got to finish my
trig problem, anyhow," he told himself. But he forced
himself not to think of his work any more. The day
was long. Bergère told him about the life of Lautréa-
mont, but Lucien did not pay much attention : Bergère
annoyed him a little. That night they slept in Caudebec.
They returned to Paris towards the end of the afternoon. All in all, Lucien was not displeased with
himself.

His parents welcomed him with open arms : " I hope
you at least said thank you to M. Bergère ? " his
mother asked. He stayed a while to chat with them
about the Normandy countryside and went to bed early.
He slept like an angel, but on awakening the next
day he seemed to be shivering inside. He got up and
studied his face for a long time in the mirror. " I'm
a pederast," he told himself. And his spirits sank.
" Get up, Lucien," his mother called through the door,
" you go to school this morning." " Yes, mamma,"
he answered docilely, but let himself drop back on to
the bed and began to stare at his toes. " It isn't right,
I didn't realize, I have no experience." A man had
sucked those toes one after the other. Lucien violently
turned his face away.

He dressed and went out but he did not have the
heart to go to the lycée. He went down the Avenue
Lamballe as far as the Seine and followed the quais.
The sky was pure, the streets smelled of green leaves,
tar and English tobacco. A dreamed-of time to wear

clean clothes on a well-washed body and new soul. The people had a moral look ; Lucien alone felt suspicious and unusual in this springtime. " The fatal bent," he thought, " I started with an Oedipus complex, now I'm a pederast ; where am I going to stop ? " Evidently, his case was not yet very grave : he did not derive much pleasure from Bergère's caresses. " But suppose I get in the habit ? " he thought with anguish. He would become a tarnished man, no one would have anything to do with him, his father's workers would laugh when he gave them orders. Lucien imagined his frightful destiny with complacency. He saw himself at 35, gaunt, painted, and already an old gentleman with a moustache and the Legion d'Honneur, raising his cane with a terrible look, " Your presence here, sir, is an insult to my daughters." Then suddenly he hesitated and stopped imagining. His experience with Bergère had been a warning, nothing more He must never start again because a bad habit is taken quickly and then he must absolutely cure himself of these complexes. He resolved to have himself psychoanalysed by a specialist without telling his parents. Then he would find a mistress and become a man like the others.

Lucien was beginning to reassure himself when suddenly he thought of Bergère : even now, at this very moment Bergère was existing somewhere in Paris, delighted with himself and his head full of memories. Lucien hated Bergère with all his strength : without him, without this scandalous irremediable conscience, everything would have been all right, no one would have known and even Lucien himself would eventually have forgotten it. " If he would die suddenly ! Dear God, I pray You make him die tonight without telling

anybody. Dear God, let this whole business be buried,
You don't want me to be a pederast." He took a few
more steps, then added, as a measure of precaution,
"Dear God, make Berliac die, too."

Lucien could not take it upon himself to return to
Bergère. During the weeks that followed, he thought
he met him at every step and, when he was working
in his room, he jumped at the sound of the bell; at
night he had fearful nightmares. But Bergère made
no attempt to see him again and gave no sign of life.
"He only wanted my body," Lucien thought vexedly.
Berliac had disappeared as well and Guigard, who
sometimes went to the races with him on Sundays, told
Lucien he had left Paris after a nervous breakdown.
Lucien grew a little calmer: his trip to Rouen affected
him as an obscure, grotesque dream attached to
nothing; he had almost forgotten the details, he kept
only the impression of a dismal odour of flesh and eau-
de-cologne and an intolerable weariness. M. Fleurier
sometimes asked what had happened to his friend
Bergère: "We'll have to invite him to Férolles to thank
him." "He went to New York," Lucien finally
answered. Sometimes he went boating on the Marne
with Guigard and Guigard's sister taught him to dance.
"I'm waking up," he thought, "I'm being reborn."
But he still often felt something weighing on his back
like a heavy burden: his complexes: he wondered if
he should go to Vienna and see Freud: "I'll leave
without any money, on foot if I have to, I'll tell him
I haven't a franc but I'm a case." One hot afternoon
in June he met The Baboon, his old philosophy prof,
on the Boulevard Saint-Michel. "Well, Fleurier,"
The Baboon said, "you're preparing for Centrale?"

" Yessir," Lucien said. " You should be able," The Baboon said, " to orient yourself toward a study of literature. You were good in philosophy——" " I haven't given it up," Lucien said, " I've done a lot of reading this year, Freud, for instance. By the way," he added, inspired, " I'd like to ask you, Monsieur, what do you think about psychoanalysis ? " The Baboon began to laugh : " A fad," he said, " which will pass. The best part of Freud you will find already in Plato. For the rest," he added, in a voice that brooked no answer, " I'll tell you I don't have anything to do with that nonsense. You'd be better off reading Spinoza." Lucien felt himself delivered of an enormous weight and he returned home on foot, whistling. " It was a nightmare," he thought, " nothing more is left of it." The sun was hard and hot that day, but Lucien raised his eyes and gazed at it without blinking : it was the sun of the whole world and Lucien had the right to look it in the face ; he was saved ! " Nonsense," he thought, " it was nonsense ! They tried to drive me crazy but they didn't get me." In fact he had never stopped resisting : Bergère had tripped him up in his reasoning, but Lucien had sensed, for instance, that the pederasty of Rimbaud was a stain, and when that little shrimp Berliac wanted to make him smoke hasheesh Lucien had dressed him down properly : " I risked losing myself," he thought, " but what protected me was my moral health ! " That evening, at dinner, he looked at his father with sympathy. M. Fleurier had squared shoulders and the slow heavy gestures of a peasant with something racial in them and his grey boss's eyes, metallic and cold. " I look like him," Lucien thought. He remembered that the Fleuriers, father to son, had been captains of industry for four generations : " Say what you like, the family exists ! " And he thought proudly of the moral health of the Fleuriers.

Lucien did not present himself for the examinations at the Ecole Centrale that year and the Fleuriers left very shortly for Férolles. He was charmed to find the house again, the garden, the factory, the calm and poised little town. It was another world : he decided to get up early in the mornings and take long walks through the country. " I want," he told his father, " to fill my lungs with pure air and store up health for next year." He accompanied his mother to the Bouffardiers and the Besses and everyone thought he had become a big, well-poised and reasonable boy. Hébrard and Winckelmann, who were taking law courses in Paris, had come back to Férolles for a vacation. Lucien went out with them several times and they talked about the jokes they used to play on Abbé Jacquemart, their long bicycle trips, and they sang the *Artilleur de Metz* in harmony. Lucien keenly appreciated the rough frankness and solidity of his old friends and he reproached himself for having neglected them. He confessed to Hébrard that he did not care much for Paris, but Hébrard could not understand it : his parents had entrusted him to an abbé and he was very much held in check ; he was still dazzled by his visits to the Louvre and the evening he had spent at the Opera. Lucien was touched by this simplicity ; he felt himself the elder brother of Hébrard and Winckelmann and he began to tell himself that he did not regret having had such a tormented life : he had gained experience. He told them about Freud and psychoanalysis and amused himself by shocking them a little. They violently criticised the theory of complexes but their objections were naïve and Lucien pointed it out to them, then he added that from a philosophical viewpoint it was easy to refute the errors of Freud. They admired him greatly but Lucien pretended not to notice it.

M. Fleurier explained the operation of the factory to Lucien. He took him on a visit through the central buildings and Lucien watched the workers at great length. " If I should die," M. Fleurier said, " you'd have to take command of the factory at a moment's notice." Lucien scolded him and said, " Don't talk like that, will you please, old papa." But he was serious for several days in a row thinking of the responsibilities which would fall on him sooner or later. They had long talks about the duties of the boss and M. Fleurier showed him that ownership was not a right but a duty : " What are they trying to give us, with their class struggle ? " he said, " as though the interests of the bosses and the workers were just the opposite. Take my case, Lucien, I'm a little boss ; what they call small fry. Well, I make a living for 100 workers and their families. If I do well, they're the first ones to profit. But if I have to close the plant, there they are in the street. *I don't have a right*," he said forcefully, " to do bad business. And that's what I call the solidarity of classes."

All went well for more than three weeks ; he almost never thought of Bergère ; he had forgiven him : he simply hoped never to see him again for the rest of his life. Sometimes, when he changed his shirt, he went to the mirror and looked at himself with astonishment :

" A man has desired this body," he thought. He passed his hands slowly over his legs and thought : " A man was excited by these legs." He touched his back and regretted not being another person to be able to caress his own flesh like a piece of silk. Sometimes he missed his complexes : they had been solid, heavy, their enormous sombre mass had balanced him. Now it was finished, Lucien no longer believed in it and he felt terribly unstable. Though it was not so unpleasant, it was rather a sort of very tolerable disenchantment, a little upsetting, which could, if necessary, pass for *ennui*. " I'm nothing," he thought, " but it's because nothing has soiled me. Berliac was soiled and caught. I can stand a little uncertainty : it's the price of purity."

During a walk, he sat down on a hillock and thought : " For six years I slept, and then one fine day I came out of my cocoon." He was animated and looked affably around the countryside. " I'm built for action," he thought. But in an instant his thought of glory faded. He whispered, " Let them wait awhile and they'll see what I'm worth." He had spoken with force but the words rolled on his lips like empty shells. " What's the matter with me ? " He did not *want* to recognize this odd inquietude : it had hurt him too much before. He thought, " It's this silence . . . this land . . ." Not a living being, save crickets laboriously dragging their black and yellow bellies in the dust. Lucien hated crickets because they always looked half dead. On the other side of the road, a greyish stretch of land, crushed, creviced, ran as far as the river. No one saw Lucien, no one heard him ; he sprang to his feet and felt that his movements would meet with no resistance, not even that of gravity. Now he stood beneath a curtain of grey clouds; it was as though he existed in a vacuum. " This silence . . ." he thought. It was more than silence, it was nothingness. The countryside was extraordinarily calm and soft about Lucien, inhuman : it seemed that it was making itself tiny and was holding its breath so as not to disturb him. " *Quand l'artilleur de Metz revint en garnison . . .* " The sound died on his lips as a flame in a vacuum : Lucien was alone, without a shadow and without an echo, in the midst of this too discreet nature which meant nothing. He shook himself and tried to re-capture the thread of his thought. " I'm built for action. First, I can bounce back : I can do a lot of foolishness but it doesn't go far because I always spring back." He thought, " I have moral health." But he stopped, making a grimace of disgust ; it seemed so absurd to him to speak of " moral health " on this white road crossed by dying insects. In rage, Lucien stepped on a cricket ; under his sole he felt a little elastic ball and, when he raised his foot, the cricket was still alive : Lucien spat on it. " I'm perplexed, I'm perplexed. It's like last year." He began to think about Winckelmann who called him " the ace of aces " ; about M. Fleurier who treated him like a man ; Mme Besse who told him, " This is the big boy I used to call my little doll ; I wouldn't dare say it now ; he frightens me." But they were far, far away and it seemed the real Lucien was lost, that there was only a white and perplexed larva. " What am I ? " Miles and miles of land, a flat, chapped soil, grassless, odourless, and then, suddenly, springing straight from this grey crust, the beanpole, so unwonted that there was even no shadow behind it. " What am

I ? " The question had not changed since the past vacation ; it was as if it waited for Lucien at the very spot he had left it ; or, it wasn't a question, but a condition. Lucien shrugged his shoulders. " I'm too scrupulous," he thought, " I analyse myself too much."

The following days he forced himself to stop analysing : he wanted to let himself be fascinated by things, lengthily he studied egg cups, napkin rings, trees and store fronts ; he flattered his mother very much when he asked her if she would like to show him her silver service ; he thought he was looking at silver and behind the look throbbed a little living fog. In vain Lucien absorbed himself in conversation with M. Fleurier ; this abundant, tenacious mist, whose opaque inconsistency falsely resembled light, slipped *behind* the attention he gave his father's words : this fog was himself. From time to time, annoyed, Lucien stopped listening, turned away, tried to catch the fog and look it in the face : he found only emptiness ; the fog was still *behind*.

Germaine came in tears to Mme Fleurier : her brother had broncho-pneumonia. " My poor Germaine," Mme Fleurier said, " and you always said how strong he was ! " She gave her a month's vacation and, to replace her, brought in the daughter of one of the factory workers, little Berthe Mozelle who was seventeen. She was small, with blonde plaits rolled about her head ; she limped slightly. Since she came from Concarneau, Mme Fleurier begged her to wear a lace coiffe, " That would be so much nicer." From the first days, each time she met Lucien, her wide blue eyes reflected a humble and passionate adoration and

Lucien realized she worshipped him. He spoke to her familiarly and often asked her, "Do you like it here?" In the hallways he amused himself making passes at her to see if they had an effect. But she touched him deeply and he drew a precious comfort from this love; he often thought with a sting of emotion of the image Berthe must make of him. "By the simple fact that I hardly look like the young workers she goes out with." On a pretext he took Winckelmann into the pantry and Winckelmann thought she was well built: "You're a lucky dog," he concluded, "I'd look into it if I were you." But Lucien hesitated: she smelled of sweat and her black blouse was eaten away under the arms. One rainy day in September M. Fleurier drove into Paris and Lucien stayed in his room alone. He lay down on his bed and began to yawn. He seemed to be a cloud, capricious and fleeting, always the same, always something else, always diluting himself in the air. "I wonder why I exist?" He was there, he digested, he yawned, he heard the rain tapping on the window-panes and the white fog was unravelling in his head: and then? His existence was a scandal and the responsibilities he would assume later would barely be enough to justify it. "After all, I didn't ask to be born," he said. And he pitied himself. He remembered his childhood anxieties, his long somnolence, and they appeared to him in a new light: fundamentally, he had not stopped being embarrassed with his life, with this voluminous, useless gift, and he had carried it in his arms without knowing what to do with it or where to set it down. "I have spent my time regretting I was born." But he was too depressed to push his thoughts further; he rose, lit a cigarette and went down into the kitchen to ask Berthe to make some tea.

She did not see him enter. He touched her shoulder and she started violently. " Did I frighten you ? " he asked. She looked at him fearfully, leaning both hands on the table and her breast heaved : after a moment she smiled and said, " It scared me, I didn't think anybody was there." Lucien returned her smile with indulgence and said, " It would be very nice if you'd make a little tea for me." " Right away, Monsieur Lucien," the girl answered and she fled to the stove : Lucien's presence seemed to make her uncomfortable. Lucien remained on the doorstep, uncertain. " Well," he asked paternally, " do you like it here with us ? " Berthe turned her back on him and filled a pan at the spigot. The sound of the water covered her answer. Lucien waited a moment and when she had set the pan on the gas range he continued, " Have you ever smoked ? " " Sometimes," the girl answered, warily. He opened his packet of Cravens and held it out to her. He was not too pleased : he felt he was compromising himself ; he shouldn't make her smoke. " You want . . . me to smoke ? " she asked, surprised. " Why not ? " " Madame will scold me." Lucien had an unpleasant impression of complicity. He began to laugh and said, " We won't tell her." Berthe blushed, took a cigarette with the tips of her fingers and put it in her mouth. Should I offer to light it ? That wouldn't be right. He said to her, " Well, aren't you going to light it ? " She annoyed him ; she stood there, her arms stiff, red and docile, her lips bunched around the cigarette like a thermometer stuck in her mouth. She finally took a sulphur match from the tin box, struck it, smoked a few puffs with eyes half shut and said, "It's mild." Then she hurriedly took the cigarette from her mouth and clutched it awkwardly between her five fingers. "A born victim," Lucien thought. Yet, she thawed a little when he asked her if she liked her Brittany ; she described the different sorts of Breton coiffes to him and even sang a song from Rosporden in a soft, off-key voice. Lucien teased her gently but she did not understand the joke and looked at him fearfully : at those times she looked like a rabbit. He was sitting on a stool and felt quite at ease : "Sit down," he told her . . . "Oh no, Monsieur Lucien, not before Monsieur Lucien." He took her under the arms and drew her to his knees. "And like that ? " he asked. She let herself go, murmuring, "On your knees ! " with an air of ecstasy and reproach with a funny accent and Lucien thought wearily, "I'm getting too much involved, I shouldn't have gone so far." He was silent : she stayed on his knees, hot, quiet, but Lucien felt her heart beating. "She belongs to me," he thought, "I can do anything I want with her." He let her go, took the teapot and went back to his room : Berthe did not make a move to stop him. Before drinking his tea, Lucien washed his hands with his mother's scented soap because they smelled of armpits.

"Am I going to sleep with her ? " In the following days Lucien was absorbed by this small problem ; Berthe was always putting herself in his way, looking at him with the great sad cyes of a spaniel. Morality won out : Lucien realized he risked making her pregnant because he did not have enough experience (impossible to buy contraceptives in Férolles ; he was too well known) and he would cause M. Fleurier much worry. He also told himself that later he would have less authority in the factory if one of the workers' daughters could brag he had slept with her. " I don't have the right to touch her." He avoided being alone with Berthe during the last days of September. " So," Winckelmann asked him, " what are you waiting for ? " " I'm not going to bother," Lucien answered dryly. " I don't like ancillary love." Winckelmann, who heard the word ancillary love for the first time, gave a low whistle and was silent.

Lucien was very satisfied with himself : he had conducted himself like a *chic type* and that repaid many errors. " She was ripe for it," he told himself with a little regret, but on reconsidering it, he thought, " It's the same as though I had her : she offered herself and I didn't want her." And henceforth he no longer considered himself a virgin. These slight satisfactions occupied his mind for several days. Then they, too, melted into the fog. Returning to school in October, he felt as dismal as at the beginning of the previous year.

Berliac had not come back and no one had heard anything about him. Lucien noticed several unknown faces. His right-hand neighbour whose name was Lemordant had taken a year of special mathematics in Poitiers. He was even bigger than Lucien, and with his black moustache, already looked like a man. Lucien met his friends again without pleasure : they seemed childish to him and innocently boisterous : schoolboys. He still associated himself with their collective manifestations but with nonchalance, as was permitted by his position of *carré*. Lemordant would have attracted him more, because he was mature ; but, unlike Lucien, he did not seem to have acquired that maturity through multiple and painful experiences: he was an adult by birth. Lucien often contemplated, with a full satisfaction, that voluminous, pensive head, neck-less, planted awry on the shoulders: it seemed impossible to get anything into it, neither through the ears, nor the tiny slanting eyes, pink and glassy: " a man with convictions," Lucien thought with respect; and he wondered, not without jealousy, what that certitude could be that gave Lemordant such a full consciousness of himself. " That's how I should be; a rock." He was even a little surprised that Lemordant should be accessible to mathematical reasoning; but M. Husson convinced him when he gave back the first papers: Lucien was seventh and Lemordant had been given a " 5 " and 78th place; all was in order. Lemordant gave no sign; he seemed to expect the worst. His tiny mouth, his heavy cheeks, yellow and smooth, were not made to express feelings: he was a Buddha. They saw him angry only once, the day Loewy bumped into him in the cloakroom. First, he gave a dozen sharp little growls, and blinked his eyes: " Back to Poland," he said at last, " to Poland, you dirty kike, and don't come crapping around here with us." He dominated Loewy with his whole form and his massive chest swayed on his long legs. He finished up by slapping him and little Loewy apologised: the affair ended there.

On Thursdays, Lucien went out with Guigard who took him dancing with his sister's girl friends. But Guigard finally confessed that these hops bored him. " I've got a girl," he confided, " a *première* in Plisnier's, Rue Royale. She has a friend who doesn't have anybody: you ought to come with us Saturday night."

Lucien made a scene with his parents and got permission to go out every Saturday; they left the key under the mat for him. He met Guigard around nine o'clock in a bar on the Rue Saint-Honoré. "You wait and see," Guigard said, "Fanny is charming and what's nice about her is she really knows how to dress." "What about mine?" "I don't know her; I know she's an apprentice dressmaker and she's just come to Paris from Angoulême. By the way," he added, "don't pull any boners. My name's Pierre Daurat. You, because you're blond, I said you were part English; it's better. Your name's Lucien Bonnières." "But why?" asked Lucien, intrigued. "My boy," Guigard answered, "it's a rule. You can do what you like with these girls but never tell your name." "All right," Lucien said, "what do I do for a living?" "You can say you're a student, that's better, you understand, it flatters them and then you don't have to spend much money. Of course, we share the expenses; but let me pay this evening; I'm in the habit: I'll tell you what you owe me on Monday." Immediately Lucien thought Guigard was trying to get a rake-off. "God, how distrustful I've become!" he thought with amusement. Just then Fanny came in, a tall, thin brunette with long thighs and a heavily rouged face. Lucien found her intimidating. "Here's Bonnières I was telling you about," Guigard said. "Pleased to meet you," Fanny said with a myopic look. "This is my girl friend Maud." Lucien saw an ageless little woman wearing a hat that looked like an overturned flower pot. She was not rouged and appeared greyish after the dazzling Fanny. Lucien was bitterly disappointed but he saw she had a pretty mouth

—and then there was no need to be embarrassed with her. Guigard had taken care to pay for the beers in advance so that he could profit from the commotion of their arrival to push the two girls gaily toward the door without allowing them the time for a drink. Lucien was grateful to him : M. Fleurier only gave him 125 francs a week and out of this money he had to pay his carfare. The evening was amusing ; they went dancing in the Latin quarter in a hot, pink little place with dark corners and where a cocktail cost five francs. There were many students with girls of the same type as Fanny but not as good-looking. Fanny was superb : she looked straight in the eyes of a big man with a beard who smoked a pipe and said very loudly, " I hate people who smoke pipes at dances." The man turned crimson and put the lighted pipe back in his pocket. She treated Guigard and Lucien with a certain condescension and sometimes told them, " You're a couple of kids," with a gentle, maternal air. Lucien felt full of ease and sweetness ; he told Fanny several amusing little things and smiled while telling them. Finally, the smile never left his face and he was able to hit on a refined tone of voice with touches of devil-may-care and tender courtesy tinged with irony. But Fanny spoke little to him ; she took Guigard's chin and pulled his cheeks to make his mouth stand out ; when the lips were full and drooling a little, like fruit swollen with juice or like snails, she licked them, saying " Baby." Lucien was horribly annoyed and thought Guigard was ridiculous : Guigard had rouge near his lips and finger marks on his cheeks. But the behaviour of the other couples was even more negligent : everyone kissed ; from time to time the girl from the check-

room passed among them with a little basket, throwing streamers and multicoloured balls, shouting, " *Olé,
les enfants, amusez-vous, olé, olé !* " and everybody
laughed. At last Lucien remembered the existence of
Maud and he said to her, smiling, " Look at those
turtle doves . . ." He pointed to Fanny and Guigard
and added, " *nous autres, nobles vieillards . . .*" He
did not finish the phrase but smiled so drolly that
Maud smiled too. She removed her hat and Lucien
saw with pleasure that she was somewhat better than
the other women in the dance hall ; then he asked her
to dance and told her the jokes he played on his pro-
fessors the year of his baccalaureat. She danced well ;
her eyes were black and serious and she had an intelligent look. Lucien told her about Berthe and said he
was full of remorse. " But," he added, " it was better
for her." Maud thought the story about Berthe was
poetic and sad ; she asked how much Berthe earned
from Lucien's parents. " It's not always funny," she
added, " for a young girl to be in the family way."
Guigard and Fanny paid no more attention to them ;
they caressed each other and Guigard's face was
covered with moisture. From time to time Lucien
repeated, " Look at those turtle doves, just look at
them ! " and he had his sentence ready. " They make
me feel like doing it too." But he dared not say it
and contented himself with smiling ; then he pretended
that he and Maud were old friends, disdainful of love,
and he called her " brother " and made as if to slap
her on the back. Suddenly, Fanny turned her head and
looked at them with surprise. " Well," she said, " first-
graders, how're you doing ? Why don't you kiss,
you're dying to." Lucien took Maud in his arms ; he

was a little annoyed because Fanny was watching them : he wanted the kiss to be long and successful but he wondered how people breathed. Finally, it was not as difficult as he thought ; it was enough to kiss on an angle, leaving the nostrils clear. He heard Guigard counting " one-two-three-four——" and he let go of Maud at 52. " Not bad for a beginning," Guigard said. " I can do better." Lucien looked at his wrist watch and counted : Guigard left Fanny's mouth at the 159th second. Lucien was furious and thought the contest was stupid. " I let go of Maud just to be safe," he thought, " but that's nothing, once you know how to breathe you can keep on for ever." He proposed a second match and won. When it was all over, Maud looked at Lucien and said seriously, " You kiss well." Lucien blushed with pleasure. " At your service," he answered, bowing. Still he would rather have kissed Fanny. They parted around half past twelve because of the last métro. Lucien was joyful : he leaped and danced in the Rue Raynouard and thought " It's in the bag." The corners of his mouth hurt because he had smiled so much.

He saw Maud every Thursday at six and on Saturday evening. She let herself be kissed but nothing more. Lucien complained to Guigard, who reassured him. " Don't worry," Guigard said, " Fanny's sure she'll play ; but she's young and only had two boys ; Fanny says for you to be very tender with her." " Tender ? " Lucien said, " get a load of that ! " They both laughed and Guigard concluded, "That's what you've got to do." Lucien was very tender. He kissed Maud a lot and told her he loved her, but after a while it became a little monotonous and then he was not too

proud of going out with her : he would have liked to
give her advice on how she should dress, but she was
full of prejudices and angered quickly. Between kisses,
they were silent, gazing at each other and holding
hands. " God knows what she's thinking with those
strict eyes she has "; Lucien still thought of the same
thing : this small existence, sad and vague, which was
his own, and told himself, " I wish I were Lemordant ;
there's a man who's found his place ! " During those
times he saw himself as though he were another person : sitting near a woman who loved him, his hand
in hers, his lips still wet from kisses, refusing the
humble happiness she offered him : alone. Then he
clasped Maud's fingers tightly and tears came to his
eyes : he would have liked to make her happy.

One morning in December, Lemordant came up to
Lucien ; he held a paper. " You want to sign ? " he
asked. " What is it ? " " Because of the kikes at the
Normale Sup, they sent the *Oeuvre* a petition against
compulsory military training with 200 signatures. So
we're protesting ; we need a thousand names at least :
we're going to get the *cyrards*, the *flottards*, the *agros*,
the *X's*, and the whole works." Lucien was flattered.
" It is going to be printed ? " " Surely in *Action*.
Maybe in *Echo de Paris* besides." Lucien wanted to
sign on the spot but he thought it would not be wise.
He took the paper and read it carefully. Lemordant
added, " I hear you don't have anything to do with
politics : that's your business. But you're French and
you've got a right to have your say." When he heard
" you've got a right to have your say " Lucien felt an
inexplicable and rapid joy. He signed. The next day
he bought *Action Française* but the proclamation was

not there. It did not appear until Thursday; Lucien found it on the second page under the headline: YOUTH OF FRANCE SCORES IN TEETH OF INTERNATIONAL JEWRY. His name was there, compressed, definite, not far from Lemordant's, almost as strange as the names *Flèche* and *Flipot* which surrounded it; it looked unreal. "Lucien Fleurier," he thought. "A peasant name, a real French name." He read the whole series of names starting with F aloud and when it came his turn he pronounced it as if he did not recognize it. Then he stuffed the newspaper in his pocket and went home happily.

A few days later he sought out Lemordant. "Are you active in politics?" he asked. "I'm in the League," Lemordant said. "Ever read *Action Française*?" "Not much," Lucien confessed, "up to now it didn't interest me but I think I'm changing my mind." Lemordant looked at him without curiosity, with his impenetrable air. Lucien told him, in a few words, what Bergère had called his "Disorder". "Where do you come from?" Lemordant asked. "Férolles. My father has a factory there." "How long did you stay there?" "Till second form." "I see," Lemordant said, "it's very simple, you're uprooted. Have you read Barrès?" "I read *Collette Baudoche*." "Not that," Lemordant said impatiently, "I'll bring you the *Déracinés* this afternoon. That's your story. You'll find the cause and cure." The book was bound in green leather. On the first page there was an "*ex libris* André Lemordant" in gothic letters. Lucien was surprised; he had never dreamed Lemordant could have a first name.

He began reading it with much distrust: it had been

199

explained to him so many times : so many times had
he been lent books with a " Read this, it fits you
perfectly." Lucien thought with a sad smile that he
was not someone who could be set down in so many
pages. The Oedipus complex, the Disorder : what
childishness, and so far away ! But, from the very
first, he was captivated : in the first place, it was not
psychology—Lucien had a bellyfull of psychology—
the young people Barrès described were not abstract
individuals or declassed like Rimbaud or Verlaine, nor
sick like the unemployed Viennese who had themselves
psychoanalysed by Freud. Barrès began by placing
them in their milieu, in their family : they had been
well brought up, in the provinces, in solid traditions.
Lucien thought Sturel resembled himself. " It's true,"
he said, " I'm uprooted." He thought of the moral
health of the Fleuriers, a health acquired only in the
land, their physical strength (his grandfather used to
twist a bronze sou between his fingers) : he remembered
with emotion the dawns in Férolles : he rose, tiptoed
down the stairs so as not to wake his family, straddled
his bicycle, and the soft countryside of the Ile de
France enveloped him in its discreet caresses. " I've
always hated Paris," he thought with force. He also
read the *Jardin de Bérénice* and, from time to time,
stopped reading and began to ponder, his eyes vague ;
thus they were again offering him a character and a
destiny, a means of escaping the inexhaustible gossip
of his conscience, a method of defining and appre-
ciating himself. And how much more he preferred the
unconscious, reeking of the soil which Barrès gave him,
to the filthy, lascivious images of Freud. To grasp it,
Lucien had only to turn himself away from a sterile

and dangerous contemplation of self : he must study the soil and subsoil of Férolles, he must decipher the sense of rolling hills which descended as far as the Sernette, he must apply himself to human geography and history. Or, simply return to Férolles and live there : he would find it harmless and fertile at his feet, stretched across the countryside, mixed in the woods, the springs, and the grass-like nourishing humus from which Lucien could at last draw the strength to become a leader. Lucien left these long dreams exalted and sometimes felt as if he had found his road. Now he was silent close to Maud, his arm about her waist, the words, the scraps of sentences resounding in him : " renew tradition ", " the earth and the dead ", deep, opaque words, inexhaustible. " How tempting it is," he thought. Yet he dared not believe it : he had already been disappointed too often. He opened up his fears to Lemordant : " It would be too good." " My boy," Lemordant answered, " you don't believe everything you want to right away : you need practice." He thought a little and said, " You ought to come with us." Lucien accepted with an open heart, but he insisted on keeping his liberty. " I'll come," he said, " but I won't be involved. I want to see and think about it."

Lucien was captivated by the camaraderies of the young *camelots* ; they gave him a cordial, simple welcome and he immediately felt at ease in their midst. He soon knew Lemordant's " gang ", about twenty students almost all of whom wore velvet berets. They held their meetings on the second floor of the Polder beerhall where they played bridge and billiards. Lucien often went there to meet them and soon he realized they had adopted him, for he was always greeted with shouts of "*Voilà le plus beau!*" or "Our National Fleurier!" But it was their good humour which especially captured Lucien: nothing pedantic or austere; little talk of politics. They laughed and sang, that was all; they shouted or beat the tables in honour of the student youth. Lemordant himself smiled without dropping an authority which no one would have dared question. Lucien was more often silent, his look wandering over these boisterous, muscular young people. "This is strength," he thought. Little by little he discovered the true sense of youth in the midst of them: it was not in the affected grace Bergère appreciated; youth was the future of France. However, Lemordant's friends did not have the troubled charm of adolescence: they were adults and several wore beards. Looking closely, he found an air of parenthood in all of them: they had finished with the wanderings and uncertainties of their age; they had nothing more to learn, they were made. In the beginning their lighthearted, ferocious jokes somewhat shocked Lucien: one might have thought them without conscience. When Rémy announced that Mme Dubus, the wife of the radical leader, had her legs cut off by a truck, Lucien expected them to render a brief homage to their unfortunate adversary. But they all burst out laughing and slapped their legs, saying: "The old carrion!" and "What a fine truck driver!" Lucien was a little taken aback but suddenly he understood that this great, purifying laughter was a refusal: they had scented danger, they wanted no cowardly pity and they were firm. Lucien began to laugh too. Little by little their pranks appeared to him in their true light:

there was only the shell of frivolity; at heart it was the affirmation of a right: their conviction was so deep, so religious, that it gave them the right to appear frivolous, to dismiss all that was not essential with a whim, a pirouette. Between the icy humour of Charles Maurras and the jokes of Desperreau, for instance, there was only a difference of degree. In January the University announced a solemn meeting in the course of which the degree of *doctor honoris causa* was to be bestowed on two Swedish mineralogists. "You're going to see something good," Lemordant told Lucien, giving him an invitation card. The big amphitheatre was packed. When Lucien saw the President of the Republic and the Rector enter at the sound of the *Marseillaise*, his heart began to pound; he was afraid for his friends. Just then a few young people rose from their seats and began to shout. With sympathy Lucien recognized Rémy, red as a beet, struggling between two men who were pulling his coat, shouting "France for the French!" but he was especially pleased to see an old gentleman, with the air of a precocious child, blowing a little horn. "How healthy it is," he thought. He keenly tasted this odd mixture of headstrong gravity and turbulence which gave the youngest an air of maturity and the oldest an impish air. Soon Lucien himself tried to joke. He had some success and when he said of Herriot, "There's no more God if he dies in his bed," he felt the birth of a sacred fury in him. Then he gritted his teeth and, for a moment, felt as convinced, as strict, as powerful as Rémy or Desperreau. "Lemordant is right," he thought, "you need practice, it's all there." He also learned to avoid discussions: Guigard, who was only a republican,

overwhelmed him with objections. Lucien listened to
him politely but, after a while, shut up. Guigard was
still talking, but Lucien did not even look at him any
more : he smoothed the fold in his trousers and amused
himself by blowing smoke rings with his cigarette and
looking at women. Nevertheless, he heard a few of
Guigard's objections, but they quickly lost their weight
and slipped off him, light and futile. Guigard finally
was quiet, quite impressed. Lucien told his parents
about his new friends and M. Fleurier asked him if
he was going to be a *camelot*. Lucien hesitated and
gravely said, " I'm tempted, I'm really tempted."
" Lucien, I beg you, don't do it," his mother said,
" they're very excitable and something bad can happen
so quickly. Don't you see you can get into trouble or
be put in prison ? Besides, you're much too young to
be mixed up in politics." Lucien answered her only
with a firm smile and M. Fleurier intervened, " Let him
alone, dear," he said gently, " let him follow his own
ideas ; he has to pass through it." From that day on
it seemed to Lucien that his parents treated him with
a certain consideration. Yet he did not decide ; these
few weeks had taught him much : in turn, he considered the benevolent curiosity of his father, Mme
Fleurier's worries, the growing respect of Guigard, the
insistence of Lemordant and the impatience of Rémy,
and, nodding his head, he told himself, " This is no
small matter." He had a long conversation with
Lemordant and Lemordant well understood his reasons
and told him not to hurry. Lucien still was nostalgic :
he had the impressions of being only a small gelatinous
transparency trembling on the seat in a café and the
boisterous agitation of the *camelots* seemed absurd to

him. But at other times he felt hard and heavy as a rock and he was almost happy.

He got along better with the whole gang. He sang them the *Noce à Rebecca* which Hébrard had taught him the previous vacation and everyone thought it was tremendously amusing. Lucien threw out several biting reflections about the Jews and spoke of Berliac who was so miserly: " I always asked myself: why is he so cheap, it isn't possible to be that cheap. Then one day I understood: he was one of the tribe." Everybody began to laugh and a sort of exaltation came over Lucien: he felt truly furious about the Jews and the memory of Berliac was deeply unpleasant to him. Lemordant looked him in the eyes and said, " You're a real one, you are." After that they often asked Lucien: " Fleurier, tell us a good one about the kikes." And Lucien told the Jewish jokes he learned from his father; all he had to do was begin, " Vun day Levy met Bloom . . ." to fill his friends with mirth. One day Rémy and Patenôtre told how they had come across an Algerian Jew by the Seine and how they had almost frightened him to death by acting as if they were going to throw him in the water: " I said to myself," Rémy concluded, " what a shame it was Fleurier wasn't with us." " Maybe it was better he wasn't there," Desperreau interrupted, " he'd have chucked him in the water for good ! " There was no one like Lucien for recognizing a Jew from the nose. When he went out with Guigard he nudged his elbow : " Don't turn around now: the little short one, behind us, he's one of them ! " " For that," Guigard said, " you can really smell 'em out." Fanny could not stand the Jews either; all four of them went to Maud's room

one Thursday and Lucien sang the *Noce à Rebecca*.
Fanny could stand no more, she said, " Stop, stop, or
I'll wet my pants," and when he had finished, she gave
him an almost tender look. They played jokes on him
in the Polder beerhall. There was always someone
to say, negligently, " Fleurier who likes the Jews so
much . . ." or " Leon Blum, the great friend of
Fleurier . . ." and the others waited, in stitches, holding their breath, open-mouthed. Lucien grew red and
struck the table, shouting, " God damn . . . ! " and
they burst out laughing and said, " He bit ! He didn't
bite—he swallowed it ! "

He often went to political meetings with them and
heard Professor Claude and Maxime Real Del Sarte.
His work suffered a little from these new obligations,
but, since Lucien could not count on winning the
Central scholarship anyhow, that year, M. Fleurier was
indulgent. " After all," he told his wife, " Lucien
must learn the job of being a man." After these
meetings Lucien and his friends felt hotheaded and
were given to playing tricks. Once about ten of them
came across a little, olive-skinned man who was crossing the Rue Saint-André-des-Arts, reading *Humanité*.
They shoved him into a wall and Rémy ordered,
" Throw down that paper." The little man wanted to
act up but Desperreau slipped behind him and grabbed
him by the waist while Lemordant ripped the paper
from his grasp with a powerful fist. It was very
amusing. The little man, furious, kicked the air and
shouted " Let go of me ! Let go ! " with an odd accent
and Lemordant, quite calm, tore up the paper. But
things were spoiled when Desperreau wanted to let the
man go : he threw himself on Lemordant and would

have struck him if Rémy hadn't landed a good punch behind the ear just in time. The man fell against the wall and looked at them all evilly, saying " *Sales Français!* " " Say that again," Marchesseau demanded coldly. Lucien realized there was going to be some dirty work : Marchesseau could not take a joke when it was a question of France. " *Sales Français!* " the dago said. He was slapped again and threw himself forward, his head lowered. " *Sales Français, sales bourgeois,* I hate you, I hope you croak, all of you, all of you!" and a flood of other filthy curses with a violence that Lucien never imagined possible. Then they lost patience and all had to step in and give him a good lesson. After a while they let him go and the man dropped against the wall : his breath was a whistle, one punch had closed his left eye and they were all around him, tired of striking him, waiting for him to fall. The man twisted his mouth and spat : " *Sales Français! Sales Français!* " " You want some more ? " Desperreau asked, breathless. The man didn't seem to hear : he looked at them defiantly with his left eye and repeated, " *Sales Français, sales Français.* " There was a moment of hesitation and Lucien realized his friends were going to give it up. Then it was stronger than he was ; he leaped forward and struck with all his might. He heard something crack and the little man looked at him with surprise and weakness. " *Sales* . . ." he muttered, but his puffed eye began to open on a red, sightless globe ; he fell to his knees and said nothing more. " Get to hell out," Rémy hissed. They ran, stopping only at Place Saint-Michel : no one was following them. They straightened their ties and brushed each other down.

The evening passed without mention of the incident and the young men were especially nice to each other : they had abandoned the modest brutality which usually veiled their feelings. They spoke politely to each other and Lucien thought that for the first time they were acting as they acted with their families ; but he was enervated : he was not used to fighting thugs in the middle of the street. He thought tenderly of Maud and Fanny.

He could not sleep. "I can't go on," he thought, "following them like an amateur. Everything has been weighed. I *must* join!" He felt grave and almost religious when he announced the good news to Lemordant. "It's decided," he said, "I'm with you." Lemordant slapped him on the shoulder and the gang celebrated the event by polishing off several bottles. They had recovered their gay and brutal tone and said nothing about the incident of the night before. As they were about to leave, Marchesseau told Lucien simply, "You've got a terrific punch !" and Lucien answered, "He was a Jew."

The day after that he went to see Maud with a heavy malacca cane he had bought in a store on the Boulevard Saint-Michel. Maud understood immediately : she looked at the cane and said, "So you did it ? " "I did it," Lucien smiled. Maud seemed flattered ; personally, she favoured the ideas of the Left, but she was broad-minded. "I think," she said, "there's good in all parties." In the course of the evening, she scratched his neck several times and called him, "My little *Camelot*." A little while after that, one Saturday night, Maud felt tired. "I think I'll go back," she said, "but you can come up with me if

you're good : you can hold my hand and be nice to
your little Maud who's so tired, and you can tell her
stories." Lucien was hardly enthusiastic : Maud's room
depressed him with its careful poverty : it was like a
maid's room. But it would have been criminal to let
such an opportunity pass by. Hardly in the room,
Maud threw herself on the bed, saying, " Whew ! it
feels so good !." Then she was silent, gazing into
Lucien's eyes, and puckered her lips. He stretched
himself out near her and she put her hand over his
eyes, spreading her fingers and saying, " Peekaboo, I
see you, you know I see you, Lucien ! " He felt soft
and heavy ; she put her fingers in his mouth and he
sucked them, then spoke to her tenderly, " Poor little
Maud's sick, does little Maud have a pain ? " and he
caressed her whole body ; she had closed her eyes and
was smiling mysteriously. After a moment he raised
her skirt and they made love ; Lucien thought, " What
a break ! " When it was over Maud said, " Well, if
I'd thought that ! " She looked at Lucien with a tender
reproach, " Naughty boy, I thought you were going to
be good ! " Lucien said he was as surprised as she
was. " That's the way it happens," he said. She
thought a little and then told him seriously, " I don't
regret anything. Before, maybe, it was purer but it
wasn't so complete."

In the métro, Lucien thought, " I have a mistress."
He was empty and tired, saturated with a smell of
absinthe and fresh fish ; he sat down, holding himself
stiffly to avoid contact with his sweat-soaked shirt ; he
felt his body to be curdled milk. He repeated forcefully, " I have a mistress." But he felt frustrated :
what he desired in Maud the night before was her

narrow, closed face which seemed so unattainable, her slender silhouette, her look of dignity, her reputation for being a serious girl, her scorn of the masculine sex, all those things that made her a strange being, truly *someone else*, hard and definitive, always out of reach, with her clean little thoughts, her modesties, her silk stockings and crêpe dresses, her permanent wave. And all this veneer had melted under his embrace, the flesh remained. They had made a single one : he could no longer distinguish his flesh from that of Maud ; no one had ever given him that feeling of sickening intimacy, except possibly Riri, when Riri showed him his wee-wee behind a bush or when he had forgotten himself and stayed resting on his belly, bouncing up and down, his behind naked, while they dried out his pants. Lucien felt some comfort thinking about Guigard : tomorrow he would tell him: " I slept with Maud, she's a sweet little kid, old man, it's in her blood." But he was uncomfortable, and felt naked in the dusty heat of the métro, naked beneath a thin film of clothing, stiff and naked beside a priest, across from two mature women, like a great, soiled beanpole.

Guigard congratulated him vehemently. He was getting a little tired of Fanny. " She really has a rotten temper. Yesterday she gave me dirty looks all evening." They both agreed : there have to be women like that, because, after all, you couldn't stay chaste until you got married and then they weren't in love and they weren't sick but it would be a mistake to get attached to them. Guigard spoke of real girls with delicacy and Lucien asked him news of his sister. " She's fine," said Guigard, " she says you're a quitter. You know," he added, with a little abandon,

" I'm not sorry I have a sister : you find out things you never could imagine." Lucien understood him perfectly. As a result they spoken often of girls and felt full of poetry and Guigard loved to recite the words of one of his uncles who had had much success with women : " Possibly I haven't always done the right thing in my dog's life, but there's one thing God will witness : I'd rather cut my hands off than touch a virgin." Sometimes they went to see Pierrette Guigard's girl friends. Lucien liked Pierrette a lot ; he talked to her like a big brother, teased her a little and was grateful to her because she had not cut her hair. He was completely absorbed in his political activities ; every Sunday morning he went to sell *Action Française* in front of the church in Neuilly. For more than two hours, Lucien walked up and down, his face hard. The girls coming out of mass sometimes raised beautiful frank eyes towards him ; then Lucien relaxed a little and felt pure and strong ; he smiled at them. He explained to the gang that he respected women and he was glad to find the understanding he had hoped for. Besides, they almost all had sisters.

On the 17th of April, the Guigards gave a dance for Pierrette's eighteenth birthday and naturally Lucien was invited. He was already quite good friends with Pierrette ; she called him her dancing partner and he suspected her of being a little bit in love with him. Mme Guigard had brought in a caterer and the afternoon promised to be quite gay. Lucien danced with Pierrette several times, then went to see Guigard who was receiving his friends in the smoking room. " Hello," Guigard said, " I think you all know each other : Fleurier, Simon, Vanusse, Ledoux." While Guigard

was naming his friends, Lucien saw a tall young man
with red, curly hair, milky skin and harsh black eyelashes, approaching them hesitantly, and he was overcome with rage. "What's this fellow doing here?"
he wondered. "Guigard knows I can't stand Jews!"
He spun on his heels and withdrew rapidly to avoid
introductions. "Who is that Jew?" he asked Pierrette
a moment later. "It's Weill; he's at the Hautes
Etudes Commerciales; my brother met him in fencing
class." "I hate Jews," Lucien said. Pierrette gave a
little laugh. "This one's a pretty good chap," she said,
"take me into the buffet." Lucien drank a glass of
champagne and only had time to set it down when he
found himself nose to nose with Guigard and Weill.
He glared at Guigard and turned his back, but Pierrette
took his arm and Guigard approached him openly:
"My friend Fleurier, my friend Weill," he said easily,
"there, you're introduced." Weill put out his hand
and Lucien felt miserable. Luckily, he suddenly remembered Desperreau: "Fleurier would have chucked the
Jew in the water for good." He thrust his hands in
his pockets, turned his back on Guigard and walked
away. "I can never set foot in this house again," he
thought, getting his coat. He felt a bitter pride.
"That's what you call keeping your ideals; you can't
live in society any more." Once in the street his pride
melted and Lucien grew worried. "Guigard must be
furious!" He shook his head and tried to tell himself
with conviction, "He didn't have the right to invite
a Jew if he invited me!" But his rage had left him;
he saw the surprised face of Weill again with discomfort, his outstretched hand, and he felt he wanted a
reconciliation: "Pierrette surely thinks I'm a swine.

I should have shaken hands with him. After all, it didn't involve me in anything. Say hello to him and afterwards go right away : that's what I should have done." He wondered if he had time to go back to Guigards'. He would go up to Weill and say, " Excuse me. I wasn't feeling well." He would shake hands and say a few nice words. No. It was too late, his action was irreparable. He thought with irritation, " Why did I need to show my opinions to people who can't understand them ? " He shrugged his shoulders nervously : it was a disaster. At that very instant Guigard and Pierrette were commenting on his behaviour ; Guigard was saying, " He's completely crazy ! " Lucien clenched his fists. " Oh God," he thought, " how I hate them ! God, how I hate Jews ! " and he tried to draw strength from the contemplation of this immense hatred. But it melted away under his look ; in vain he thought of Jean Luis who got money from Germany and hated the French ; he felt nothing more than a dismal indifference. Lucien was lucky to find Maud home. He told her he loved her and possessed her several times with a sort of rage. " It's all screwed up," he told himself, " I'll never be *anybody*." " No, no," Maud said, " stop that, my big darling, it's forbidden ! " But at last she let herself go : Lucien wanted to kiss her everywhere. He felt childish and perverse ; he wanted to cry.

At school, next morning, Lucien's heart tightened when he saw Guigard. Guigard looked sly and pretended not to see him. Lucien was so enraged that he could not take notes : " The bastard," he thought, " the bastard ! " At the end of the class, Guigard came up to him ; he was pale. " If he says a word," thought

Lucien, "I'll knock his teeth in." They stayed side by side for an instant, each looking at the toes of their shoes. Finally, Guigard said in an injured voice, "Excuse me, old man. I shouldn't have done that to you." Lucien started and looked at him with distrust. But Guigard went on painfully, "I met him in the class, you see, so I thought . . . we fenced together and he invited me over to his place, but I understand, you know, I shouldn't have . . . I don't know how it happened, but when I wrote the invitations I didn't think for a second . . ." Lucien still said nothing because the words would not come out, but he felt indulgent. Guigard, his head bowed, added, "Well, for a boner . . ." "You big chunk of baloney!" Lucien said, slapping his shoulder, "of course I know you didn't do it on purpose." He said generously, "I was wrong, too. I acted like a rotter. But what do you expect—it's stronger than I am. I can't stand them —it's physical. I feel as though they had scales on their hands. What did Pierrette say?" "She laughed like mad," Guigard said pitifully. "And the guy?" "He caught on. I said what I could, but he took off fifteen minutes later." Still humble, he added, "My parents say you were right and you couldn't have done otherwise because of your convictions." Lucien savoured the word "convictions"; he wanted to hug Guigard: "It's nothing, old man," he told him; "It's nothing because we're still friends." He walked down Boulevard Saint-Michel in a state of extraordinary exaltation: he seemed to be himself no longer.

He told himself, "It's funny, it isn't *me* any more. I don't recognize myself!" It was hot and pleasant; people strolled by, wearing the first astonished smile of springtime on their faces : Lucien thrust himself into this soft crowd like a steel wedge ; he thought, " It's not me any more. Only yesterday I was a big, bloated bug like the crickets in Férolles." Now Lucien felt clean and sharp as a chronometer. He went into La Source and ordered a pernod. The gang didn't hang around the Source because the place swarmed with dagos ; but dagos and Jews did not disturb Lucien that day. He felt unusual and threatening in the midst of these olive-tinted bodies which rustled like a field of oats in the wind ; a monstrous clock leaning on the bar, shining red. He recognized with amusement a little Jew the J.P. had roughed up last semester in the Faculté de Droit corridors. The fat and pensive little monster had not kept the mark of the blows ; he must have stayed laid up for a while and then regained his round shape ; but there was a sort of obscene resignation in him.

He was happy for the time being : he yawned voluptuously ; a ray of sunlight tickled his nostrils ; he scratched his nose and smiled. Was it a smile ? Or rather a little oscillation which had been born on the outside, somewhere in a corner of the place and which had come to die on his mouth ? All the dagos were floating in dark, heavy water whose eddies jolted their flabby flesh, raised their arms, agitated their fingers and played a little with their lips. Poor bastards ! Lucien almost pitied them. What did they come to France for ? What sea currents had brought them and deposited them here ? They could dress in clothes from tailors on the Boulevard Saint-Michel in vain ; they were hardly more than jellyfish. Lucien thought, he was not a jellyfish, he did not belong to that

humiliated race. He told himself, " I'm a diver." Then
he suddenly forgot the Source and the dagos ; he only
saw a back, a wide back hunched with muscles going
farther and farther away, losing itself, implacable, in
the fog. He saw Guigard : Guigard was pale ; he
followed the back with his eyes and said to an invisible
Pierrette, " Well, what a boner . . . ! " Lucien was
flooded with an almost intolerable joy : this powerful,
solitary back was *his own*! And the scene happened
yesterday ! For an instant, at the cost of a violent
effort, he was Guigard, he saw the humility of Guigard
and felt himself deliciously terrified. " Let that be a
lesson to them ! " he thought. The scene changed : it
was Pierrette's boudoir ; it was happening in the
future ; Pierrette and Guigard were pointing out a
name on the list of invitations. Lucien was not there
but his power was over them. Guigard was saying,
" Oh no ! Not that one ! That would be fine for
Lucien. Lucien can't stand Jews." Lucien studied himself once more ; he thought, " I am Lucien ! Somebody
who can't stand Jews." He had often pronounced this
sentence but today was unlike all other times. Not at
all like them. Of course, it was apparently a simple
statement, as if someone had said " Lucien doesn't like
oysters " or " Lucien likes to dance ". But there was
no mistaking it : love of dancing might be found in
some little Jew who counted no more than a fly : all
you had to do was look at that damned kike to know
that his likes and dislikes clung to him like his odour,
like the reflections of his skin, that they disappeared
with him like the blinking of his heavy eyelids, like
his sticky, voluptuous smiles. But Lucien's anti-
semitism was of a different sort : unrelenting and pure,

it stuck out of him like a steel blade menacing other breasts. " It's . . . sacred," he thought. He remembered his mother when he was little, sometimes speaking to him in a certain special tone of voice : " Papa is working in his office." This sentence seemed a sacramental formula to him which suddenly conferred a halo of religious obligations on him, such as not playing with his air gun and not shouting "Tararaboom ! " He walked down the hall on tiptoes as if he were in a cathedral. " Now it's my turn," he thought with satisfaction. Lowering their voices, they said, " Lucien doesn't like Jews," and people would feel paralysed, their limbs transfixed by a swarm of aching little arrows. " Guigard and Pierrette," he said tenderly, " are children." They had been guilty but it sufficed for Lucien to show his teeth and they were filled with remorse ; they had spoken in a low voice and walked on tiptoe.

Lucien felt full of self respect for the second time. But this time he no longer needed the eyes of Guigard ; he appeared respectable in his own eyes—in his own eyes which had finally pierced his envelope of flesh, of likes and dislikes, habits and humours. " Where I sought myself," he thought, " I could not find myself." In good faith he took a detailed counting of all he *was*. " But if I could only be what I am I wouldn't be worth any more than the little kike." What could one discover searching in this mucous intimacy if not the sorrow of flesh, the ignoble lie of equality and disorder ? " First maxim," Lucien said, " Not to try and see inside yourself ; there is no mistake more dangerous." The real Lucien—he knew now—had to be sought in the eyes of others, in the

frightened obedience of Pierrette and Guigard, the
hopeful waiting of all those beings who grew and ripened
for him, these young apprentices who would become
his workers, people of Férolles, great and small, of
whom he would one day be the master. Lucien was
almost afraid, he felt almost too great for himself.
So many people were waiting for him, at attention :
and he was and always would be this immense waiting
of others. " That's a leader," he thought. And he
saw a hunched, muscular back reappear, then, immediately afterwards, a cathedral. He was inside, walking on tiptoe beneath the sifted light that fell from the
windows. " Only this time I am the cathedral ! " He
stared intently at his neighbour, a tall Cuban, brown
and mild as a cigar. He must absolutely find words to
express this extraordinary discovery. Quietly, cautiously, he raised his hand to his forehead, like a lighted
candle, then drew himself for an instant, thoughtful and
holy, and the words came of themselves, " I HAVE
RIGHTS ! " Rights : Something like triangles and
circles : it was so perfect that it didn't exist. You
could trace thousands of circles with a compass in
vain, you could never make a single circle. Generations of workers could as well scrupulously obey the
commands of Lucien ; they would never exhaust his
right to command ; rights were beyond existence, like
mathematical objects and religious dogma. And now
Lucien was just that : an enormous bouquet of
responsibilities and rights. He had believed that he
existed by chance for a long time, but it was due to a
lack of sufficient thought. His place in the sun was
marked in Férolles long before his birth. They were
waiting for him long before his father's marriage : if

he had come into the world it was to occupy that place : " I exist," he thought, " because I have the right to exist." And perhaps for the first time, he had a flashing, glorious vision of his destiny. Sooner or later he would go to the Centrale (it made no difference). Then he would drop Maud (she always wanted to sleep with him, it was tiresome ; their confused flesh giving off an odour of scorched rabbit stew in the torrid heat of springtime. " And then, Maud belongs to everybody. Today me, tomorrow somebody else, none of it makes any sense ") ; he would go and live in Férolles. Somewhere in France there was a bright young girl like Pierrette, a country girl with eyes like flowers who was staying chaste for him : sometimes she tried to imagine her future master, this gentle and terrible man ; but she could not. She was a virgin ; in the most secret part of her body she recognized the right of Lucien alone to possess her. He would marry her, she would be *his* wife, the tenderest of his rights. When, in the evening, she would undress with slender, sacred gestures, it would be like a holocaust. He would take her in his arms with the approval of everyone, and tell her, " You belong to me ! " What she would show him she would have the right to show to him alone and for him the act of love would be a voluptuous counting of his goods. His most tender right, his most intimate right : the right to be respected to the very flesh, obeyed to the very bed. " I'll marry young," he thought. He thought too that he would like to have many children ; then he thought of his father's work ; he was impatient to continue it and wondered if M. Fleurier was not going to die soon.

A clock struck noon ; Lucien rose. The metamorphosis was complete : a graceful, uncertain adolescent had entered this café one hour earlier ; now a man left, a leader among Frenchmen. Lucien took a few steps in the glorious light of a French morning. At the corner of the Rue des Ecoles and the Boulevard Saint-Michel, he went towards a stationery shop and looked at himself in the mirror : he would have liked to find on his own face the impenetrable look he admired on Lemordant's. But the mirror only reflected a pretty, headstrong little face that was not yet terrible enough. " I'll grow a moustache," he decided.

Bestselling European Fiction in Panther Books

Bestselling British Fiction in Panther Books

The Children of Violence series

MARTHA QUEST	Doris Lessing	60p	☐
A PROPER MARRIAGE	Doris Lessing	75p	☐
A RIPPLE FROM THE STORM	Doris Lessing	50p	☐
LANDLOCKED	Doris Lessing	50p	☐
THE FOUR-GATED CITY	Doris Lessing	90p	☐
ALFIE	Bill Naughton	40p	☐
ALFIE DARLING	Bill Naughton	60p	☐
FRIENDS IN LOW PLACES	Simon Raven	35p	☐
THE SABRE SQUADRON	Simon Raven	35p	☐
FIELDING GRAY	Simon Raven	30p	☐
SOUND THE RETREAT	Simon Raven	50p	☐
BROTHER CAIN	Simon Raven	40p	☐
DOCTORS WEAR SCARLET	Simon Raven	30p	☐
THE FEATHERS OF DEATH	Simon Raven	35p	☐
COME LIKE SHADOWS	Simon Raven	65p	☐
THE ROMANTIC ENGLISHWOMAN	Thomas Wiseman	60p	☐

Bestselling Transatlantic Fiction in Panther Books

THE SOT-WEED FACTOR	John Barth	£1.50	☐
BEAUTIFUL LOSERS	Leonard Cohen	60p	☐
THE FAVOURITE GAME	Leonard Cohen	40p	☐
TARANTULA	Bob Dylan	50p	☐
MIDNIGHT COWBOY	James Leo Herlihy	35p	☐
LONESOME TRAVELLER	Jack Kerouac	35p	☐
DESOLATION ANGELS	Jack Kerouac	50p	☐
THE DHARMA BUMS	Jack Kerouac	40p	☐
BARBARY SHORE	Norman Mailer	40p	☐
AN AMERICAN DREAM	Norman Mailer	40p	☐
THE NAKED AND THE DEAD	Norman Mailer	60p	☐
THE BRAMBLE BUSH	Charles Mergendahl	40p	☐
TEN NORTH FREDERICK	John O'Hara	50p	☐
FROM THE TERRACE	John O'Hara	75p	☐
OURSELVES TO KNOW	John O'Hara	60p	☐
THE DICE MAN	Luke Rhinehart	95p	☐
COCKSURE	Mordecai Richler	60p	☐
ST URBAIN'S HORSEMAN	Mordecai Richler	50p	☐
THE CITY AND THE PILLAR	Gore Vidal	40p	☐
BLUE MOVIE	Terry Southern	60p	☐
SLAUGHTERHOUSE 5	Kurt Vonnegut Jr	50p	☐
MOTHER NIGHT	Kurt Vonnegut Jr	40p	☐
PLAYER PIANO	Kurt Vonnegut Jr	50p	☐
GOD BLESS YOU, MR ROSEWATER			
	Kurt Vonnegut Jr	50p	☐
WELCOME TO THE MONKEY HOUSE			
	Kurt Vonnegut Jr	40p	☐

All these books are available at your local bookshop or newsagent, or can be ordered direct from the publisher. Just tick the titles you want and fill in the form below.

Name ....

Address ....

....

Write to Panther Cash Sales, PO Box 11, Falmouth, Cornwall TR10 9EN.

Please enclose remittance to the value of the cover price plus:

UK: 18p for the first book plus 8p per copy for each additional book ordered to a maximum charge of 66p.

BFPO and EIRE: 18p for the first book plus 8p per copy for the next 6 books, thereafter 3p per book.

OVERSEAS: 20p for the first book and 10p for each additional book.

Granada Publishing reserve the right to show new retail prices on covers, which may differ from those previously advertised in the text or elsewhere.